"I feel gratitude for being here, for being rather, for there is no need to tie oneself to the snow mountains in order to feel free. I am not here to seek the "crazy wisdom"; if I am, I shall never find it. I am here to be here, like these rocks and sky and snow, like this hail that is falling down out of the sun."

From *The Snow Leopard* by Peter Matthiessen, 1978

Claes Grundsten

TREK!

The best trekking in the world

dbp

DUNCAN BAIRD PUBLISHERS

LONDON

Previous page: Porters in Garhwal on the Curzon Trail. In the background are India's highest mountains: on the right, Nanda Devi, 25,645 feet (7,817m) above sea level; on the left, Dunagiri, 23,180 feet (7,066m) above sea level.

Trek!
Claes Grundsten

This edition published in the United Kingdom
and Ireland in 2006 by Duncan Baird Publishers Ltd
Sixth Floor
Castle House
75–76 Wells Street
London W1T 3QH

Translated by Julie Martin in association with
First Edition Translations Ltd, Cambridge, UK

Editor: Ingrid Court-Jones
Designer: Allan Sommerville
Managing Editor: Christopher Westhorp
Map artwork: Martin Thelander

British Library Cataloguing-in-Publication Data:
A CIP record for this book is available from the British Library.

10 9 8 7 6 5 4 3 2 1

ISBN-13: 9-781844-831838 ISBN-10: 1-84483-183-3

Typeset in FF Scala and Gill Sans
Colour reproduction by Scanhouse, Malaysia
Printed in Singapore by Imago

Contents

Foreword

Looking through a gap in the trees across to Vernal Falls during a walk through the Sierra Nevada in Yosemite National Park, California.

A world without people – what would that look like? Is there anywhere in the universe like our earth, but where only the wind and the leaves talk in unheard forests? Where a human voice would break a thousand million years of silence?

In such a world there would be no time. Only recurrences. The waters of the ocean would lap the beaches and splash against the rocks. Sirens would call and warning cries sound. There would be rustling in the long grass and a surge as a heavy body dived. It would be an earth of murmuring woods, a globe velvety with vegetation.

When I read Claes Grundsten's descriptions of his travels and see his pictures I wonder whether he is looking for a world without people. Does he want to tread ground so untouched that it responds to him from beneath his feet?

Claes has walked far and climbed high to reach places that have not been conquered by humans. In one or two places a couple of thousand people have gone before him in the same season. Nature photographers and climbers have gathered there. But he has walked on past the camps and the tourist debris. He seems to have been determined to get so high up that all human voices are stilled. He has walked on loose lava and blocks of ice, gasped for breath where oxygen is sparse, climbed precipices and felt his knees groan with pain on the way down. He has plodded heavily up through humid rainforests. His lungs have smarted in the winter cold and his head has swum with altitude sickness. He knows what it is like to grind on hour after hour, with rasping breath. Why has he done this?

Claes Grundsten has trekked throughout the world's continents to bring back something that only becomes beautiful in a human context. His words and pictures set us thinking unusual thoughts – about the nature of time and experiencing remote places, about a world in which such words would never get written and such photographs would never get taken if nobody ventured there.

Kerstin Ekman – *Writer*

Trek!

A STEP CLOSER TO NATURE

The trekker's routes and experiences of nature vary. In the Zion National Park in Utah we follow a narrow gorge along the Virgin River Narrows, 15 miles (25km) long. This 2,600-foot (800-metre) deep ravine is so constricted in places that the river fills the whole space and you have to splash through the water to get by.

Progress is slow when you're trekking, but just under two miles (3km) an hour is about right if you want to encounter the world on a human level. It gives us time to see and understand the reality, smell the scents, hear the sounds, touch the ground and digest the impressions. Walking brings us down to earth and it is the most primeval and natural way to travel. But walking is not the same thing as trekking. There is an essential difference between one and the other. Walking is something we do every day, but usually over only short distances. Trekking is more of a real journey into the wild, most often on paths but sometimes in more hazardous ways – and freedom is automatically part of it.

The activity of hiking along paths the world over is best summed up nowadays by using the verb "trek", a word the Boers coined in South Africa, where it meant travelling with ox carts. A modern English dictionary states that a trek is a long and difficult journey and that trekking entails an arduous migration. In a slightly narrower sense trek can also mean travelling on foot in areas where there are dangerous natural features. That is what I spend most of my time doing and what this book is about.

Trekking is a concept already well-known in my native Sweden as "fell-walking", but the English term extends that meaning because we can trek in jungles and deserts as well as through better-populated yet quite remote mountain landscapes. To travel, wherever possible, without engine power, is essential to the experiences and adventures we are looking for, so skiing and riding trips in regions where there are no roads are also counted as trekking.

Luggage will almost certainly be in the form of a backpack, but you don't always need to carry a pack or even to cook your own food. In many areas it is possible to hire porters, pack-horses and guides, and this definitely makes trekking easier, while at the same time supporting the local economy. In some places there are huts and hostels located along the trail. The availability of such shelter also helps to keep the weight of the pack down. With a light backpack, trekking in strange environments becomes a really pleasant journey. But sometimes there is no alternative to struggling along with a heavy pack. That, too, has its charm even if it is not so attractive, but carrying a well-loaded pack is often the only way you are able to trek through exciting terrain.

Most of all we like to seek out places where nature, with its flora and fauna, and its scenery, is primeval and unspoilt – at any rate as far as possible. For my part I like to look for areas which have an interesting geographical location; this is not so easily defined in words, but if a mere glance at the map arouses my overwhelming wanderlust, there's a good chance that I've hit the spot. I also like to get close to the people who live along the trails. This is no simple matter since I am a stranger, turning up with intriguing knick-knacks and unfamiliar habits. Endeavouring to understand the local people's traditional lifestyle and culture without eulogizing or moralizing is a good maxim. In spite of everything that has been said about global standardization, there is huge cultural diversity on this earth.

These days trekking is considered a form of ecotourism, a kind of respectful and environmentally aware travel, usually in small groups to unspoilt areas where one can humbly experience the landscape and the local culture. According to principles agreed on by a number of ecotourism organisations, a journey such as this should be instructive, environmentally friendly and responsible, and should contribute to the local economy. These are far-sighted goals that we must take seriously. Tourism can revolutionize and destroy places which become popular, and the trekking trails lead us to vulnerable environments. If we travel in a spirit of respect and with consideration, trekking can counteract the exploitation of landscapes and cultural environments that is happening throughout the world. As I see it, trekking is good for nature conservation since people in remote villages can earn a livelihood from a trade that demands an unspoilt environment. It is also good because those of us who travel there are happy to support the work of nature conservation.

But trekking is also an inner journey, a meeting with oneself in exotic surroundings, and sometimes in extremely rough conditions. For me trekking has become a kind of life philosophy and mental therapy. Nowadays the beneficial effects of walking for both physical and mental health are recognized. We get exercise and fresh air, and even a short, easy walk can boost our well-being. But long treks also build up our physical fitness. It is, in fact, recreation in the true sense of the word.

Of course, trekking is no new phenomenon. The inhabitants of every populated patch have gone in for migration since the dawn of humankind, but walking as an aid to well-being first began to be developed in the eighteenth century. Jean-Jacques Rousseau wrote down his thoughts on the philosophy of walking – classical words today. And the poet William Wordsworth was an early model with his writings and long walks in England's Lake District. As a result of industrialization and the migration to the cities, walking became a popular movement in the West in the centuries that followed. Tourist associations and walking clubs were formed all over the place in the second half of the nineteenth century. The destinations of tours were

A cowboy or *vaquero* rides past in the Cordillera Blanca, Peru. Encounters and contacts with local people allow us first-hand experience of the great variety of cultures to be found around the world.

usually local areas, landscapes within easy reach, mountain ranges and untouched regions within one's own country, or in the countries which one could travel to easily, mostly in Europe and North America.

It was not until the 1960s that trekking was launched as a concept for more distant travel. Possibilities opened up for many Westerners to go on walking holidays in unfamiliar environments. The first tours took place in the Himalayas and nowadays there are organized trips to most parts of the world. Trekking is on the programmes of innumerable travel companies around the globe. Their arrangements have made it considerably easier for the inexperienced to get out into exciting and inaccessible areas.

The development of modern outdoor equipment has also played a significant part. Backpacks, tents and footwear are getting better and, not least, lighter in weight all the time. Today's maps and guidebooks provide us with information about trails in ways which were inconceivable just half a century ago. That has also spurred on developments.

It is now obvious that trekking and outdoor experiences have become a way of life. "Back to nature" was Rousseau's slogan. Even those of us living in the twenty-first century can follow his lead by trekking – a step closer to nature.

TREK!

Pyrenees

THE MAD COUNT'S MOUNTAIN

Beyond the Marcadau Valley the mountain Vignemale rises proudly to 10,820 feet (3,300m) – the highest peak in the French part of the Pyrenees. Beneath it Count Henry Russell carved out caves in the nineteenth century. Today the forty-five-day-long "Haute Randonnée Pyrénéenne", or High Pyrenean Trail, runs below the peak and through the valley pictured.

Only the head of Henry Russell was visible when he was "buried alive" under a boulder one freezing night in 1880, not far from the path we are walking on. How would a mountain climber feel if there was a skull lying on the path up here? But Russell survived his act of bravado and went on to try out plenty of other crazy things.

There has scarcely been a climber who was as eccentric and so full of enthusiasm as the count born in Toulouse of an Irish father and a French mother. Russell's relationship with the mountain Vignemale in the Pyrenees developed into a real love affair. He hired it from the French state for one franc per annum and had some small caves carved out close to the peak. He lived in his inaccessible burrows for long periods, even laid out Persian carpets and held banquets in the dripping wet eyries, arranged for Catholic masses to be said on the glacier, and, as I have mentioned, had himself buried up to his neck. Henry Russell was an out-and-out romantic who explored the beauty of the mountain and the aesthetics of life. Russell's driving force was far different from that of another pioneer in the Pyrenees, his friend Charles Packe who charted the area's topography, geology and flora in a scientific way.

As the artist Björn Wessman and I pass the caves we are rather congenially following in Russell's footsteps in order to investigate and discuss the aesthetic possibilities of the mountain, for Björn as a painter and for me as a photographer. An elevated path between the Atlantic and Mediterranean, the "haute route" (high trail) of the Pyrenees leads us towards a pass beneath Vignemale, the highest peak on the French side.

The Pyrenees provide an excellent place for our meeting. Earlier treks have taught me that this barrier between Spain and France is unique. The profusion of flowers is extremely rich in the valleys and there is a lively interface between this pastoral verdure and the prison-grey barrenness of the jagged rocks higher up. These mountains are no deep-frozen ice-maidens like the Alps, they are smaller and bare like stone cherubs. No big glaciers here. In the Aigues Tortes National Park on the Spanish side grey blocks carve up the mountainous precipices. This is the nearest thing to a wilderness in the Pyrenees. The popular area around Gavarnie in France has more enticing features, with steeper and smoother mountains and wonderful beech forests. There the valleys are green with grass growing high up the sides.

Gavarnie will be our starting point. It is the end of September and the tourist invasion is over. A dead cow attracts about fifty griffon vultures as we turn towards Vignemale. The day is perfectly defined, the air is still and clear, and the late summer heat still lingers, the meadows remain green, while the leaves on the trees are beginning to take on their autumn hues. The trail winds up the slope towards a hut.

The Haute Randonnée Pyrénéenne is a long trail crossing a lot of high passes. It takes forty-five days to walk the whole length from the Atlantic to the Mediterranean. We are travelling the most popular section, between the tourist destination of Gavarnie and the freestanding Pic du Midi d'Ossau. One day west of Gavarnie and just 8,530 feet (2,600m) above sea level lies the solid stone bulk of the Refuge de Bassellance. There we take a break. If you don't want to climb Russell's beloved mountain from here, the Petit Vignemale offers a less demanding alternative. We stick to the path and wonder how this overpowering landscape could be reflected in pictures with a personal touch. For me it is interesting to hear how Björn will tackle the challenge. He has never been in such precipitous mountains before.

We continue our discussion when we spend the night in the Refuge Wallon a day or so later. This hut lies to the west of Vignemale and the landscape has become much more rugged than that around Gavarnie. In the Marcadau valley there is a dense forest of mountain pines. Knotty, gnarled and stocky trees have gained a foothold even on the very steep sides of the valley. They are photogenic and in the

In the rain we reach the Refuge Wallon, which is an old stone building, built on the tree-line in the Marcadau valley.

The dawn light reveals overblown angelica against the backdrop of the almost 4,920-foot (1,500-m) high mountain walls in the Gavarnie glacier niche. This is the most famous and dramatic location in the Pyrenees. On the other side of these peaks lies Spain. Few other mountain chains form such a sharp national frontier. The name Pyrenees may come from the Celtic word "byren" meaning back or ridge.

Lacs d'Opale at just over 7,545feet (2,300m) above sea level lie to the west from the Refuge Wallon. The sediment in the meltwater from the snow and ice gives the water its colour. There are only a few receding glaciers left. Since the middle of the nineteenth century 85 per cent of the Pyrenees' ice mass has melted away.

These gnarled specimens of the mountain pine in the Marcadau Valley are hardy, stunted trees, which give the mountain range a homely touch.

persistent rain, which has dogged us, this forest landscape reinforces the gloomy effect. As image-makers, we have no problem with this kind of harmony.

The rain makes even the hut seem sombre, with its old, grey, stone walls. The first night there are not more than ten of us there, being served with prepared food and wine. As a rule one can usually spend the night under cover on the trail along the Haute Randonnée Pyrénéenne, although it can get a little crowded. The next night is a Friday and the Wallon hut gets stuffed full of French weekend walkers. There are about fifty people crammed into the dining room, but the three wardens are good at keeping tabs on who has ordered what. Even though our upstairs room is small and the walls thin, we sleep well after a delicious dinner.

Our steps lead us on toward the Col de Cambales, while the main route of this high mountain path crosses a different pass, the Col de la Fache, that leads to Spain. (There are many variations on the Haute Randonnée Pyrénéenne, and the national boundary gets crossed several times.) Now the path leads us up to the high alpine part of the Pyrenees. The scenery becomes barren and less colourful, delighting my eyes more than Björn's. There is scarcely a single patch of snow to relieve the sea of grey rock. The mountain chain as a whole only houses a few small glaciers, but in winter the snow is plentiful and Gavarnie is one of several ski resorts. We walk to the Lacs d'Opale, the "Opal Lakes", a handful of small acid-blue pools in the midst of all the grey. For me, as a photographer, this austere simplicity of form and colour is a source of inspiration. Björn, who works in oils, would rather have the complex motifs of luxuriant vegetation. The rich diversity of the Pyrenees turns out to be satisfying to us both, and that is one of the conclusions of our trip.

Dolomites

LONG-DISTANCE PATH AND CLIMBING ROUTE

The Tre Cime di Lavaredo, or Drei Zinnen, are the icons of the Dolomites. Their almost 1,640-foot (500-m) tall north faces confront the walkers trekking along the Alta Via 4.

We are walking in shorts with a lightweight day pack on our way to the pride of the area, the scenic trio called the "Tre Cime di Lavaredo" in Italian or "Drei Zinnen" in German. The mountains display their magnificent north faces as we climb towards the Locatelli hut. This view has become something of a symbol for the Dolomites. Mountain walls such as these attracted climbers early on and by the beginning of the twentieth century there was already a group of skilled guides. One of them, Sepp Innerkoffler, became a legend before he died in dramatic circumstances during the First World War. There were battles raging around the Drei Zinnen when Innerkoffler attemptcd a night climb on the north face of the Kleine Zinne in order to run a telephone line up to the Austrian frontier post at the top. When he then went to scale the nearby peak of Paternkopfel he was shot dead by the Italians. At that time the South Tyrol was part of the Austro-Hungarian Empire. Since the Treaty of Saint-Germain in 1919, this province has belonged to Italy. In other words, the Dolomites represent an old meeting place for central and southern European cultures.

On the slope beneath the Paternkopfel there are small man-made caves which were used during the war. We climb up to them and look at the famous north faces, which are aligned when viewed from here. On our way to the hut we can see the trio from the traditional angle from the path below the mountain. The Drei Zinnen now look like three gigantic gravestones, almost 1,640 feet (500m) tall.

These extremely steep mountains in northeastern Italy were formed 25 million years ago from ancient coral reefs which were raised to the skies at the same time as the Alps came into being. The former reefs were shaped by weathering into sharp peaks with rugged slopes peppered with ledges and terraces. The rock has a hardness that is perfect for climbers, and it forms the most impressive landmark a walker can come across. At the end of the eighteenth century the French geologist Déodat de Dolomieu discovered that the rock reacted only slightly to corrosive acid. Apart from calcium there is also a lot of magnesium. In some places nature has replaced that with iron, which makes the rocks more yellow and brown than the whiter limestone. The rock was named "dolomite" after its discoverer. It is very resistant to degradation.

Their geology has made the Dolomites quite different from the Alps. The surface of the rocks is more rough than polished. The peaks are lower and not significantly glaciated, but equally radiant thanks to the constituent rock. But what makes the charm of the Dolomites irresistible in my eyes is the powerful contrast between idyllic beauty and nightmarish precipices. You can become dizzy just looking at the cliff-faces surrounding the path, yet at the same time you can walk tranquilly through the most glorious meadows.

There is no real wilderness left in the Dolomites, although such a convoluted terrain does conceal nooks and crannies where people seldom go. Although the paths have become incredibly popular and the huts are often overcrowded in the high season, you can still find deserted places and moments of solitude. In the heat of summer we reach a remote corner as we follow a path up through the woods in Val de Rinbianco, in the Sesto (Sexten) area. Alone and with no roads or buildings in sight, we reach an alpine meadow full of flowers at the Forcella del'Arghena pass. And across an uninhabited valley we can see the Rautkofel (Monte Rudo) soaring 9,185 feet (2,800m) above sea level. The mountains here are rarely higher than that, but their sharp profiles engender a kind of privacy and in this place we too feel that the landscape is untouched – a nice feeling when experiencing nature.

Further on, we reach the Alta Via 4, one of the Dolomites' eight long-distance paths. These connect the huts with one another and act as high-level trails. The numbers indicate the degree of difficulty: the lower the number the easier the walk. Number 4 is moderately difficult, 56 miles (90km) long, and can be completed in eight days. There is a variant of the paths called a climbing route or *via ferrata*, which offers a cross between walking and mountain climbing. On the steepest passages there are ladders, wires and sometimes footholds carved in the rock. With gaping voids beneath your feet, these passages can be quite hair-raising.

A day later, as we are walking another stretch of the Alta Via 4, past the Fonda Savio hut and on southward, we get to try a *via ferrata*. It leads to a pass 8,530 feet (2,600m) above sea level, in the Cadini di Misurina massif. The descent on the other side of the pass has some steep sections with steel ladders fixed to the rock, which facilitate progress, though there is nothing very titillating about climbing down here.

The mountain in front of us has several jagged pinnacles next to one another. They are shining brightly thanks to the light-coloured dolomite rock and at their foot lies an almost snow-like covering of fallen boulders. In the sun these pure rock formations form a bright and cheery landscape. The Dolomites dazzle not only mountaineers from far and wide, but also artists and writers. Gustav Mahler wrote his ninth symphony during a stay here. Henrik Ibsen too found his way to the area. Franz Kafka wrote some telling lines in a letter to a girlfriend and his words sum up the Dolomites well: "What a land this is! My God if only you were here."

The glory of the meadow flowers is enchanting, here with harebells, hawkbit, buttercups, clover and suchlike. In the background is the Rautkofel peak.

Mont Blanc

THE GRAND TOUR

The stars form a pale line in the night sky above Mont Blanc. This long-exposure photograph was taken while we were camping above Val Veni, opposite the mighty south side of the massif, which is in Italy. The elevation is 9,840 feet (3,000m) from the valley floor to the top.

A dedicated walker would probably say we are cheating, Jill and I, but it is nice not to have to start the walk with a long, steep, uphill slope. The cable railway in Les Houches carries us to the Col de Voza. At some points on the Tour du Mont Blanc you can save yourself some of the walking with the help of cable cars or buses.

On the other side we descend into the Montjoie Valley, past log cabins with overflowing window boxes. The alpine villages remind us of one thing immediately – however wild the mountains seem, we are travelling in an ancient cultivated landscape. During the first day we trudge along asphalt roads and paths that criss-cross between closely packed buildings, pastoral meadows and tall pine woods.

We are following one of the most time-honoured walking trails in the world – the Tour du Mont Blanc. The mountains around us have the reputation of being among the most beautiful, and the name "Mont Blanc" describes not just the highest peak but also a compact chain, a fifteen-mile-long (25-km) magnificent fortress of rock, snow and ice, with 400 distinct peaks and about forty glaciers that have eaten their way into the bedrock and created highs and lows to rival the Himalayas. From Chamonix it is 12,140 vertical feet (3,700 vertical metres) straight up to Mont Blanc.

Across the peaks run the national frontiers of France, Italy and Switzerland, and the mountain range is bounded by seven valleys. These form the natural lines of the Tour du Mont Blanc, abbreviated to TMB, a logo which you see on the signposts along the path. But the path does not just run along the bottom of the valleys. There are long stretches where you walk high up on the mountainsides and you cross at least six strategic passes, depending on which alternatives you choose to walk.

The first person to walk round the massif was Horace Bénédict de Saussure in 1767. He was a well-to-do scientist in Geneva who fell in love with the landscape. Later, he offered a reward for anyone who could climb Mont Blanc. That was the catalyst for what subsequently developed into mountain climbing. In 1783 Gabriel Paccard, a Chamonix doctor, made an unsuccessful attempt with Marc-Théodore Bourrit from Geneva, who later wrote a book about their adventure. In subsequent years each man returned to the heights time and again, as did many others.

A few walkers are en route from the Swiss side to the Fenêtre d'Arpette pass in the depths of the valley. That is where the frontier with France runs.

Les Drus peep out as the clouds reveal the jagged profile of this granite mountain. The books call it "the jewel in the Chamonix crown" and it is considered to be one of the most challenging of all the *aiguilles* (needles) in the Mont Blanc massif.

Paccard coveted the prize and invited Jacques Balmat, an aspiring young crystal collector, to accompany him. Close to the top the men encountered problems and Balmat wanted to turn back, but Paccard persuaded him to go on and at ten past six in the evening on 7th August 1786 the two of them stood on the roof of Europe. For a long time thereafter Mont Blanc remained the highest mountain in the world to have been climbed.

Their success made Bourrit green with envy. In an article he tried to blacken Paccard's name and claimed that Balmat had more or less dragged him to the top. Paccard took the affair philosophically but the damage was done and in the public's eyes only Balmat became a hero. He won international fame and was honoured with a statue of himself in the centre of Chamonix. Only on the occasion of the bicentennial of the first climb was a bronze monument erected in honour of Paccard.

From the Montjoie Valley we walk through the woods to the alpine meadows above the tree-line. We are travelling in the midst of a procession of walkers trudging up to the Col du Bonhomme pass. There we all rest a while, surrounded by boundless views, though it's a little awkward if you want to spend a penny! The best spot if you want to be undisturbed lies right up on a slope above the crowds. On Col des Fours we reach the highest pass on the trail, at 8,890 feet (2,710m) above sea level. From

there you can take a short detour to Tête Nord des Fours, which provides us with a view of the western flank of Mont Blanc. This is where de Saussure stood in 1781, and we do as he did, absorbing the grandiose landscape. The path leads down into the Vallée des Glaciers, the shortest of the seven valleys, but we stay on the slope to pitch our tent. The twilight invites us to camp where we can see all of the mountains. The nearest hut is down in the bottom of the valley – not an attractive position.

The next pass, the Col de la Seigne, forms the frontier with Italy. It is a very old track and was probably used by Hannibal when he brought his elephants over the Alps in 219BC. On the other side we see for the first time the imposing south slope of Mont Blanc. Since the good weather is holding out, we dare to chance a higher route than the normal path. Mont Fortin is our goal. The alternative routes add an extra spice to the TMB. You can actually tailor your walk to your own ability and the prevailing weather.

On a fairly untrodden path we scramble up toward a new pass and from there look deep into Italy. The path continues beneath a mountain that hides Mont Blanc, and then we reach a viewpoint which induces us to linger for a long time. The south face of Mont Blanc is so impressive that I would compare it with the Himalayas. Beneath our feet lies the Val Veni, green with inviting meadowlands. Like an enormous walrus head, with two small glaciers for teeth, dark rock divided like wrinkled skin with a domed forehead uppermost, the Alps' highest mountain rises 9,840 feet (3,000m) in one sweep from the valley floor. The landscape of Europe doesn't come more majestic than this. And to top it all, we have the privilege of being able to camp with this panorama as our neighbour.

As we eat breakfast in front of the tent in the hot sun, the first walkers from the Elisabeth Soldini hut down in the Val Veni go by. The TMB continues along the side of the valley opposite Mont Blanc and all the paths are easy to walk and the views more dramatic than ever. The peaks inspire us with their beguiling shapes and beautiful names: Aiguille Noire de Peuterey, Dent du Géant (Giant's Tooth), Grandes Jorasses. It is pure poetry.

In Courmayeur heavy clouds gather and the next day we take the bus to the end of the road in Val Ferret and then walk toward Switzerland. Several thunderstorms pass over the mountains and we reach the village of La Fouly in the rain. There a *gîte d'étape*, a private hostel, is our accommodation for the night. The Swiss section of the TMB is tamer in character, or at least that's how it feels as we stroll through the park-like woods in Val Ferrat toward the spa town of Chamonix. Then the landscape rises to a new crescendo, and to our delight so does the weather. We choose the high route over the Fenêtre d'Arpette pass. The tourist procession wakes again and on the last slope up to a notch in the mountain ridge we have to queue a little. But the mood is upbeat as a small crowd pushes safely between the rock walls. The path on the other side is just as steep, and further down, we walk down a lengthy slope, parallel with the dazzling Trient glacier.

Previous pages: From the Lac Blanc you can look across the Chamonix Valley straight into the heart of Mont Blanc. The Mer du Glace glacier stretches out a tongue of ice in front of the massive north face of the Grandes Jorasses, and to the left stands the Petit Dru in sharp profile.

Mont Blanc and the black tip of
Aiguille Noire du Peuterey are
reflected in little Lac Chécroui
on the Italian side.

There is one more pass before we return to France. On the Col de Balme a hut
offers much longed-for refreshment before we descend again, to the Chamonix
Valley. Unfortunately there is cloud lying over the mountains and we can see nothing
of the views, but the next day the weather is perfect again. We stride at a comfortable
pace up to the Aiguillette d'Argentière. The TMB follows the wide mountain ledges
on the Massif des Aiguilles Rouges, high above the valley. After a tricky passage, on
ladders fixed to the rock, we reach Lac Blanc (White Lake) whose shores are alive
with people. In the background stands Mont Blanc (White Mountain), packed
in snow and ice, and with our binoculars we can trace Paccard's and Balmat's
route to the top. Poor Paccard! What a farce he got himself into!

The last day rounds off the tour with a well-prepared lunch and good wine in
Brévent, which according to many has the best view of Mont Blanc. From there we
walk steeply down to Les Houches to complete the circle of the great Alpine tour.

Crete

THE SHEPHERDS' HEIGHTS

The mists rise from the deep Samaria Gorge as we follow a narrow stony path 4,920 feet (1,500m) above sea level. Juniper and cedar thickets grow on the slopes of the light-coloured mountains in Lefka Ori.

Let's go to Crete for a holiday in the sun, suggests my wife. I think that's a great idea provided we do more than just lie on the beach. Mountain walking for instance. So this sudden whim leads us to embark on a charter plane with boots on our feet and a backpack full of outdoor gear. Our destination is Chania, a town on the western half of the island. There we check in to the hotel room included in the trip, which is to be our "base camp".

Crete is a splendid island for walkers. There are impressive mountain landscapes, which are perhaps the most dramatic Greece has to offer. The highest massif is Psiloritis, 8,060 feet (2,456m) above sea level situated in the centre of the island, but it is Lefka Ori, (the White Mountains) further west that have made their name as the walkers' promised land, a trackless area about 18 miles by 18 miles (30km by 30km). The tallest point is called Pékhnes, which is just 10 feet (3m) lower than Psiloritis. People joke about the fans who want to build a big cairn on top to make Lefka Ori the highest peaks on Crete.

The mountains are made of limestone. The higher sections are covered with snow in winter and the pale rock reflects the sun's light so strongly that the mountains look white even in summer. Hence their name. More than thirty peaks are over 6,560 feet (2,000m) high and the whole range displays a strong relief against the Mediterranean, which is just 6 miles (10 km) to the south. About fifty deep ravines cut into the limestone; the most famous of these is Samaria Gorge, which is a popular destination for day trips.

We are here in the first week of November and Samaria Gorge is closed for the season, but that doesn't matter to us because our goal is the White Mountains. With a hire car we drive to the end of the road at Xiloskalo, where the tour down to the well-known gorge begins. From here you can also follow a path that leads across Lefka Ori. To begin with we plod along a winding, stony path to the Kallergi hut, which offers board and lodging if you book in advance.

The weather is sunny and sweat runs off us as we trudge up the slopes with our backpacks packed for camping. The view from the hut is impressive, particularly looking down to the depths of Samaria Gorge. The mountains we can see have rounded crowns but steep sides. A scrubby *maquis* consisting of brushwood and thorny plants is spread thinly across the slopes.

The stony path leads us deeper into the remote Lefka Ori where the mountains look disconcertingly similar and the topography lacks sharp profiles. Long, undulating, bare ridges dominate the panorama in every direction. The landscape looks deserted and when a few elderly shepherds come walking toward us, laughing merrily, we are surprised. In halting German we try to understand one another. They seem to be on their way down, their work done. There are plenty of sheep and – above all – goats, but unfortunately the grazing of the animals has taken its toll on the natural vegetation. When the shepherds have passed we are once again alone in the barren mountain landscape, until we suddenly see three hunters of birds just a few miles further on. Communication with them is just as primitive, but we understand that they, too, are on their way down. We had not expected to meet local

Cypress trees grow wild on the mountain slopes. This tree is common throughout the Mediterranean region.

A shepherd lying down to rest on the thorny bushes of the *maquis*. The main form of animal life in the mountains is goats, whose eating habits make considerable inroads into the vegetation.

inhabitants up here. When they disappear, silence reigns as dusk falls quickly and we find a suitable place to camp among the dry bracken, a stone's throw from the path.

Lefka Ori is demanding walking territory. There is water in only a few wells so you have to carry plenty with you – the altitude, the heat and the exertion all make you thirsty. The weather can be changeable. Under the summer sun it is scorching hot, but sometimes storms can turn the walk into a rugged adventure. There are not many paths and often they are completely unmarked. Away from them it is easy to get lost. All of these factors make for a wild region, and thus an attractive one for walkers – in my view, at any rate.

At dawn the next day we are sitting on a rock, looking down into Samaria Gorge, where wisps of cloud swirl around. Then, we walk on along the path called the "Europe Trail", which continues some tens of miles across the mountains to the village of Anapolis. When we reach a saddle between the peaks of Mávri and Melidaú we can see that the landscape is nothing more than a broad, high, alpine desert with smooth and beautiful earth-coloured slopes, sparse plants, a lot of stone and rounded mountains. Lefka Ori is, quite simply, a side of Crete very different from the one shown in the tourist brochures.

Pirin Mountains

UNEXPECTED CIRCUS TOUR

From Vichren mountain we can look across the deserted granite landscape of the national park to the triangular peak of Kamenica, at 9,260 feet (2,822m) above sea level. In the foreground lies a mountain hollow or *cirque*.

"Pirin has the most rugged mountains in Bulgaria," says our guide Kostadin. "I go trekking there as often as I can. The woods are wonderful and the mountains steep. There are lots of lakes below the precipices, like small sparkling jewels. We Bulgarians love lakes and there aren't many in this country. For us this area is an untamed landscape."

My companion and I nod politely. It is a joy to hear local patriots declaim their enthusiasm and Kostadin seems to know what he is talking about. He offers a lot of tips as we eat our lunch poring over a map, but we are going to trek by ourselves and cross the mountains in a week. The Pirin traverse follows the ridges running north to south, across the storm-lashed range of mountains which lie between the cultivated parts of the country. For those who don't know any better, the landscape looks surprisingly alpine and unspoilt. Here granite shale and limestone lie side by side. The limestone is pale in colour and the granite peaks loom dark. While the limestone area is adorned with rare plants, the granite terrain is botanically poor.

Kostadin drives us to Vichren hut, which lies on the periphery of this alpine landscape. Where the mountainsides narrow to a deep valley there stands a haunted castle of stone, surrounded by pine forest. Being mid-June, the season has scarcely begun. We set off on an afternoon walk, following a steep path past pine thickets. The colours are muted, the grass bleached like straw, the mountainsides chequered with patches of snow. The early summer is a spartan yet bustling time. Carpets of wild crocus grow in a meadow. The path leads up to a basin below steep mountain walls. The contours in Pirin are sharp, thanks to small niche glaciers, long since disappeared, which have carved out the landscape. We walk from the basin up to a little plateau and then there is only the pale limestone cone of the summit ahead of us.

From Bulgaria's second highest mountain, Vichren, 9,565 feet (2,915m) above sea level, we can see what a fantastic area we are about to explore. Peak after peak extends to the south in the granite area, like an untamed Balkan empire, not endless but undulating and uplifting. And in the other direction runs the narrowest of ridges leading to the pyramid-shaped limestone peaks to the north.

Here on Vichren we start our traverse of Pirin and walk south into the granite area. From the hut the path winds between thickets of mountain pine and leads into a basin-like glacier niche. On the map this is called the "Bandiriski Cirkus" or *cirque* and we decide to christen the Pirin crossing the "circus tour", which takes you into a basin, over a mountain and down into a basin on the other side.

It begins to rain then stops again, but the clouds are here to stay. From the valley it is 1,310 feet (400m) up to the top of Vazela, where the path continues at a higher level. We tramp across mushy snow up to the ridge and then the thunder starts to rumble. Suddenly this place feels menacing. We immediately abandon the high path and cross straight down into the next cirque, accompanied by several claps of thunder. There, we pitch our tent beside a small tarn at the same time as it begins to snow lightly and the thunder dies away. We feel snug here and have no complaints.

The improvised route continues beneath the ridge where the path runs. We scramble on to another glacier niche and join up with the path again. Immediately the next climb begins while the clouds draw in again, and just for a moment we are conscious of the void beneath us. In spite of the 7,875-foot (2,400-m) altitude the mountain pine still keeps us company – even at the top we find a specimen between the barren rocks. These bushes imbue the landscape with a unique character.

The Pirin traverse is a real switchback and the topography is fun. The mountains are neither too easy nor too hard. They lie like pearls on a string and are not too big to cross in an hour or so with a full pack. They offer the walker rapid changes of scene, but we can't see much today, we just feel the variations in our legs and bodies.

The Tevnoto Ezero lake is the heart of Pirin. The ice has not yet melted and the thick snow together with the raw weather means that we appreciate the hut close to the shore. In the main room we meet a middle-aged man who can speak English. Alexander Marinov has studied in the USA and is besotted with Pirin. "I'm going up Mount Orlovec to see the three lakes in the Kremenski cirque," he says. He shows us a postcard on the wall. "That's it, the most beautiful place in the whole of Bulgaria. Have you seen Kamenica yet?" We shake our heads, not even sure where it is. "An imposing house of a mountain," he says. "You can see it from the doorway."

The next day dawns in sparkling light and finally Kamenica emerges, a veritable cathedral of dark rock, 9,260 feet (2,822m) above sea level. We stroll around our barren surroundings, walk up the easy climbs and study the plants that have ventured out between the patches of snow: dwarf primula, spring snowflake and masses of crocus.

Alexander suggests a different route from the one we had intended. "To the south, the Pirin traverse is tamer and less interesting," he says and marks a more rewarding route on the map. We leave Tevno Ezero right away and head west, across a pass into the Kasja Dolina valley, where we camp in beautiful meadows surrounded by precipitous mountains. This is a place that typifies wilderness.

Previous pages: A snowfall in June has powdered the landscape in the Glavniski cirque. Pirin takes its name from the Slav god of thunder, Perun. According to myth, he was crossing the land with a sack full of huge rocks which proved too heavy for him and fell to the ground, forming Pirin.

The Tevno Ezero hut lies in the heart of the area. In summer it is often full of walkers. Bulgarians love to walk in the mountains.

Our route now takes us through inhabited areas and the path leads to fertile land on which cattle graze. As we round a grass mound, three big sheepdogs jump to their feet and rush at us drooling. Luckily, I have a sturdy staff with me and, as the beasts get close, I swing it round and automatically counter-attack, surprising myself as much as them. The dogs stop short and bark hungrily while I throw stones. That drives them away, but they follow us for a short distance, growling.

The Kamenica hut is well hidden in the forest. From there a jeep track leads down to a little village from where a road continues to the town of Sandanski. A few national park wardens are sitting in the empty building. One of them can speak German and tells us of a shortcut, but we miss that and after a while the wardens appear again in their Russian-made jeep. They offer us a lift and tell us they are looking for poachers. The jeep continues on to Sandanski, which we reach just in time for the evening bus to Sofia. The end of our tour, which has been almost as much improvised as planned, is unexpectedly simple.

Isle of Skye

BLUE SKY ABOVE THE ISLE OF CLOUDS

In the clear evening we see the light fading over the grazing grounds at Glenbrittle and Sgurr Alasdair, the highest peak in the Black Cuillin. Norwegian Vikings occupied Skye for 400 years and called it Skuy Island, which means the "Isle of Clouds". In Gaelic its name is Eilean a' Cheo.

"There are only two kinds of weather," says climber Bob Whittow as we meet on a peak in the Black Cuillin. "Most days it's rain. That's what you have to expect. Then, when the weather changes like it has today, you're happy and you forgive the climate."

I know what he means. The "black mountains" in the Black Cuillin are basking in steady high pressure and the trek into the massif is turning into a carefree odyssey. It begins with an early call in Glenbrittle, at the foot of the mountain. The Black Cuillin lies on the south side of the Isle of Skye, which is part of the Inner Hebrides. Here, there are the most dramatic mountains in Great Britain. Climbers flock to the rock-faces and walkers are drawn here, too. The jagged massif and the pastoral grazing grounds falling away towards the Atlantic form a rare combination of coast, human habitation and fells.

I am here on holiday with my family and I have a day to myself. My route is called a traverse and it follows the rocky ridges that form a horseshoe round the deep valley cauldron of Coire Lagan, in the depths of which lies a charming little pool. The traverse leads from one peak to another, up and down the narrow cuttings between them. For long stretches it passes along narrow rocky ledges. At the highest point it rises almost 3,280 feet (1000m) above Glenbrittle, and the walking varies between steep climbs and easy scrambles. Since I am walking without a rope, extra care must be taken on the most exposed passages. My equipment consists of a "bum bag" with a camera and a tiny backpack with a thermos flask and sandwiches; I am dressed in a T-shirt, shorts and boots.

Thanks to this thin clothing and light pack I feel a rare closeness to the mountains. Usually one is laden down for peak walks. The rock is almost scorching hot and the landscape is showing its best side in the fine weather. Black Cuillin is synonymous with wild features – tangled slopes and jagged pinnacles. The Atlantic, with its islands and the sea horizon in the other direction, is the embodiment of freedom. Together the scenes bolster my feelings of personal independence and humility in the face of nature. Also, when I can climb simply without rope or safety gear (which often weigh you down) and can feel the rock with my hands as I hoist myself up without acrobatics, I feel a physical affinity with the mountain. This simplicity on a challenging mountain, the beauty of the landscape, and the weather contribute to an experience of nature the like of which I have never had before.

Sgurr Alasdair is the highest peak in the massif, 3,260 feet (993m) above sea level. There I meet Bob Whittow and three other climbers. They have driven out to Skye from Edinburgh to take advantage of the weekend's high pressure. "A chance like this is not to be missed for any self-respecting climber," he says. The group is going the same way as me, so we join forces.

The Black Cuillin is made up of the hard, dark rock, gabbro, which gives the area its special character. Its unique quality becomes clear when you compare it with nearby massifs, which are rounder and lighter in colour – especially the Red Cuillin with its sharp granite domes. Of the two types of rock found in the island's wet climate, it is gabbro that weathers best – that is why it has jagged peaks. Gabbro is magnetic and it upsets compasses. In some places soft volcanic magma has penetrated the cracks in the gabbro, forming gaps in the ridges.

I reach one of the gaps, below the top of Sgurr Mhic Coinnch. On the other side the Scots press on, without a rope, along a ramp called Collies Ledge, which runs diagonally up the mountainside to the highest part of the peak. This passage looks dangerous but the metre-wide ramp proves to be safe to walk on even without a rope, although the drop sets the butterflies fluttering in my stomach.

Place names around here are of Gaelic origin. Sgurr Alasdair means "Alexander's peak", after the sheriff Alexander Nicholson who was the first to climb it, in 1873. This peak is one of twenty in the Black Cuillin which rise over 3,000 feet (914m) above sea level. That is a magic number in British mountaineering! In this country people talk respectfully of "munros", which means mountains over 3,000 feet. The term comes from Sir Hugh Munro, who in 1891 issued a table of Scotland's peaks above that height. He wanted to bring order and method to the topography but little suspected the effect his tables would have. He started a new sport – climbing munros. A mountaineer in Great Britain must set foot on as many munros as possible. Sir Hugh identified 545 peaks of the magic height and 277 of these are considered freestanding massifs. Even I manage to collect five munros on this one glorious day.

Bob tries to get me to climb one more, the Inaccessible Pinnacle, which is a phallic rock column perched on the shoulder of yet another munro called Sgurr Dearg. It can only be reached by climbing a short but very exposed path. We have a heated discussion about the risks of mountaineering before I decline the offer of joining their roped team. My interest in demanding climbing is not so great when the family is waiting for me down in the tent. So we go our separate ways.

A climber stands on the brink on Sgurr Alasdair. The mountain in the background is called Bla Bheinn or sometimes Blaven, meaning the Blue Mountain. It lies 5 miles (8 km) away and in the far distance the hills of the Scottish mainland can be seen.

Sarek

VALLEY OF THE ELKS

The Bielloriehppe fell rises 4,265 feet (1300m) above the fertile delta of Rapadalen. Sarek has three big delta areas that are built up from the sediment produced by melting glaciers. In the thick birch forest at the valley bottom wildlife is abundant.

At last we can see one of the kings of Rapadalen really close by. The big elk bull comes lumbering through a forest of gnarled birch trunks. Stately and resolute, he comes straight toward us, seemingly indifferent to our presence. No need to stand stock still as he passes just over ten yards (9m) away from us, to continue on between the stunted trees in his wild kingdom. We can whisper to one another and swap camera positions, and he doesn't care a jot. His broad, spade-shaped antlers sway a little, but the mighty body yields to nothing. This is his country. It is the rutting season and reticence has gone by the board. A combatant with burnished antlers is lying in the grass a few miles further on. Around him stands a circle of wildlife photographers. Everyone wants a close-up of this regal bull.

In Sarek National Park live perhaps the biggest of Europe's elks. The vegetation there offers them excellent grazing and they thrive protected in their inaccessible fell valleys, where hunting was banned as early as 1909, when Sweden created the first national parks in Europe. With that, Sarek became a legend – referred to as the last wilderness, a paradise for wildlife and an Eldorado for trekkers, it was eventually named a World Heritage site. Sarek's southern parts have deep valleys with luxuriant forest, marshy delta landscapes and a wealth of fauna. In the north it is more barren and the valleys are treeless, with heath, meadow and stony ground, and less wildlife. But above all Sarek has steep mountain massifs, glaciers, roaring rivers and blue-green lakes – constituting an imposing landscape that defies description.

For a long time Sarek has meant a great deal to me. This is where I learned to trek and to appreciate wildlife. After almost forty years and so many journeys in the area that my memory can no longer distinguish them all, and after trekking through fantastic mountain regions on other continents, I still consider Sarek to be one of the world's outstanding areas for trekking. I feel at home here, which of course colours my view, but Sarek also has many magnificent qualities that everyone can appreciate.

The contrasts. In a short space the paths range between high and low altitudes. The plateau at Luottolako is sterile, like a desert near the North Pole. The birch forest in Rapadalen, 6 miles (10km) away, grows as tangled as a tropical rainforest.

The light. Constantly changing with the seasons. Light summer nights with the midnight sun. Dark winter days with the northern lights.

The weather. Usually changeable, exposed to Atlantic storms with a lot of rain, quite a lot of sunshine, heatwaves and sometimes snowfall, even in the summer.

Emptiness. No huts to stay in, no marked trails. Trips become minor expeditions. You have to carry everything in backpacks and you need to allow at least a week.

But most of all Sarek is topography – exciting topography. The shape of the land is ideally suited to trekking, you can see that from the map. Sarek generates enticing cartography. The high fells with their glaciers are concentrated in the composite massifs that border the valleys. This gives the map of Sarek some similarity to town maps, if such a comparison can be made for a natural wilderness. The valleys are like roads, they cross one another and are in turn narrow then wide, while the mountains stand like apartment blocks between them. It's an attractive area on the map, but the trips really bring it to life.

That is why my companions and I do not stay in Rapadalen to track the wildlife. Bears and wolverines are also found here, but we are here as trekkers and want to walk through Sarek. We wish to see the variations in the landscape from one valley to the next, find new patches of wild strawberries, climb peaks, look out over and get to know the whole area. The knowledge that the animals have a sanctuary makes us happy. Seeing them is a bonus, but it is the mountains that drive us on.

A few days later we go on a new journey in Jilavagge, one of the national park's least visited valleys. At this time of year – September – the place is completely empty.

Previous pages: While dusk lays its mist over Sarek's fells, two walkers have climbed to the top of Gådoktjåhkkå, 6,325 feet (1,928m) above sea level to the south of Rapadalen. Among the peaks it is easy to distinguish Sadelberget (Saddle Mountain) in the middle. Sarek's famous pioneer, Axel Hamberg, stood here in 1901. We can still see the same view that he saw. A timeless landscape.

An elk bull with burnished antlers moves majestically across one of Rapadalen's marshes. During the winter most of the elks leave Sarek and go down to the pine forests further east.

In the autumn the water levels are often low. A rambling path follows the shore of the lagoons and rivers in Rapadalen.

In the height of summer a couple of thousand people travel through the most popular valleys, but when the mountains are powdered with snow and winter is approaching, very few people come this way. So now is the best time: no mosquitoes, just vibrant autumn colours and crystal clear days.

We climb high up in the fells and try to identify familiar old peaks from a hitherto unseen angle. When one peak has been spotted, it is easier to identify the others. Mountainous terrain makes you want to work out where you are. That is one of the driving forces behind trekking. That, plus the wildlife draw us back to Sarek time after time. Only the short-lived jet trails across the sky indicate that the area is part of a populated planet.

Kebnekaise

THE FROSTY FELL

The desolate January daylight is as bitter as it is blue. On the left, Tarfaladalen, Kebnekaise's stately north peak, is clad in icy armour, while the overnight hut can be glimpsed in the valley below. The northern Lapp spelling for Sweden's highest mountain is Giebnegaise.

The thermometer is showing -30°C, and Nikkaluokta, the gateway to Kebnekaise, is living up to its reputation as the coldest place in Lapland. The air scorches, scratching the face like cats' claws and burning like brandy in the throat. The cold of the fells stings and is quite unlike the raw cold which prevails on the coast at far higher temperatures.

We are here, Örjan Nyström and I, in the middle of January to ski to Sweden's highest mountain. Of our own volition, perhaps we should add. At this time of year it's easy to believe that only masochists would be found on the fells, but midwinter has a charm of its own. The weak light creates a strange kind of day and the emptiness is bracing. There are not many people about. If you meet someone it is natural to fall into conversation. We meet Lasse Sarri as he comes in on his snow-scooter. "The weather has been mild this year," he says. "A couple of weeks ago we had torrential rain. It's very changeable nowadays".

There is a reindeer herd in the valley and during the day he has helped to drive them together. But generally you don't find many reindeer herdsmen in Lapland.

Two days later the temperature has risen by 30 degrees. We travel from the empty tourist complex at the foot of Kebnekaise up to Tarfaladalen. The skiing is heavy going, the visibility poor. The snow keeps giving way and we have to trudge forward, lifting our knees high. From a hut where we will spend the night we later take a trip up to Storglaciären (the Big Glacier). The snow has become firmer and the going is tougher, but the grip is better. In spite of the clear skies the temperature remains within a reasonable range, at about -15°C. At altitudes above 3,280 feet (1,000m) above sea level, the cold is rarely as extreme as down in Nikkaluokta at 1,640 feet (500m). Cold air is heavy and sinks down.

A fox's tracks punctuate the frozen crust beneath Södra Klippberget (South Rocky Mountain). We climb steeply up to the glacier and suddenly feel as if we are in the Himalayas. On the vertical mountain wall below Kebnekaise the snow hangs like whipped cream. It makes the mountain resemble an ice-clad, rocky citadel in the highest mountain range in the world.

The highest section of the glacier adjoins the upper sections of the Isfall glacier and the Kebnepakte glacier. Together they form a highland landscape of ice with two saddle passes offering a gently undulating ski route at 4,920 feet (500m). It looks tempting. As the scant daylight fades we glide on our skis to the outermost pass where we linger for a moment on a narrow snow ridge that turns into a steep, convex, north-facing slope. Down in the depths lies Lake Tarfal under its white blanket, and on the other side of this narrow valley lies the most immense peak of them all, Kaskasapakte, swathed in hoar frost. The landscape is surprisingly alpine for Lapland, but by turning our heads 180 degrees towards the east, we can see a change of character and it becomes more typical. Behind the Norra Klippberget (North Rocky Mountain) the lowlands stretch out in wave upon wave of softly rounded undulations. We think we can make out the outline of Mount Dundret in the far distance, surely 93 miles (150km) away.

Örjan has skied a little way away from me and stopped; silhouetted against the snowy ridge he looks like the only person in the world. There is no other two-legged creature between us and Nikkaluokta, 12 miles (20km) away, of that we are sure. It's probably just as empty for many miles to the west, as far as the Norwegian coast. And not a breath of wind disturbs the peace which prevails.The frozen colours of the sky heighten the feeling of isolation and vulnerability. There is warmth in our souls but cold in our bodies after standing still for too long.

A long downhill slope awaits us. It is only two o'clock in the afternoon, but if we want to beat the darkness we need to get a move on. The Isfall Glacier slopes down steeply, like a smooth piste. We slalom between the ice towers and the Södra Klippberget and finally reach the hut, barely able to see.

When we leave Tarfala a few days later, the weather is clear, cold and still. Our journey turns into a lesson in the physics of cold. At the start, at 3,610 feet (1,100m), it is -10°C. In the Laddtjovagge valley which lies 1,310 feet (400m) lower, the thermometer shows -15°C, and then the temperature drops to -25°C as we continue our way east. In spite of the cold, or rather thanks to the cold, we have been blessed with the kinder side of the midwinter climate of the fells: its wonderful daylight and inner peace. We daren't contemplate the bad side. Just a week later we read in the newspaper of dreadful, hurricane-force winds, 260 feet (80m) a second, in Tarfadalen. A house next to the one we slept in was blown to pieces by the wind. Just think ...

It is -35°C when we meet the reindeer herdsman Lasse Sarri. He is one of thirteen brothers and sisters in the Sarri family. Their father, Nils Sarri, established the settlement of Nikkaluokta in 1910, with a few other Lapp families.

Laugavegur

A TRAIL OF COLOURS

The 60-mile (100-km) long river of Markarfljot has a colourful, almost 655-foot (200-m) deep, canyon close to Laugavegur. It was probably formed by a catastrophic flood 2,500 years ago. Today, meltwater from Myrdalsjökull runs through the gorge.

"Landmannalauger" means "a hot bath for country folk" and that is precisely how we start – with a dip. The weather is bleak but that's fine when you've just reached a hot spring! The mountains form a ring of picturesque heights around this natural hot tub. From the spring runs a hot stream that joins a cold one, and in this mixture of waters you can choose your own bath temperature. We sit in the water like frogs for a long time and nobody climbs out into the bitter wind until their skin has begun to turn to sponge.

This place in the interior of Iceland is where Laugavegur begins. Here there are not only hot springs but an entire natural art gallery. Behind it stands Torfajökull, a rumbling volcano with two smaller plateau glaciers on its "crown". In the last hundred thousand years its many eruptions have sculpted and painted a landscape, the like of which we have never seen. A rock called rhyolite is responsible for the colours. It derives from a magma that has crystallized slowly at great depths beneath the earth's crust. It has been further embellished by trapped gases. Where we are walking the heights are washed in wonderful pastel colours, often pale yellow, pink or grey-blue. And where the magma has been thrust to the surface, it has cooled so quickly that black volcanic glass – obsidian – has formed. We can see that, too.

Rust-red patches around iron-bearing, percolating water are also part of this spectrum, as are narrow bands of verdigris-coloured moss and olive-coloured mats of another kind of moss growing on the dark lava gravel. There are also sulphur springs that form pale pustules on the ground. It all makes up an enormous patchwork quilt.

From the first moment we realize that Laugavegur is a trail for beauty-lovers, and we start our trek with a day trip around Landmannalauger. We walk into the narrow cleft of Stóra-Brandsgil, which has ragged scree slopes in all shades of brown. Here the landscape looks like the planet Mars. We then have an easy climb up the blue-black mountain of Bláhnúkur. From the top we have an overview of the pattern of the landscape. The crumbly mountainsides are striped with small ravines where there are lines of unmelted snow; between the stripes you can glimpse the whole range of rhyolite. Nature has rarely created a more beautiful work of art.

Previous pages: The landscape is barren where the path swings close to Kaldaklofsfjöll and its glacier. The mountain is part of the ring of ridges which form Torfajökull's great collapsed crater or caldera. There has been no eruption in these parts since the fifteenth century.

The combination of strong colours, suggestive shapes and austere vegetation is photogenic. This trio of melting snow, iron-oxide deposits and green moss is found at Jökulgil.

When we have walked up the path from Laugahraun we can see a big lava field to the north and the steaming hot springs billowing up on the edge of it. Beyond the lava field lies Landmannalauger where our walk started.

Icelandic trekkers consider Laugavegur to be a truly royal trail. In the 1960s members of Iceland's tourist association discovered the remarkable landscape around the Torfajökull. They started organizing regular walks, and a few decades later the idea for a trail from Landmannalauger to Thorsmork came to fruition. The great glacial rivers were one obstacle that had to be overcome. Bridges, as well as huts, were built. In 1978 Laugavegur was inaugurated and quickly became popular.

The first stage takes us to Reykjafjöll mountain. The path picks its way across open, stony ground. On the whole, the trail is so easy to walk that you scarcely need to watch where you are putting your boots. Today's section is barely 6 miles (10km), but it rises 1,640 feet (500m) and at the beginning crosses a thick layer of lava. This is called Laugahraun and extends close to Landmannalauger. The volcano erupted in 1480. Since then mosses and lichens have clothed the angular boulders. Where the lava cover ends, the vapour from a sulphur spring billows and steam spurts out of small holes. We can hear it hissing and smell rotten eggs.

From this seething place the path climbs up a steep scree slope to a deserted high plateau that is part of the highest section of Torfajökull. The weather deteriorates and there is a passing flurry of snow before we reach the hut of Hraftinnusker on the other side of a saddle between two ridges. The hut is full of other walkers but that is no problem for us because we have our tent.

During the night the cloud cover lifts and our journey continues in better weather across a new stony plateau enclosed by pale ravines. Directly to the west, far beyond the multicoloured ground close by, the Hekla volcano rises but the path goes on to the south, up to a new pass with even more steaming springs. There we cross a natural boundary in the landscape. The terrain suddenly changes shape. Further on it is more undulating, darker in colour and in the far distance rises Myrdalsjökull, an impressive dome of shimmering ice. Between the hump-backed mountains in that direction we can also see a big lake that looks interesting. After a steep descent we reach Alftavatn (the Lake of the Mute Swans), where a hut marks the end of this leg of the trek.

Here Laugavegur crosses a fairly well-used gravel path, and a few jeeps are parked by the hut. We could have done without them, and as the next leg runs parallel with the road we choose our own route along the south side of Alftavatn. Further on, however, we find that the Blafjallakvisl constitutes far too great an obstacle and we follow the river back to the road. Our own path turns out to be a major detour, but in consolation we get to see the west side of Storasula, a very unusual mountain. The slopes are covered with such densely growing moss that it clothes the mountain in a livid green jacket.

After following the road for 3 miles (5km) and seeing jeeps driving by with clouds of dust in their wake, the path turns off onto an empty and desolate stony desert where we walk in gentle curves between sterile hills. The day ends with a long descent to the hut at Botnar. In a fertile little gorge by a stream below the hut you can camp among grass, angelica and other flowers.

From here you can take an excursion to the Markarfljot river which has carved the land into a spectacular, several-hundred-feet deep and very colourful gorge where fulmars swoop between the ledges. We walk forward to the very edge, which makes us feel dizzy, and wonder why this immense canyon is not one of the best known in the world. The answer is, of course, that it is rather inaccessible and is not often seen.

The next leg leads us via a sturdy bridge that has been built over a side branch of the gorge. The river thunders awe-inspiringly beneath our feet. Ahead of Thorsmork we have to wade through a few rivers, but that is easy with the low water level, and finally we enter thicker vegetation. The leafy birch forest is a sight for sore eyes, as we have begun to long for some greenery.

Laugavegur officially ends in Thorsmork, but our journey is not over yet. We continue on up to the pass between Eyjafallajökull and Myrdalsjökull and the landscape now becomes even more alpine. The path is bordered by precipitous slopes and deep ravines, and in the background dazzling ice fields shimmer. On the last day we stroll down to the most beautiful waterfall on the island. The Skogá river flows full-width over a rocky ledge and drops 195 feet (60m) to the coastal plain below. Not exactly Niagara, but still an impressive curtain of water falling headlong down, gladdening the heart of anyone who loves nature. By extending our journey with these two extra days at Skogáfoss, we experience the full gamut of changing scenes between the interior of Iceland and the Atlantic coast. It is worth absolutely every minute.

The Skogáfoss waterfall thunders down and sprays a fine mist over the onlooker. This is where our journey ends, close to the circular path which goes right round Iceland.

High Atlas

THE BERBERS' MOUNTAIN

The moon lights up the new snow on the peaks of this 13,125-foot (4,000-m) high mountain ridge called Mgoun, and the star-strewn sky creates streaks on the twenty-minute photographic exposure. Almost 3,280 feet (1,000m) below the peaks stretches the high plateau of Tacheddid.

We've heard of Toubkal, the highest peak in Morocco and the Atlas Mountains, but where's Mgoun? Björn Esping, who suggested this tour, shows me a map of the mountain range. We know that Mgoun, at 13,325 feet (4,060m) above sea level, is the second highest peak, and we finally locate it near Marrakech. Hamish Brown, a British expert on the area whom Björn has contacted, recommends that we trek here. In this part of the Atlas Mountains the Berbers still live in the traditional way, their villages undisturbed by roads. The landscape is different from Toubkal, where the peaks are steep and consist of hard crystalline shale. Mgoun is built up of easily weathered sedimentary rock. That is why there are extensive ridges and long slopes, and also deeply carved canyons. Remarkable, I think, as I become more and more fascinated by the narrow gorges.

It takes a whole day to drive by Land Rover from Marrakech to our starting point – the village of Agouti in the Bougoumez valley. From here our journey is organized by our guide, Muhammed. One cook, four muleteers and five mules are provided by the village and we four trekkers only need to carry a little backpack each. Our group straggles out of the cultivated land of the valley and on into a narrower valley which points us towards snow-powdered mountain tops. We are immediately struck by the sharp contrasts. The Bougoumez valley looks fertile, even now in October when the apples are being harvested. On the other hand the mountainsides seem terribly barren, with fallen brown scree and dark cliffs. During our journey we realize that this contrast between the valley bottom and the heights is typical of the Atlas Mountains, whose name comes from the Greek god who held up the firmament and was turned into Mount Atlas.

As in the Himalayas, a lot of people use the paths. The Berbers are an old ethnic group in the High Atlas. They came here possibly via the Straits of Gibraltar, but their origins are uncertain. In the village of Ait Said young girls are threshing grain. Others are washing clothes in a stream; others still, just walking. Past the village the landscape becomes more desolate. Dense thickets surround us for a long time but open up as we get higher and further into the mountains.

On the path we meet an uninterrupted stream of Berbers, who make up the majority of the population in Morocco. They have their own language, although many of them speak Arabic. Their culture has existed in the Atlas Mountains for around 5,000 years.

A young Berber girl walks between the clay-brick houses in Megdaz, 6,430 feet (1960m) above sea level. The village is considered one of the most beautiful in the Atlas Mountains. The houses are a bright ochre colour and blend into the mountainside, but they seldom withstand the sporadic, sudden downpours for more than fifty years.

A flock of sheep is grazing on a meadow, watched by a lone shepherd near a stone hut. There are gnarled juniper trees on the steep slopes.

Before its gets dark we take a look at the small ravine in which the Assif Arous valley ends. Canyons are often interesting features, but in this mountain chain they are treacherous. If there is heavy rain the water level can rise rapidly and wash away everything from the depths of the ravine. There are sometimes fatal accidents, and lingering between the overhanging walls of Assif Arous feels both exciting and uncomfortable. Some people would perhaps call it claustrophobic.

The valley is uninhabited at 6,560 feet (2,000m) above sea level, which we reach the next day. On a mountainside there are purple minerals in the brown scree, and when rain begins to fall the palette of colours makes the landscape somehow look ominous. We walk gently up to a pass. The pagoda-like top of Ighil-n-Ikkis stands out from the veils. Over the long ridge of Jbel Tarkedid and the 10,665-foot (3,250-m) high pass we reach an unexpectedly wide plateau surrounded by high peaks. This is where the nomads spend the summer, but by this time of year they have left the area. Winter is on its way, and it snows abundantly during the night, which we spend in an icy cold stone hut. In the dawn light we see the rare sight of a snow-white Africa. On the other side of the plateau stands a row of high, rounded fells and shimmering

Mgoun is a tempting goal for a day's trek, but one of our company has an upset
stomach so we rest instead of climbing the mountain.

One high pass later and we are down in Oued Tessaout, which is the biggest
ravine in this part of the High Atlas. Knotty cedars grow in places on the steep, dry
slopes around the opening of the canyon. However, the stony world we have entered
is largely infertile. From our base camp we can explore the ravine and follow the river
upstream, surrounded by 2,295-foot (700-m) high rock palisades. Using the rope in
our pack we start to climb from the innermost nook up to the high plateau we have
left, but we turn back when we reach a waterfall, break camp and walk the other way,
out of the ravine. The landscape changes suddenly. The valley widens and becomes
really green. In one place the inhabitants have diverted the river water into ingenious
channels to water their small fields. We reach Amezri, a large but trackless village.
Shouts are heard from people working in the fields and we are met by curious
children as we reach the houses.

In this way our journey continues westward along the Tessaout river for a couple
of days. In fine weather we walk across open land in the valley bottom, through
groves of deciduous trees and travel from village to village. We pass Berbers washing,
threshing, digging, walking and riding. And all the time we are surrounded by
the rugged, brown Atlas Mountains, which here and there slump a little or draw
themselves up to imposing heights. Muhammed takes care of our contact with the
villagers. The houses sometimes cling to the cliffs like clay eyries and we learn that
the most substantial are called *casbahs* and were previously home to princes and
potentates. They are square with high defensive towers in all four corners. In the
seventh century, Morocco was invaded by Arabs who disseminated Islam among the
population. However, in the High Atlas the women are unveiled. Mountain life is
hard, we see women carrying heavy loads of wood or digging with bent backs in the
fields where they grow maize.

Further on, the valley becomes even wider and, with the prevailing low water
level, the river bed is like an avenue covered with cobblestones. A traffic of mules and
wandering Berbers moves along the dry bed of the watercourse. At the village of Ait
Ali-n-Ita a tributary joins the river, and the two stony river valleys converge like a road
junction. We stay here a couple of nights in an inn on the edge of the river bed. On
a day trip we climb the side valley to Megdaz, the most beautiful and ancient Berber
village in the whole of the Atlas Mountains.

In the evening the host throws a party for us. He offers *mechoui*, a whole lamb
roasted slowly in a clay oven. The meat is served with the traditional Moroccan
couscous. Several middle-aged men sit on a balcony, singing loudly to the exciting
music of the drums, while the young girls of the village dance, wearing brightly
coloured dresses and bright green rubber boots on their feet – an incongruous sight.
During our travels in the High Atlas we encounter both the Berber culture and
dramatic natural scenery.

Mount Kenya

CIRCUIT OF A SOLITAIRE

Behind a giant senecio plant the eastern flank of Mount Kenya is gilded by the morning sun. To the Kikuyu people the mountain is known as Kirinyaga (the Great Light Height). Their god Ngai sat on the top after creating the world. The mountain is sacred to the Masai, too. The highest point is where the first Masai came to earth with cattle from heaven.

Sometimes it just seems natural. You decide to walk round a mountain and look at it from every angle. Particularly if that mountain is freestanding and constitutes a solitary landmark. Mount Kenya is just such a mountain. This bold and ice-laden alpine peak is unique; it does not belong to a folded mountain chain and does not lie at high latitude. It is a sharply defined massif just below the equator. And it still looks as if it belongs in the Alps.

During my first trip at the end of the 70s, I walk right around it. There are a few of us trekking the most popular route from Naro Moru through the Teleki valley and clockwise around the mountain via the Hausberg Pass. After a night in the primitive Kami hut with mice running over the sleeping bags, we try to move on over a pass between the Gregory and Lewis glaciers, but are halted by rock-hard ice. Instead, the Simba Pass becomes our route to the high Austrian hut, which we leave in the early hours of this wonderful morning when our trip is to reach its zenith at Point Lenana. We walk along the edge of the Lewis glacier and see how the highest pinnacle is beginning to burn like a giant torch in the first light of the sun. Just an hour later and 655 feet (200m) higher, we are standing on the third highest peak of Mount Kenya, almost 16,405 feet (5,000m) above sea level. When we squint toward the south we can see a tiny little bump on the horizon. That is Kilimanjaro, more than 186 miles (300km) away. Later in the day we go down to the Teleki valley and complete the circuit. Twenty-four hours further on and we are back at Naro Moru, our starting point – we have seen the loneliest alpine peak on earth from all four points of the compass.

In mountaineering, what we have just done is called "orbiteering". Walking in a circle around prominent peaks has religious antecedents. There are a number of sacred mountains in the world that pilgrims walk around as a form of religious worship. "Orbiteering" is, of course, a more secular pastime, but it is also a particularly fine way to express your love for the mountains.

In spite of its alpine appearance Mount Kenya is a volcano. That explains the mountain's lonely position. The tip is formed from a volcanic plug, made up of the

Close to the Austrian hut we look down on Thomson Tarns in the deserted Hobbley valley. There are about thirty small pools in the valleys which radiate out from the top of Mount Kenya.

From Point Lenana it is only half a mile across the melting Lewis glacier to the precipitous slopes of Nelion. In 1979 news spread throughout the world of a middle-aged, barefoot African man who spent several days at the top of Nelion. He said he had been sent from God. Climbers were amazed – to get there normally requires climbing gear and considerable experience of mountains.

hard rock syenite, which solidified in the barrel of the volcano a couple of million years ago. The sides were worn down and the lava gravel was carried away by running water. From the savannah around the mountain, one can deduce the original shape of the volcano to have been a bow-shaped, approximately twenty-five-mile (40-km) long elevation with a pointed top on the highest section. What you see are the rock walls of Mount Kenya's highest peaks.

The missionary Johan Ludwig Krapf saw the mountain like that in 1849, but it took forty years before a European returned to it. Count Samuel Teleki von Szek led an expedition that tried to climb Mount Kenya, but he only got as far as the valley which bears his name. After a few more attempts by other people, it was the geographer Halford Mackinder and two alpine guides who, in 1899, were the first to conquer the mountain. At the same time Mackinder named the mountain's main summits. The highest peak, at 17,055 feet (5,199m) above sea level, was called Batian after a legendary Masai chief. The second highest was named after his brother Nelion, and it is only 33 feet (10m) lower than Batian, separated from it by a 164-foot (50-m) deep gorge that Mackinder called the "Gate of Mists". The third highest peak reaches a height of 16,350 feet (4,985m) and was given the name of Lenana, after Batian's son.

Mount Kenya is a compact mountain area with three access routes. Twenty years after my trip in the 70s, I return with Björn Esping to walk the most beautiful route from east to west. We start in the small town of Chogoria, where we manage to procure two porters. Together we travel by jeep through the rainforest up to the entrance of the national park on the forest border. Our plan is to stay here for an extra day to acclimatize ourselves better to the altitude. That gives us time to take a day trip around beautiful Lake Ellis, which lies beside the trail in an open hollow surrounded by sloping grassy meadows. Beyond the water-hole, undulating hills stretch out to the east. In the west we see the highest peaks putting on their daily cloak of cloud. Almost every afternoon Mount Kenya is swathed in mist, which lifts in the evening.

Two stages later, at the Halls Tarn campsite, we take a short detour to the Temple, a little, flat hill with vertical drops to the dizzying canyon of the Gorges valley. From an exposed ledge, with legs dangling in the void, you can look down into the abyss to the circular Lake Michaelson, and directly across the void you can see rugged peaks with names such as Macmillan Peak and Delamere Peak. There are some South Africans at the campsite. An older man in the group is so happy he is almost crying when we talk to him. Ever since childhood he has dreamt of Mount Kenya, which is now so close. His delight is infectious and we understand his attraction to the mountain. Mount Kenya has strong charisma.

The steep summit rises provocatively straight up in front of us. The path winds in extended loops between the stunning giant plants. This massif is known for its almost forest-like stock of East African senecio. In the rosette of leaves of one of these strange giant plants we see a rock hyrax eating the fruit. Although these fearless animals look like overgrown guinea pigs, they are most closely related to the elephant.

The path leads us up a testing scree slope and over a saddle before we finally stand in front of the Austrian hut, which is basically a primitive refuge. When we walk to Point Lenana at dawn I notice that the glacier has shrunk considerably since my last visit. This time I walk around the mountain anticlockwise. From the top we walk down the north side to a small pool, Harris Tarn, and then scramble steeply across to the Kami hut where we camp rather than do battle with the mice in the hut. The path then takes us past Two Tarn, with the much-admired view that makes the whole south side of Mount Kenya look like an impregnable fortress: the Tyndall and Darwin glaciers hang like snow-white shields in the middle of the rock walls.

Further on I see something that was not there on my previous visit. In Teleki Valley they have built a big stone house called the Teleki Valley Lodge. A similar facility, the Shipton hut, has also been built in Mackinder Valley, north of the mountain. The number of trekkers on Mount Kenya is steadily increasing and so is the litter, but on the whole there don't seem to have been any great changes over the two decades since I was last here.

KENYA

Mount Elgon

AN UNFINISHED JOURNEY

Koitoboss watches over blooming heathland flowers and a recumbent, uprooted tree. The peak is the highest on the Kenyan side and is part of the ring of mountains around Elgon's crater. The volcano has long been dormant and is thought once to have been higher than Kilimanjaro. The name refers to its resemblance in shape to a woman's breast.

Suddenly, our trip takes an unexpected turn. The national park wardens stop the safari bus as we are on our way to the starting point of our trek. They get out and we follow them, but just as the view starts to call for the camera, we are told to jump in again, and with a roar the bus turns round. In the gravel of the road we can see the tracks of boots and cloven hoofs. Cattle poachers are ahead of our vehicle and the wardens say the poachers are heavily armed. If anyone follows them they shoot, the wardens tell us. By a hairsbreadth we have avoided a possible exchange of fire and even sudden death. The sharp eyes of the wardens are our salvation.

In the headquarters of the national park there is consternation when we return. The wardens have a visible respect for these poachers and leave them be. Later we learn that the poaching raid was already known about. A gang from Uganda, on the other side of the mountain, has wrought havoc for a week among the cattle owners in Kenya. The thieves hide in the forest with their prey during the day and then drive the animals up the mountain by moonlight, which is bright just now. "They will probably cross the border tonight," says the head of the national park, who doesn't want to stop us trekking.

And we would like to go through with our planned tour. Mount Elgon is a high, single volcano on the border between the two countries. There is a large uninhabited area here for trekking, but it is unknown to most who climb East Africa's most famous mountains, Mount Kenya and Kilimanjaro. Forgotten areas with attractive topography and interesting locations on the map have a special allure. You get curious and long to discover what secrets they hide.

Elgon is an extinct volcano that erupted 10 million years ago and has turned into a collapsed crater. What is left is a ring of peaks that are steep in places. The base of the volcano was very broad and Elgon is tens of miles in diameter. The higher parts are a desolate wilderness. On the long slopes a dense rainforest grows, while fertile agricultural land stretches out at the foot of the mountain. We are aiming for the highest peak on the Kenyan side, Koitoboss, 13,735 feet (4,187m) above sea level.

As few trekkers walk here, the national park has long been used as a transport route by poachers. The authorities in Kenya had overcome the problem, we were told, and we hadn't given it a thought when we arrived in February 1997. For safety's sake the park director promises us an escort of two armed wardens. From the headquarters we travel in the safari bus to the starting point, where the road ends at an altitude of 11,155 feet (3,400m). Through gaps in the forest we see glimpses of Koitoboss, looking like a fortress, and as we reach the tree-line the landscape becomes almost pastoral, with open heath vegetation. That is where the tracks of the poachers appear.

The next morning we set off again, escorted by an army lorry with eight military-looking park wardens. Four of them accompany us on our trek from the turning point, the others wait there. The path leads up through well-grown stands of lobelia and senecio, the strange, giant plants of the East African mountains. We walk slowly and reach a pass at 13,125 feet (4,000m). From there we can see over a hidden mountain kingdom. The upper section of Elgon is an unusually large collapsed crater – a caldera. But you don't get the feeling of a crater, the volcano looks more like a deserted expanse of hills, with undulating ridges in most directions. Only Koitoboss stands out like a steep rock beside the pass.

During a trip to Uganda in 1878, Henry Stanley became the first foreigner to see Elgon. This desolate view from the crater's rim reveals the part of the great collapsed crater that lies mainly in Uganda. That is where you find the highest point, Wagagai, at 14,175 feet (4,321m) above sea level. There is also better scope for trekking in that part. The first woman to reach the highest point was Ingeborg Lindblom, from Sweden, when she took part in a Swedish botanical expedition in 1920.

Björn Esping has photographed me and our escort of armed national park wardens on our trip in the footsteps of cattle poachers up to the Elgon crater.

It seems unreal that the poachers could have walked through here with their weapons, but the wardens are very nervous, spying anxiously in every direction, and they don't want to go any further. The path's final stretch to the top passes a cave where they might be hiding, according to the wardens. But we are sceptical and think it more likely that the wardens are not interested in climbing. The peak is high and the air thin and what is there for them on a steep mountain peak?

We remain on the pass for just a couple of hours, which is not long to absorb the interesting and beautiful landscape. We turn back along the same path, robbed of our peak and with an odd incident under our belts. During the journey down, the vehicle stops where the poachers had lain hidden beside the road. Across a wide area, only a few hundred metres in front of the place where we turned round, the vegetation is trampled. It is only then that we understand how serious the situation had been. But even though we escaped unscathed and we're glad about that, our trip was a setback, as we got to spend far too little time on Elgon.

Kilimanjaro

THE ROAD TO NIRVANA

The two people in front of the little icefield of the Arrow glacier indicate the scale of this 165-foot (50-m) high cliff called Breach Wall. The west side of Kilimanjaro is significantly steeper than the east, where most trekkers follow the Marangu route. To the left of the glacier is the hardest trail, called Western Breach.

"And then he knew that there was where he was going." That is what it says at the end of the short story *The Snows of Kilimanjaro* by Ernest Hemingway. The mountain is magnetic. Not just because it is Africa's highest. Kilimanjaro is also an unusually well-made volcano. And high volcanoes have one thing that other mountains don't – a crater in the sky.

The first time I climbed Kilimanjaro, I took the popular Marangu trail with two friends. After three days' trekking we left the Kibo hut at half past one in the morning and trudged up an exhausting slope of lava gravel to see the sunrise over the crater. At the highest point you can read a metal plaque dated 1961, signed by President Julius Nyerere: "We, the people of Tanganyika, will light a candle on top of Mount Kilimanjaro, which will shine beyond our borders, giving hope where there is despair, love where there is hate, and dignity where before there was only humiliation."

Only those who can conquer themselves can climb Kilimanjaro. You have to use your utmost determination. And at the top, your feelings are so overwhelming that you want to shout out to the whole world "I did it!"

The mountain is a challenge to committed trekkers, but you don't need to be a mountaineer. You can walk the whole way up. There's no need to worry about avalanches, rock falls or rough going on rock and ice. On the other hand you have to be prepared for problems with the lack of oxygen. You can run out of steam. The last bit on the lava gravel is a pure endurance test. The short time you need for the climb makes Kilimanjaro a tougher challenge than the Everest trail.

When I return to Kilimanjaro many years later, my companion is the guide Samuel Mosha, known as Sami. He claims to be the son of one of the porters who took part in the first ascent of Kilimanjaro. I am doubtful at first – it sounds incredible. Sami notices this and is annoyed. Later I read his father's name on the memorial plaque listing those who took part in the first ascent. Toma Mosha was a virile 85-year-old when Sami was born. In his youth he accompanied the German geographer Hans Meyer on his second and most successful expedition to the mountain. While the porters waited at a lower level on 6th October 1889, Meyer and one guide from the Alps reached the highest point, which they christened Kaiser Wilhelm Peak. The name was changed to Uhuru Peak when Tanzania became an independent nation.

In the thirteenth century a Chinese chronicler reported that there was a high mountain in the interior of Africa. The first European to mention the same thing was the Spaniard Fernando de Encisco in 1519. In the mid-nineteenth century the British "Africa expert" William Cooley heard tell of a high peak called Kirimanjara, which meant "red stones", but he never got there. In 1848 the missionary John Rebman wrote of a white African peak in his diary. He asked a guide what the colour came from. The guide said the cold, which led Rebman to write "... The most wonderful memory ran through my head, that this was a familiar old European guest called snow." When the discovery was made public in Europe it caused uproar. Cooley dismissed the snow as a crazy idea, but after the first attempted ascent in 1862 Charles New was able to report that there really was snow up there.

Kilimanjaro is a young volcano with three extinct cores, set in an oval base 37 miles (60km) long. Two million years ago the land began to sink in this part of the Great Rift Valley and a million years later volcanic magma flowed out of the cracks. The western volcano, Shira, collapsed into a caldera after a short period of activity and even the eastern one, Mawenzi, died out; only the solidified fire-pipe remained as a jagged rock formation. Of the original three volcanoes only Kibo continued to grow, eventually becoming the symmetrical cone that is the symbol of Kilimanjaro.

Our guide Samuel Mosha usually manages about ten tours to the peak per year. He started as a porter before becoming an authorized guide.

The evening mists roll over the Great Barranco valley and its strange vegetation. The high mountains in East Africa have their own indigenous species of tree-like giant senecio. The trek on Kilimanjaro is a fascinating journey from rainforest to high alpine desert.

Sami has co-opted two boys to lug the food and gear. We follow the Machame trail (also known as the "Whisky Route") which is normally four days' walking from the west to the slope up to the Uhuru peak. The rhythm is extremely slow. "Pole, pole." "Gently, gently" in Swahili. We climb "in slow motion" through the dense rainforest. After about 9 miles (15km) the view opens out at the Machame camp. The next leg leads steeply up to the Shira plateau where the forest ends. On day three we head toward the foot of Kibo, but then veer off to the southeast and walk down into the Great Barranco valley. We lose several hundred metres' height, which is mentally draining but good for our adaptation to the altitude. Walk high sleep low, is the rule.

Sami is a heavy smoker. During our trek he gets through a packet a day and claims that the cigarettes reduce the need for oxygen, which sounds doubtful. His smoker's cough worries me at times. But the paradoxical truth is that quite a few smokers have actually climbed Kilimanjaro, while many well-trained athletes have had to turn back. Altitude sickness is an unpredictable affliction.

As the clouds lift an imposing landscape takes shape. The western side of Kibo is very much steeper than the east. Here there is a high cliff called Breach Wall. The mountain seems to have little in common with the timid volcanic cone that greets trekkers on the Marangu trail.

Sami suggests that we change our itinerary and walk the most difficult of the three routes to Kilimanjaro's summit. It is called Western Breach. I have no problem with that. With our slow tempo the acclimatization has worked well. Kilimanjaro is a snail's world. It's better to sing the praises of slowness than to be fast.

From Barranco we follow a path to Arrow Glacier Camp just below the mountain wall. Here, the porters turn back to meet us the next day on the other side of the mountain. The last leg begins in the middle of the night. A very steep gravel slope leads to steep cliffs below the crater. This is where the torment begins. In the light of my headlamp I try to pinpoint something to hold on to. I am gasping for breath, my legs are heavy and I suddenly understand everyone who says that Kilimanjaro is pure madness. If you can think at all, you want to spend the rest of your life at sea level. Pole, pole. Gently, gently. We trudge on, hour after hour and spur ourselves on to the steepest section of the wall where it takes a little simple climbing to continue on. And as light begins to dawn we recover our breath by the Furtwängler glacier inside Kibo's crater. The glacier stands on gravel like some stranded iceberg with a 49-foot (15-m) high ice wall. The cold is biting. It must be -10°C, while the blue blackness of the night slowly turns to orange on the horizon.

When there is more light we gather our strength for the final part of the ascent. There are 655 feet (200m) left, the toughest of the whole trip. We plod on up the slope below Uhuru Peak in a zigzag. Sami first, then me. Thirty steps forward, then rest. Then the same again. And again. And again. The gradient is steep, our pulses are racing and our breathing is like bellows. But we are moving onwards and upwards and just as the sun emerges like a tomato from behind the ragged

Previous pages: A few walkers follow the rim of the crater towards Stella Point after a successful ascent. In front of them lies the boundless view towards the rugged satellite peak of Mawenzi, 16,800 feet (5,120m) above sea level and the sea of cloud over the savanna. A legend among the Wachagga people has it that Kibo and Mawenzi were wives of the god Ruwa. One day Kibo got cross and hit Mawenzi with a wooden cudgel and that is how the mountain came to look as it does.

From the savanna in the south, Kilimanjaro rises almost 16,405 feet (5,000m) in a single sweep. At the very top are the basins of three craters like Russian dolls one inside the other. Kibo is considered a dormant volcano, but in the 1940s there were fears of a fresh eruption.

silhouette of Mawenzi, we are standing on the highest point of Kilimanjaro, at 19,340 feet (5,895m) above sea level. We feel like heroes. Everything becomes easier and the tropical dawn dazzles us with its suddenness. In a few minutes the darkness turns to strong light and the cold is transformed to pleasant warmth.

Normally Kilimanjaro offers something unusual for high mountains, namely an easy descent, but this time Uhuru Peak is covered with strange pipe ice. A white bed of nails covers the crater's rim and Sami tells us that it formed after the rain of El Niño the previous spring. The whole Kibo crater is white with snow and the sun's vertical rays have carved out metre-high spines in the snow cover. The previous time I walked on bare gravel the whole way. Now we walk jerkily across the pipe ice, down to Stella Point where a steady flow of walkers from the Marangu trail meets us.

On the scree slope further down I suddenly feel weak and tumble down the scree as if I were drunk. I am dehydrated and have to drink the little water I have left. Slithering on the gravel I reach the Barufa hut and am forced to sleep for two hours before we can continue. In the afternoon we meet the porters further down. They have pitched the tent by the Mweka hut. The tension eases while tiredness numbs every limb. What am I thinking? Nothing at all. I'm just in a state of easy intoxication – call it contentment, happiness or perhaps nirvana.

Ruwenzori

DRAMA IN THE MOUNTAINS OF THE MOON

For once the peaks of Mount Stanley are free from cloud. The one to the right is Margherita, the highest point in the Ruwenzori Mountains at 16,730 feet (5,100m) above sea level. In the foreground, at 13,120 feet (4,000m) above sea level, the giant senecio grows above Freshfield Pass.

Why would I want to trek through one of the world's rainiest mountain massifs? My honest answer would be just *because*, or rather because of the consequences. As the Ruwenzori has such a wet climate it is one of the most difficult massifs in the world to explore, and the vegetation has run amok. This is where Africa's biggest glacier is located, yet it was not until the nineteenth century that a European got a glimpse of the peaks. And what is more, the Ruwenzori is actually Africa's only real mountain chain – the legendary Mountains of the Moon at the source of the Nile.

Even the ancient Greeks wondered where the Nile started. Herodotus believed the water came from melting snow. Aristotle claimed that the source was a silver mountain, and after studying ancient manuscripts in the library in Alexandria, the geographer Ptolemy drew a diagrammatic map of Africa in 150 BC. Far to the south, deep in the interior of the continent between two tributaries of the Nile, he marked *Lunae Montes finis orientalis*. Aristotle's silver mountain had become the Mountains of the Moon. Thereby was born a legend that intrigued travellers, slave traders and explorers for almost two thousand years.

When Europeans explored central Africa in the mid-nineteenth century, the Mountains of the Moon were high on the agenda. The explorers found Mount Kenya and Kilimanjaro at an early stage and the question was: could these be the *Lunae Montes*? No, they were too far away from the river and the quest continued. John Hanning Speke came to Lake Victoria in 1861 and saw the outlet of the Nile. He thought that the volcanoes in Virunga further south were the Mountains of the Moon, but they didn't have permanent snow fields. Nobody believed him.

Twenty years later, the most famous adventurer of the colonial era, Sir Henry Morton Stanley, joined the hunt. During an expedition to the border country between Uganda and the Congo in 1888, he wrote in his diary:

"While looking to the southeast (...) my eyes were directed by a boy to a mountain said to be covered with salt, and I saw a peculiar shaped cloud of the most beautiful silver colour (...) I became conscious that what I gazed upon was not the image or semblance of a vast mountain, but the solid substance of a real one, with its summit

The summit of Great Tooth, 16,240 feet (4,950m) above sea level, stands out above the Stanley plateau glacier. Ruwenzori's legendary mystery and, as we discovered, alpine landscape, caused many explorers and mountaineers to follow the first climbers who reached the top in 1906. A hundred years ago the ice cover on the mountain was far thicker. But the Stanley glacier is still Africa's biggest.

On our way up to the Elena hut we can look out over Lake Bujuku. The legendary mountain explorers Eric Shipton and Bill Tillman camped by the lake in 1932. Shipton writes: "Ruwenzori would lose a good deal of its beauty, mystique and charm if it lost the eternal clouds and moisture."

covered with snow (...) I have discovered the long lost, snowy Mountains of the Moon."

Thereupon he coined the name Ruwenzori, which was his own amalgamation of several local names. The meaning is "mountains which give birth to rain".

The young guide Philimon, a park warden, Lasse Österström and I walk from the village of Nyakalengija through the rainforest to the Nyabitaba hut. The path is muddy, it is often blocked with slippery boulders and is sometimes very steep. Our porters arrive later at the hut, fourteen men from the Bakonjo people.

The path continues into the Kujuku valley and climbs a further 2295 feet (700m). A very strange forest surrounds us, and towards the end of the second day, to our delight, a very high snowy mountain appears through the foliage. At the John Matte hut Margherita, the highest peak, is visible for the first time.

We have been dreading the third leg with its tussocky bogs, the lower and upper Bigo bogs, but they are not as exhausting as we thought. The bogs are no harder to cross than the terrain we have just left behind. We are already used to having mud up to our crotch! Below Mount Speke the valley makes a bend and we plod up to an even narrower, wilder ravine and reach a deep cauldron below Margherita. The rudimentary Bujuku hut is today's goal.

Usually the cloud cover over the Ruwenzori lifts in the evening and the nights are clear until dawn. The next day as we climb up to Elena hut, the base for an attempt to climb the peak, at 14,895 feet (4,540m) above sea level, it is still warm. We now exchange mud and greenery for a barren and stony world with solid sheets of ice and rugged peaks. The temperature cools rapidly at the same time as the terrain becomes steeper.

The clear, starry night augurs well, but a problem has arisen. Lasse has an upset stomach. He stays behind at the Elena hut as at dawn I walk toward Ruwenzori's highest peak with Philimon and another guide. For a little while the Stanley plateau glacier glows, then it's on with the sunglasses. With crampons and an ice axe we tramp across the glacier to an elegant pass, a snowy saddle between the highest peaks, Alexandra and Margherita. From the pass you can look straight down into the world's second largest rainforest, in the Congo, 13,125 feet (4,000m) beneath our feet. This is where the real climbing begins.

The first rockface is not entirely easy. Philimon climbs first. He throws down a rope, which I hook on to my harness and then use to ease myself up onto a ledge. When I look outwards, feelings of dizziness bubble up from the pit of my stomach. It's certainly airy, but the onward climb is less exposed and where the rockface ends we are standing on a snow-covered ridge that leads gently up to the highest point. Fantastic. Every peak in the chain is free from cloud and that's probably a one in a thousand chance.

When we get back to the Elena hut, Lasse is feeling better. Our trek continues during the afternoon. At the Scott-Elliot pass we rejoin the path and walk along a demanding stretch across big boulders in a lunar landscape. The narrow valley is surrounded by thousand-metre cliffs. The passage beneath Mount Baker is the most dangerous of the whole trip. There is a risk of rocks falling from the heights. We increase our speed and reach the hut by the idyllic Kitandara lakes.

Lasse has got worse again, but we have to go on over Freshfield Pass to get down into the Mubuku valley, which leads out of the mountain range. This strenuous leg is a struggle for him. On the other side there are precipitous descents and a long walk over squelching bogs. The path passes several rocky recesses, which were used for overnight stops. The day ends at the Guy Yeoman hut, which is noticeably cleaner than the others.

During the evening Lasse's condition gets so much worse that we are really worried. Rescue missions in Ruwenzori are complicated. It is hard to get hold of a helicopter and the only realistic way to evacuate a sick person is on a stretcher. We decide to call for help. The park warden has a walkie-talkie, and from the edge of a steep mountainside he gets in touch with the Ruwenzori Mountain Service in Nyakalengija. A rescue mission is set up and while we continue slowly down, a gang of stretcher-bearers comes up from the village. At the bridge over the Mubuku valley some strong men are waiting. Six fleet-footed men then carry the stretcher with

Previous pages: There is nothing else quite like this fairytale vegetation. All the rain is responsible for this luxuriance, and although the vegetation belts correspond to those of other African mountains, those on Ruwenzori are not concentric. The massif is not a single, freestanding peak but is divided by valleys at various heights. Here in the Bujuku valley, 9,840 feet (3,500m) above sea level, grows a heath forest with its characteristic giant lobelias and other smaller plants.

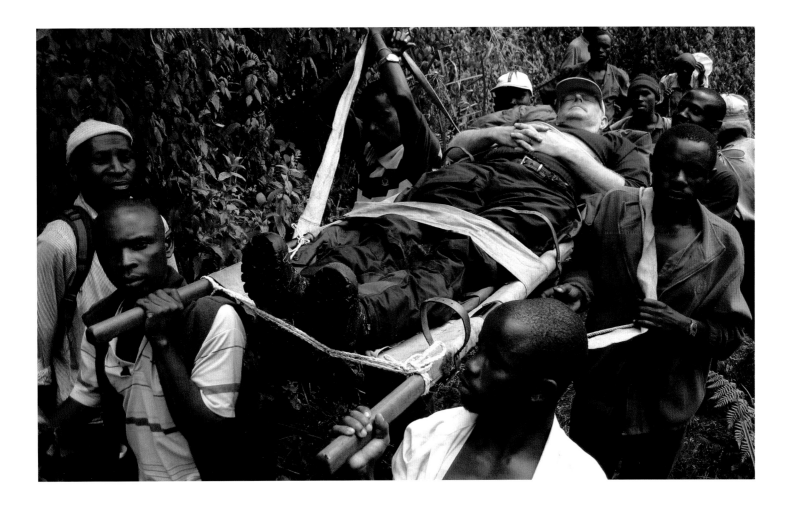

A rescue patrol from the Ruwenzori Mountain Service comes to our aid on the last day when Lasse Österström is so sick that he hasn't the strength to walk.

Lasse on it down a path that is one of the world's most inaccessible. Our porters take turns in helping, too. They rush through mud, up and down slopes, across long scrambles, yet with a firm grip the whole time and without stumbling. And they are laughing and chanting. "Da da one, da da two, da da three, money money." What a procession!

Afterwards Lasse tells us that the 7 miles (12km) on the stretcher through the rainforest have been an unforgettable experience. Whenever he comes to he sees the tree tops rushing by. But he is still unwell. In Nyakalengija we complete the expedition, say thank you and pay for an excellent rescue service, then travel by car to Kasese to buy medicine and check in at the Margherita, the best hotel. Rest at last and Lasse is finally better. In spite of this dramatic trip, the words of the mountaineer Freshfield hit the mark for both of us: "You may be familiar with the Alps and the Caucasus, the Himalayas and the Rockies, but if you have not explored the Ruwenzori, you still have something wonderful to see."

Fish River Canyon

FOOTSLOGGING THROUGH RIVERS

This part of Fish River Canyon is called Walls of Jericho and we reach it after two days' trekking. Over there at the foot of the mountain you can turn off on to the only escape route from the canyon.

We pass a grave on our way. A metal plate showing the date 14th June 1905 says: "Hier ruht in Gott Leutnant Thilo v. Trotha" (Here lies in peace Lieutenant Thilo v. Trotha). He was 27. A few plastic flowers lie on the imposing cairn. Why such respect in the middle of the wilderness, we wonder, and feel an urge to find out.

The grave lies in Africa's least known wonder, the second biggest canyon in the world after the Grand Canyon. Here, the Fish river has carved out a deep gorge between wide, high plateaux – an enormous, deep canyon, 56 miles (90km) long and just over 1,640 feet (500m) deep in the central part. The whole canyon system is 99 miles (160km) long and up to 19 miles (30km) wide. Trekking through this chasm along the winding river is one of the great African treks, but it is only possible during the dry season between May and August when water levels are low. The trip has to be booked well in advance; you need to provide an up-to-date medical certificate and there must be at least three people in the group, otherwise the national park wardens will not let you in. The only requirement Anders Eriksson and I meet is that we have our medical certificates. We hope to join some other walkers, just as it suggests in the guidebook.

When we wake in our hotel we learn that a South African group is to start out on the trip. In the early hours we go looking for them, but can't see anyone at all. Suddenly, a jeep turns up with five women who look as if they are going trekking.

"Are you from South Africa and heading for Fish River Canyon?" I ask, and the first one who gets out nods. "Could we go with you to the start please? There are only two of us and they won't let us in otherwise. We can walk on our own for the rest of the trip."

"That's OK," she replies.

We get a lift to the starting point 56 miles (90km) away. Through the window a lunar landscape is visible, in shades of brown and grey. Almost no vegetation. This is an impressive sight under a burning sun. Wide open spaces extend to the distant mountains and there is nothing in the landscape to suggest a giant canyon. At Hobas we reach an entrance to the national park. Our medical certificates are carefully

By several of the river's deep meanders we cut across desert sand, here below the Klippspringer Ridge.

The many pools along the river bed reflect the surrounding mountains, most of which are nameless.

examined by the wardens, who hang on to the papers. Nobody is allowed in without them. The biggest risk is heat stroke.

It is still 6 miles (10 km) to the canyon, which is hidden. But unannounced, like a crevasse in a glacier, a crevice opens up below the sheer mountainsides and I am gripped by the same strange feeling as at the Grand Canyon. Good gracious, where did that colossal hole come from! But here there are no hordes of people, no stinking cars, no roaring planes, no trace of civilisation apart from the primitive roads we've come on. Immediately opposite, the stony desert continues on towards distant highlands that shimmer in the heat haze. The canyon has sharp contours thanks to the flat terrace mountains and all the small, vertical ravines that score their slopes. Not a patch of green as far as the eye can see.

First, we have to walk 1,640 feet (500m) down to the river. The upper part of the slope is airy and has a few iron steps to hang on to. Just an hour later we are standing by the sluggish, brown watercourse. Hot sand lies along the bank. In spite of all the sediment the water is drinkable, which is a prerequisite for the whole trip. In this baking heat our thirst is almost unquenchable.

The bends in the river arouse our curiosity. Few trails are as demanding as those that follow a watercourse. Fish River is Namibia's longest and flows 404 miles

(650km) from the springs in the north to where it joins the Orange river on the border with South Africa. As the name suggests, it is rich in fish, but we didn't bring any fishing tackle with us in order to save weight. Stupid, perhaps, because now we have to eat freeze-dried food for several days.

Before dusk falls we have waded easily through the stream, something we shall be repeating countless times. Out of habit we pitch a tent, but because of the heat we lie outside our sleeping bags. When we see the women the next day they talk of a night under the stars.

"The constellations are unbelievable, but above all we didn't want to carry unnecessary gear, such as a tent", they say candidly.

At Palm Springs hot water is trickling out of a spring and a stand of tall palms grows. Here the gorge is at its full height, with walls that look higher, steeper and closer together than before. We camp down in an immense basin where the river collects its water in a pool reflecting the sunlit mountainsides.

After twelve hours on our backs, we are well rested for the next day's adventures. When the sun finds its way into our hidden world we set off toward a new bend in this immense slalom the river has carved out. Although there are huge distances with no real change in the landscape, the trek is not monotonous. On the contrary. The desire to explore is unusually strong. You wonder what is beyond the next bend, and advance with extra effort. Sometimes we are walking on sand, sometimes on stretches of boulders. Sometimes we climb past a bluff or walk on smooth slabs, and on the inside bends we cross slightly bigger areas of flat terrain where the bush vegetation has found a foothold beneath the rock walls. Sometimes, as at Zebra Pools, we bathe in the cool green river.

Hartmann's mountain zebra is found down here. It is timid and we only see its droppings. Leopards and kudu also live in this abyss, largely unseen. The animals we have most contact with are baboons – we hear their cries and a few groups pass us. But it is not the wildlife that makes the trip memorable. What we prize most highly is the intimate contact with the canyon and the desert landscape, and the trail's natural path along the river.

Fish River Canyon arose in a fault that began to be carved out by running water 350 million years ago. Fifty million years later inland ice was laid down across the area and ice erosion also contributed to the shaping of the canyon, which is considerably older than the "young" Grand Canyon in the USA. There is sandstone and shale in the upper layers of rock and deep down in the bottom there is a hard bedrock, thousands of millions of years old, consisting of gneiss and quartzite. In some places bands of black diabase or pale quartz can be seen in the rock walls. Beautiful patterns are formed, but the range of colours is sober. Sand, stone and rock are what you see most. Not a landscape for people, you might think. But the people of the region have been coming here for a long time, because of the water and the access to game. Although southern Namibia is one of the driest areas on earth,

Previous pages: From this viewpoint we can look down on our earlier route past Palm Springs, 1,640 feet (500m) below. Here Africa's "Grand Canyon" reaches its full height. On the rock walls there are bands of light and dark quartz and diabase.

Where the gorge begins to widen Four Finger Rock stands out like a mountain plucked from the Dolomites. On the ridge in the foreground lies the lonely soldier's grave.

50,000 year-old settlements have been found in the canyon. During the nineteenth century there was a war over this territory between the Nama and Herero tribes. The fighting ceased when Germany colonized Namibia at the end of that century, but the Nama people later started a rebellion against the colonial power. Confrontations occurred down in Fish River Canyon. We are reminded of this by the grave.

Toward the end of the trip the canyon becomes tamer. The sides are sloping, apart from the jagged peaks of Four Finger Rock, as we scramble past the lonely grave and reach Ai-Ais where dinner with the South Africans awaits us.

"Fish River Canyon is a test of manhood for trekkers in southern Africa," they sum up.

"It's a test for Scandinavians, too," we chime in.

And I find the answer to the riddle of the grave before we leave. A little German book sold by the hotel records the tragic fate of Thilo von Trotha. He came from a famous Prussian family. As a child he lived in Schleswig Holstein and subsequently saw service in South Africa. In 1904 he married a woman several years his senior and together they bought a farm in Namibia where they intended to settle. The book calls them nature-lovers. One year later, at a campsite south of Four Finger Rock he was shot dead by a Nama warrior in an ambush.

Lycian Way

BETWEEN SEA AND MOUNTAIN

On the way down to the beach at the village of Kabak you can see why the area is known as the Turquoise Coast. The trail leads through the steep mountains that line the winding coastal strip.

For one week in April four old friends and I have taken a cheap flight to the south coast of Turkey to follow a section of the Lycian Way. We fancy a coastal trek, with a "swimmer-friendly" sea on one side of the path and steep mountains on the other.

Already at the first stage, south of the town of Fethiye, we are amazed, perhaps because we had no special expectations. Our knowledge of the area known as the Turquoise Coast is scant. From high look-out points the Mediterranean shimmers to the west, and to the east Mount Baba Dagi rises in one sweep from the water, almost 6,560 feet (2,000m) above sea level. Steep limestone cliffs make the landscape light and wildly jagged, but there is another big surprise for us further on – a ravine that is spectacular in the truest sense of the word. As darkness falls we walk from an inn in the village of Faralaya to the edge of Butterfly Valley. And there we can look down into the abyss. Everyone is rooted to the spot. The ravine is deeper than it is wide, with a precipice that drops down more than 1,640 feet (500m) to a flat valley floor. Where it opens to the sea, the waves wash over a little beach – there is a gap of not more than 700 feet (200m) between the two rock walls. In that enclosed gorge, clouds of butterflies flutter, tempted there by buddleia, the butterfly bush. The pathway down is dangerous, there have been accidents, but the next day we use ropes fastened to the rock to help us over the steepest sections, where one false step can be fatal. The ascent is safer and quicker. We manage not to slide on the rock.

We continue our trek across meadows bright with glorious spring flowers. One of the first places in the next village is Mama's Restaurant, where we make an impromptu stop. A cheery matron serves beer while her daughter heats flat bread over an open fire. After a rest, Kabak Beach and a refreshing swim await us.

Here we leave the sea for a detour through the mountains. The path climbs 1,970 feet (600m) to a pass and continues on to Alinca. All at once the landscape becomes more unspoilt. We stride up through a dense pine forest and walk carefully down hairpin bends on rugged, almost ochre-coloured, limestone summits. More than halfway up a slope there is a dug-out well surrounded by planted olive trees; we decide that this is an excellent campsite and stop here for the night. Beside the spring

there is flat land where we can pitch the tent – after we have scraped away all the goat droppings. The goats, which are the animals we see most on our trek, are grazing higher up. Many of the villagers are goatherds although beekeeping is also popular.

The air has become stuffy, but it rains less now than it did twenty years ago. The local wells are drying up, causing major problems. Fortunately, ours is full and offers us the chance of a delightful break. We have a tent, camping stove and freeze-dried food. Although we could have found accommodation, the extra weight gives us great freedom. It is important to us to be able to stop in the middle of the mountains.

In Gey we're happy to choose an inn. Nobody speaks English but hospitality needs no words. The village is located on a slope from which you can see the several promontories of Yedi Burun pointing toward the Mediterranean, hence its name, which means "the seven noses". I walk there by myself in the evening. The dense scrub or *maquis* makes it difficult to get through. The ground is stony and overgrown with prickly holly bushes. Where the rock is exposed, there are facets with sharp edges that are hard on the shoes, typical of limestone weathered by rain.

From Gey the path leads back to the sea. We pass terraces where wheat is grown, and high above a creek we follow an indentation in the mountains. The drama of the landscape continues. Behind the next pass lies Bel, and there an alternative stretch of the Lycian Way rejoins us. The parallel route begins at a fork we have already passed and leads past the famous ruins of Sidyma, further inland. We branch on to this secondary path and turn back northwards. Now we are leaving the coast and as the path leads into the forest we lose contact with the sea.

Previous pages: A yacht has anchored off Butterfly Valley, in Turkish "Kelebek Vadisi". From the village of Faralaya, where we are standing, you can climb down an exposed path to the valley floor – "with butterflies in your tummy".

In Mama's Restaurant, in the village of Kabak, a bread called *yufka* is being made. It is stuffed with cheese and onions and served like a kind of pie.

Between Faralaya and Kabak the path leads over meadows bright with carpets of poppy, yellow doronicum and other flowers.

The name of the village with the ruins is Dodurga. In the background we can see the Toros mountains. The mosque has a courtyard and there are pieces of ancient stone columns and smaller blocks with inscriptions. The archaeological remains lie around, as do so many pebbles, between the houses and are used by the villagers as building material. These ancient monuments are obviously not protected. The imam is a middle-aged and very friendly man. He would like us to camp in front of the mosque. That solves the problem of where to spend the night.

Sidyma was a town as early as 200BC. A century before that, Alexander the Great marched over the Teke peninsula. Some parts of the trail follow the tracks of the great leader. Later the area was conquered by the Romans. During Roman times the towns in Lycia were united in a federation in which each town was self-governing.

The most important monument we see is a collection of graves of impressive size, built like small temples and several metres tall. They stand on a natural saddle where the path continues down into the valley toward Bogazici, our destination. As we stroll between these old sarcophagi, it is as if the whole trip has taken a new turn. Up till now we have just admired the magnificent landscape and enjoyed the great contact we have had with the villagers, but it is in Sidyma that we first fully appreciate what venerable land we have walked over.

Altai Mountains

THE REAL SHANGRI-LA

On our way up the slopes of Mount Malchin the view stretches to the long Potunini glacier and the Tavan Bogd massif in the national park of the same name. Considering they are as far from the sea as you can get, the mountains are remarkably heavy with snow. Altai means "golden mountains" in Mongolian.

August 2003. On a day trip in Central Asia, three of us are climbing higher and higher up a mountain until we finally ascend the 10,825-foot (3,300-m) high unnamed peak – the first to conquer it. Our guide, Canat, is certain of it, when he hears where we've been. And what we can see really does look like *terra incognita*. We are as far away from the sea as you can get, over 1,865 miles (3,000km) as the crow flies. This area is often called the Altai knot, an ancient crossroads for the peoples and religions of this continent and today a meeting place for three national borders: Mongolia, Russia and China. I have never set foot in a more remote place.

Altogether we are a group of twelve walkers in the Altai mountains, and in some places we follow paths where no foreigners have ever trod. My role is to lead the group, but the person who shows us the way is Canat, who lives in Ölgy, the little Mongolian provincial capital where our tour starts. After a whole day's journey west across the steppes – 155 miles (250km) in a Russian off-roader – we reach the national park of Tavan Bogd; the name means "the five holy mountains". The next day we trek 9 miles (15km) to the Potunini glacier, the biggest in the Altai.

An Asian tent, a yurt, stands next to the tongue of ice protruding from a chain of steep peaks. In it, the local chieftain, Rentsen, is playing chess with Shagdar, who is merry. Both are Kazakhs and live in this inaccessible region. At the moment they are looking after the camels that carry our equipment. The air is quite thin, affecting several of our company, and therefore we divide into two groups for day-treks in different directions. I walk with a few of them to Malchin Uul (Shepherd's Peak), a dark landmark a mile or so west of our campsite at 13,245 feet (4,037m) above sea level. The mountain stands alone, but near the great procession of craggy, white summits. Today a reassuring tranquillity pervades the landscape, while the sun shines without a puff of wind.

An atmosphere of mystery such as you rarely experience in other areas hangs over this desolate mountain chain. Frozen alpine peaks, high ridges and undulating plateaux extend in all directions. Close by we see Khuiten Uul (Frost Summit) completely enveloped in snow. At 14,350 (4,374m) above sea level, it is Mongolia's

A Kazakh hunter with his trained golden eagle. In the late autumn the birds are used to hunt small game and foxes. In western Mongolia the Kazakhs are the dominant ethnic group. There are about 400 hunters.

The nature of the landscape changes as our caravan of camels passes across the flat grass steppe east of the high mountains in Tavan Bogd.

highest mountain. Right beside it, on the summit of the almost equally high Nairandal Uul (Friendship Peak), the three national borders meet. On the Chinese side a snow-laden alpine world predominates. To the east, in Mongolia, the land is folded like a scrubbing board with long, treeless ridges. And to the west, in Russia, we can see a wide plateau extending to distant towering mountains, the massif of Gora Belukha, the highest peak in the Altai mountains.

Perhaps over there lies Shambhala, the promised land of the Tibetan holy writings. At any rate that is what the world-famous Russian artist and Tibetan expert Nicholas Roerich thought at the beginning of the twentieth century. Shambhala subsequently became the inspiration for James Hilton's myth of Shangri-la in the novel *Lost Horizon*. Hilton believed the location was in Tibet, but I would rather believe that Shangri-la lies within my sight, preferably to the south in the glittering network of snowy mountains within the Chinese province of Xinkiang. The peaks there have undoubtedly never been climbed and most of the valleys never visited by foreigners. That must be where the promised land lies!

Rentsen and Shagdar take care of the beasts of burden. A Tuvan called Dash Davaa has joined them when we leave the Potunini glacier and follow the river eastwards to the foot of a smaller mountain, Shiveet Hairhan Uul. Here, there are

rock carvings made by the Huns in 200BC. It was the Huns who forced China to build the Great Wall and who invaded Europe during the time of their "great migration". Canat is keen to show us these ancient pictures on the smooth rock.

Not far away we pitch camp by an idyllic mountain tarn. In the evening our guide drinks home-made vodka with Dash Davaa. In our mountain tent we don't notice a thing, but in the morning a weary Canat tells us that the Tuvans came to demand an apology. The reason is that a foreign woman he was guiding a few weeks before, in spite of being warned, disregarded their tradition that forbids women to ride an uncastrated stallion.

"We must show the nomads respect," says Canat.

Now our direction of travel changes and we head south toward a high pass that is only used by the local folk in exceptional circumstances and has never previously been attempted by Westerners. The whole caravan, with camels, riders and trekkers, moves along a wide valley framed with rounded but high mountain ridges. The day ends with a strenuous slope up to a mountain cirque just below the pass. At night there is heavy snowfall and in the morning we wake to a bright new world. The camels are lying chewing the cud on dark patches of ground where their bodies melt the snow. The tent is sagging with the weight of the snow, which shines in the sun, and everyone in camp is moving about in chilly expectation of Ainagull serving breakfast in the mess tent. Dash Davaa and Rentsen are worrying that our six camels will slip on the steep path.

While the animals wait until the sun has melted the snow, we trek on ahead. After a steep climb of about 985 feet (300m) we reach an awe-inspiring high plateau, and although the weather has become a little overcast it feels quite awe-inspiring to be walking here like a pioneer, wandering through the unknown heart of Asia. A mile or so across the plateau we reach heights of about 9,840 feet (3,000m) above sea level. Then, we walk steeply down to a narrow valley below high mountain walls. This leads us on to a wider main valley and, as if by metamorphosis, we reach really fertile lands where the Akzu Valley opens out its smooth cradle. The landscape becomes pleasantly idyllic without quite losing the dramatic features. We stroll on down as the weather continues to improve. Larch woods clothe the lower slopes of the mountains; the brush of late summer has painted the moors red and brown. At the bottom of the valley a network of rivulets makes a glittering pattern. A high barrier of uplands rises directly from the watercourse. To the south it gives way where the valley leads toward the Mongolian steppes. To the north the topography is sharper and the summits precipitous. They have tall craggy walls and in that direction we can see the back of the rugged snowy mountains of Tavan Bogd. The Akzu valley is as good a Shangri-la as any other place you could conceive.

Only a few hunters come here, far away from civilization. We wander around in the area for a day. On pastoral and ungrazed meadows many beautiful plants have almost finished flowering, and the larch trees in the woods are old and thickened.

Previous pages: From the top of a mountain never previously climbed we can see a Shangri-la of virgin valleys and mountains. The Akzu valley immediately below us is not even inhabited by nomads and our route follows the river. The unnamed mountains on the other side of the valley border on the Chinese province of Xinkiang.

Our beasts of burden graze in the dawn light by the lake of Khoton Nur. In Mongolia there are plenty of domesticated camels, but the few wild ones left are threatened with extinction – about 400 live in the Gobi Desert.

On the unnamed mountain above our campsite we make our aforementioned first ascent, almost 6,560 feet (2,000m) up.

At the next campsite everyone appreciates the chance for a dip in what Canat calls the Green Lake. Not far from there we leave our Shangri-la and the valley opens out on to the Mongolian steppes. Yurts start appearing like flecks of snow on the open landscape. Our journey now leads us through an area that in summer is populated by nomads and domesticated animals. Horses, yaks and goats are visible all over the plain and we are met with tremendous hospitality. Both Tuvans and Kazakhs live here, two separate ethnic groups of distinct appearance and culture. The Tuvans are in the minority, their lives an extreme blend of the old and the new: camels and jeeps, shamans and snooker players, yurts and satellite dishes.

For a long time we trek beside the long Khoton Nur lake. North across the water we can see exceptionally barren steppes and jagged mountain ridges. On our side there is more vegetation with stands of trees, and above the trees the Altai mountains rise like a wall along the border with China, 310–370 miles (500–600km) further to the southeast. At the southern end of the lake Canat's off-roaders appear. Our journey ends here in the middle of the Mongolian steppes. In the river that drains the lake we enjoy some incomparable casting for grayling. But that is another story.

Khentii Nuruu

THE TAIGA'S SACRED LAKE

Our pathfinder Chinggis wades through the Tuul Gol river, close to its source. The river is one of the highest streams to feed into the Yenisey. Beyond the mountain ridge, as the crow flies, there lie 310 miles (500km) of trackless wilderness up to the trans-Siberian railway.

We mount the horses, a little caravan with five pack horses, three Westerners and four Mongolians. The spirit of the people of the steppes pervades the area, but practical considerations soon take over, especially for me as I have only ridden once or twice before. The horse notices my uncertainty and suddenly bolts while I hold tight to the saddle so as not to fall off. A Mongolian rider quickly catches up and stops us. The horse and I are overwrought. but when calm is restored the caravan moves on and after just a third of a mile or so (500m) the horses are wading up to their bellies in the Tuul Gol river – with us on their backs. Fantastic, I think, as we reach the other side, and I am even more delighted when our pathfinder, Tulga, says that my black stallion and I will make a good team before the journey ends. Hearing that boosts my confidence.

Our goal is Hagin Har Nuur, one of the few lakes in the desolate mountain chain of Khentii Nuruu, to the northeast of the town of Ulan Bator. The mountains, which reach up to 9,185 feet (2,800m) above sea level, are still speckled with snow, even now in the early summer. Along some of the precipices there are masses of natural stone hoodoos and the valleys open up to meadow, moorland and bog. The most impressive sight is the forest on the low-lying parts of the mountains – it has never been cut. This area is home to the southernmost part of the immense Siberian taiga. Here the great woodland extends from the steppes in Mongolia to the trans-Siberian railway in the north – more than 300 miles (500km) of trackless, almost uninhabited, terrain, a boundless wilderness with quantities of bears, lynx, wolverines, wolves, elk, red deer and sable. Who said Mongolia is nothing but steppes?

We are riding through a pastoral valley bottom, across flourishing grassland where numbers of untethered horses graze, surrounded by wooded uplands. The landscape and the animals belong together, like strawberries and cream, and in my imagination I can see some wild warlord with warriors on horseback looming up in the short grass. But peace prevails here. Now in June, all kinds of flowers are blooming. We see orange globeflowers and silky anemones in the meadows, and in the forest there is a lot of bergenia, which I recognize from my garden at home.

At our third campsite we are surrounded by mountain ridges in the Khentii Nuruu range. The forest is one of the southernmost outposts of the Siberian taiga. This peak is 8,615 feet (2,626m) above sea level.

A few hunters ride past and on into these uninhabited areas, which are rich in wildlife and provide good hunting grounds for the nomads further south.

On the second day our journey takes us up a high mountainside, but in the end the gradient becomes so steep that we have to lead the horses up to the "obo" of the pass, a holy cairn that is found at well-chosen sites in this country. The Mongols usually stop and walk three times around them clockwise. Often they throw stones or gifts on to the heap. When we have done that, Ichee, who speaks good English, says he's going to look after the horse and disappears off into the forest. What horse? we wonder.

"That is what Mongolians say when they mean a call of nature," he replies brightly.

We get into the saddle again and continue down the slope on the other side of the pass, to the edge of a bog where we stop for the night. From there the ride leads across bands of marshy land, which is a struggle for the horses. Mine gets stuck in a waterhole, strains until he almost bursts and careers off like a bullet from a gun as I almost take a nose-dive over his head.

In the forest we have to ride slalom between the tree trunks and suddenly one of my kneecaps hits a fir tree. I throw myself off the horse in pain and he gallops off and has to be caught by Tulga. "No," he says, "you don't learn to ride in five minutes." Just sitting in the saddle for a few days is not enough, but it's beginning to feel good to ride in the wilderness and get that great animal to go where I want.

At Hagin Har Nuur, a shallow
lake teeming with fish, dusk is
falling. The name means "Black
Lake" and it is considered a holy
place by the Mongols.

The Mongolian pathfinders choose the campsite with care, which we can understand. The place must be practical and thoughtfully located with access to water, wood and beautiful countryside. We stop by a little lake and immediately Tulga begins to unsaddle the horses. Food is prepared on a wood-fired metal stove. Later on we eat *buuz*, a kind of meat-filled pasta.

At daybreak I stroll alone around the lake and find wolf droppings in two places. A few tufted ducks are swimming in the water. Scarlet grosbeaks whistle tunefully, a yellow wagtail hops around on the ground while nutcrackers fly excitedly to and fro in the coniferous forest where thick larch trees thrive alongside fir trees. The countryside is pristine and radiates a harmonious balance.

Hagin Har Nuur is now within our reach and when we finally glimpse the lake after five days and around 60 miles (100km) on horseback, it is a silken jewel shining behind a curtain of trees. Before us is a shallow pool, teeming with fish, set beneath soft mountain ridges. We stop and pitch camp on the southern shore.

Since time immemorial the Mongols have had a kind of religious relationship with nature and many dream of coming to Hagin Har Nuur. However, few actually have been here and we may be the first Westerners. The lake is known in Mongolia as a divinely endowed and almost unattainable place. In the thirteenth century Ghengis Khan declared nearby Mount Burkhan Khaldun sacred and he banned hunting and fishing in its vicinity.

In wildernesses on this scale the seasons rule and wild animals are the only inhabitants. Even though I only see droppings and tracks of the bigger animals, they are constantly in my thoughts. A map confirms how far we are off the beaten track, and that imbues the landscape with even greater charm. The location affects the way I perceive the lake. Asia's watersheds are close. The mountain chain contains the sources of two of the earth's mightiest watercourses, the Yenisey and the Amur.

We leave Hagin Har Nuur and ride into a narrow valley that leads to meadows beneath the ruins of a seventeenth-century monastery. In these enormously remote forests Mongol monks, adherents of the Tibetan form of Buddhism, were able to hide when the Chinese conquered their kingdom. The monastery was built by an influential *lama* and now what remains is overgrown with roots and plants.

By the tents our horses are grazing languidly. They seem quiet enough in spite of all the predators around. However, after I have been off walking on my own for a couple of hours, Ichee becomes anxious and comes after me. I look out over the immense deserted country that we have only nibbled at the edges of. "There are so many bears and wolves in the forest," he says later.

We still have a few days riding to escape the mountains. The ridges gradually become lower at the same time as the valleys broaden into plains. Now I ride at a gallop and I feel sorry to dismount from my four-legged friend for the last time. We have returned to the start after a circular tour of 124 miles (200km) in one of the biggest trackless wildernesses of the pine forest belt in the northern hemisphere.

Garhwal

A LITTLE EXPEDITION

Once we have crossed the Kuari Pass, wet November snow covers the mixed oak and pine forest on Dakwani, at 9,840 feet (3,000m) above sea level. After one unsuccessful attempt, Lord Curzon finally stood here in 1905 and we follow his trail, which leads over another pass across the ridge in the background.

Nilsingh is a short, middle-aged man with a black moustache and a kindly face. He moves deliberately and quickly, like a ferret. There is always a warm smile on his lips. From the first moment I feel a bond with him, in spite of his limited command of English.

Nilsingh is to be the cook on our trek. With a natural air of authority he is now organizing the porters who've turned up. There seem to be more than we had expected. The reason lies in the terrain. We see bulky gas cylinders, a Calor gas stove made of cast iron, a heavy-duty ridge tent and a large company tent. In addition there is gear for us two trekkers, plus a week's rations for everyone.

"Small expedition," says Nilsingh, worried yet reassured at the same time.

We've no objection. Walking with fifteen porters and getting to know them a little may bring us closer to the mountain-dwellers. Some are middle-aged, others younger. The range of personalities is mixed. Shy and self-confident, happy and surly, tall and short. They all seem helpful, but none speaks English. The guide's name is Kushal. With his modern sports clothing he resembles a ski instructor.

Our trek begins with a steep climb from the Indian ski resort of Joshimath. Above the forest the mountains unfold before us. We immediately feel uplifted, but a quotation from the old Hindu writings of Skanda Purana is better than any words of ours: "Not even a hundred generations of gods would be enough for me to describe the greatness of Himachal. As the dew evaporates in the morning sun, so it is with human sins in sight of Himachal." Many Indians call this mountain range Himachal, which means "snowy mountains". "Himalaya" is Sanskrit, and translates as "home of the snowy season." We are soon to learn that both these descriptions of the earth's mightiest mountain chain are true.

Our route leads over the Kuari Pass. We follow the Curzon Trail, which is named after a British viceroy in India, who, toward the end of the nineteenth century unsuccessfully tried to cross from the south. For a trail it is rather high, but 11,695 feet (3,565m) above sea level is not such an impressive height in this environment where the surrounding mountains are over 22,965 feet (7,000m) high. The region

Dawn at the campsite of Gurson Bugyal. All the mountains north of Joshimath emerge like sharp-edged crystals. To the right of the picture is Nilkanth, 21,640 feet (6,596m) above sea level.

From the third pass we can see north to the sunlit mountainside and the village of Pana, where we spent the night. The high snowy mountains of the Himalayas are revealed to us for the last time.

where we are trekking is Garhwal, in the Indian province of Uttar Pradesh. The area is also called Uttarakhand, and sometimes Kumaon. "Himalaya" is a very broad geographic term. There are several mountain ranges often grouped together under this heading. They extend across several nations and regions. Sometimes people mean the whole set of mountain massifs in Central Asia. But strictly speaking, Himalaya refers to the continuous chain of mountains, 1,245 miles (2,000km) long, between the rivers of the Indus in Pakistan and the Brahmaputra in Assam.

When we have traversed the side of the valley a little way, the view becomes amazingly beautiful. According to our guidebook it is one of the most splendid mountain views in the world, and we are inclined to agree. The path runs high up on a slope above the tree-line and to the north we can see a grid of steep, snowy mountains. That is the high Himalaya. In the eastward extension of the valley we can also see into the national park where India's highest mountain, Nanda Devi, is found at 25,645 feet (7,816m) above sea level.

The Himalayas present a landscape that is at the same time magnificent and terrifying, but the Curzon Trail is a comparatively easy tour. Mostly you walk below the tree-line and you never reach any extremely high points. Nonetheless, we have to puff and pant quite a lot when we cross the Kuari Pass, which translates as the

"threshold". The descent southward is extremely precipitous and very hard on the knees. As all walkers know, long, steep downward slopes are far harder work than uphill ones. In the Himalayas that is abundantly clear.

The nature of the view now changes. The steep, snowy mountains disappear from view and in front of us we see a deeply carved valley pointing toward long, forested, faraway ridges. There we can see a mountain chain extending between the plains and the Himalayas, lower and rounder in shape. The weather is also changing. A cold front is coming in from the plains via the Ganges, and we only just make it down from the pass before heavy wet snow begins to fall. This is no surprise in November, as snow can fall at any time in the higher altitudes. The season has come to an end and we are the only walkers out on the trail.

Our campsite is a clearing far below the pass, surrounded by a mixed forest of oak and pine as well as rhododendron bushes. Waiting for our food, we sit with the porters who huddle around a fire while the snow falls. They call us *sahib*s and we are served as such, as custom demands. Every meal is roughly the same menu. Dinner starts with hot soup. Then there is rice and boiled vegetables accompanied by flat Indian bread, *chapatti*s and *poppadom*s. The latter are hard crisp wafers that are highly spiced. To finish we have a dessert from a tin.

The next morning the ground is covered in snow. The weather has improved, but the air is biting cold. We turn to the porters' fire again. They are in an upbeat mood, their chatter lively and cheery. Some of them head off as an advance guard and make tracks in the snow. We follow later. The forest is magnificently beautiful with all the white snow on the branches. It is a long-drawn-out descent to the snow-free area around the village of Pana, which lies in a sunlit mountain glade. We spend the night in a disused school, where the porters dry out their big tent and their clothes over an open fire inside the building.

Hill-dwellers like these make time stand still. A medieval tempo governs their lives. Cowbells and barking dogs mingle with children's cries and crowing cocks. Even in the early dawn people are about. Smoke curls up from the slate roofs of the square clay houses, and the same leisurely procedures are carried out this morning on every other morning. Water has to be fetched, cattle driven to their grazing and food prepared.

Our trek continues down into the deep valley bottom where there is an airy suspension bridge over the Brithi Ganga river. We stop in the middle of the bridge and look at the high snowy mountains to the east, upstream, but in other directions our vision is severely restricted by the valley slopes clad in dense jungle. On the other side of the bridge the path leads up through this forest. We reach the village of Ghangri, where happy children appear, and for the rest of the day the climb continues slowly up through the forest. Our campsite is a clearing with no view.

Another pass awaits us, this time at the lower altitude of 6,560 feet (2,000m). Up there we catch a glimpse of the high mountains to the north for the last time. The path now leads to more domesticated areas. In the sloping meadows around the village of Rahmni the women are making hay, and close to the Nandakini river we catch up with two walkers who had tried to cross the Kuari Pass but were stopped by the snowfall.

There is a teahouse by the river. It forms a natural meeting place for people on the trail. Beneath a roof with no walls, two energetic cooks are boiling rice and frying eggs.

We sit at a table, drink tea and watch the stream of hill-dwellers and animal caravans passing by. After a short rest we have just a few miles left until we reach the village of Ghat, the end of our journey.

In the evening it is time for us two *sahib*s to distribute tips to the porters, which is the custom. They are in a good mood as they come forward, one by one, to receive their reward. However, at the same time, a feeling of sadness seems to pervade the whole group. For the past week we have lived side by side and have surmounted obstacles together. In spite of the language barrier and enormous differences in our lifestyles and frames of reference, a little bond has grown between us. We like to think so, anyway.

Mount Everest

THE HIGHEST JOURNEY

Mount Everest – its name comes from the man who headed the Survey of India Office in the mid-nineteenth century. From Kala Pattar we can see the classic route to the legendary peak. It leads through the ice up to the South Pass on the right, and from there along the south ridge to the summit. That is the way Edmund Hillary and Norgay Tensing walked as pioneers in 1953. The first attempts at the ascent were made from the other side, in Tibet. In 1924 George Mallory and Andrew Irvine mysteriously disappeared on the path. Exactly seventy-five years later Mallory's body, mummified by wind and cold, was sensationally found. He had slipped a short distance down the north face. Whether he had already been to the highest point remains an open question that, if answered, might rewrite history.

Kala Pattar at last! After several days trekking in increasingly thin air, we are standing on a narrow ridge and we can see the world's highest mountain pointing up toward the sky, towering over the other giants like an overgrown lad on the back row of the school photo. Mount Everest is not a particularly beautiful mountain when seen from here but it is the highest, and in my bemused state I can only think one thought – Everest is Everest.

With this scenery before your eyes you quickly forget some of the disturbing impressions gained on the way here. The trail to Everest is bordered by small, simple hotels. Here and there it grinds to a halt because of a snaking queue of trekkers, porters and animal caravans. Noisy helicopters buzz between the mountains every day, and in the biggest village, Namche Bazar, there are pizzerias, discotheques and Internet cafés. On Kala Pattar you can overlook all this for one simple reason: because Everest is Everest. The world's highest mountain is so powerful, remarkable, enticing and magnificent that you can accept the effects of tourism with equanimity.

Memories surface. On my first trip to the area in 1972 we didn't see many walkers. We spent the night in the Sherpas' homes. You don't do that any more. And above Pheriche, the highest mountain close to Everest, there was only myself and my travelling companion Rolf Bardon. On Kala Pattar we stood alone. Now, thirty years on, I can see the same view again but this time with about twenty unknown people who are crowded on to the ridge. A string of people are on their way up and for several days I have seen how tourism has changed the area. Nevertheless, I am just as overpowered as the first time.

Mount Everest holds an attraction like no other mountain. The media interest is sustained by many ingredients. The height, the risks, the deaths, the magnificent landscape, alpine history, honour, intrigue, the mountain's symbolic value. And more and more people are drawn to this temple of the world's most magnificent scenery. The Everest Trail is one of the most written about on earth.

In the village of Namche Bazar, at 9,840 feet (3,500m), I meet Uddhab Dhungana, local manager of the Sagarmatha National Park. He hangs out in the park's visitors' centre, which is located on an outcrop above the settlement. From here you can see due north through the grandiose valley that leads to the foot of Mount Everest. Only the topmost cone of the highest mountain is seen in the far distance. Beneath it runs the river of Dudh Kosi, which has carved out one of the world's deeper ravines, a stroke of rare magnitude. On the other side rises Mount Thamserku in one sweep, 11,485 feet (3,500m) from the shimmering stream deep down in the chasm up to the snow-capped crown.

"The national park was founded in 1976", says Uddhab Dhungana. The initiative came from Sir Edmund Hillary, the first man to climb Mount Everest. He is highly respected here and called "the king of Khumbu". Hillary had noticed that the area's forests were threatened by the climbing expeditions and the beginnings of trekking tourism. Too much wood was being taken. The number of trekkers was increasing rapidly, the reason being the airfield in Lukla, which he himself had initiated. The airfield is two days' walk south of Namche Bazar and has a rugged landing strip on the mountainside. For the pilots it is like landing on an aircraft carrier. When it was completed in 1968 there were big changes. By flying you can avoid the long trek from Kathmandu. Everest became much closer.

Hillary managed to gain support for the idea of a national park in spite of all the difficulties. The area is a populated region, not a wilderness, and for a long time the Sherpas were suspicious of the project, even though the park was launched by their admired friend. Ultimately, they were convinced of its benefits and today there are not many who complain.

The shapely cone of Ama Dablam rises behind the Imja Khola river. We can see it for a long time as we approach Everest. Like all the mountains in Khumbu it has a religious significance for the Sherpas. Ama means "mother" and Dablam is an amulet which *lamas* wear. This peak is reckoned to be one of the most beautiful in the world.

Dawa Tenzing was a legendary Sherpa guide who was already around when Mallory disappeared in 1924. Later he became a leader ("sirdar") for several of the major expeditions after the Second World War. This picture was taken in 1972. In the film *Solitary Journey* Dawa remarked that "where foreigners see mountains we see ourselves. The mountains are the bones and we are the blood." He passed away in 1988.

On our way back from the centre I pass a fenced plantation of trees on the slope above the village. It makes me wonder about the future of the national park. The forest can undoubtedly be saved but what kind of experience will it be if the trekkers continue to multiply? Perhaps the flow will reach a natural limit. In its way, the lack of oxygen protects the area. About half of all those who try to reach Kala Pattar are forced to turn back before they get there because of altitude sickness.

It takes us eight days to walk up to Everest from the airfield in Lukla. We follow the rushing stream of Dudh Kosi to its sources and notice how the landscape changes. For the first two days we walk through pine forests in the deeply carved river valley. Steep peaks can be made out, unbelievably high above us in the firmament, like suns at their zenith. At an altitude of 11,810 feet (3,600m) above the village of Namche Bazar we reach alpine moorlands where the view opens out. We see lammergeyers sailing elegantly through the air and long-haired tahr graze precariously on the mountainsides. Some of the most beautiful mountains on earth are around us – for example, Ama Dablam, Taboche, Cholatse, Pumori, Kantega, Thamserku. And we can see that the national park contains far more than just the world's highest mountain. Even if Mount Everest were not there the trek is worth all the effort.

Previous pages: I have climbed up on to a ridge alone to photograph the blue twilight on the west face of Ama Dablam. How can one not become a mountain-lover with sights like this? Nature, the atmosphere and the whole mood just demand reverence.

The village of Namche Bazar lies in a south-facing basin at 11,810 feet (3,600m) above sea level. It is the main centre and marketplace in Khumbu, which is the name of the district south of Everest. Sherpas came here from Tibet in the sixteenth century. The word Sherpa means "people from the east".

Dingboche, 14,270 feet (4,350m) above sea level, is a summer village. Here trekkers can now stay in small lodges built alongside the old stone barns. The Sherpas keep long-haired yaks because when trade with Tibet was significant, caravans of these animals carried goods across the high passes.

But we really want to reach the highest mountain and see the biggest protrusion from the earth, the most extreme point on our planet – Everest, the furthest outpost on the way to the cosmos. And we succeed. A divine experience of the natural world.

For the Sherpas the mountain is sacred. They originated from Tibet and in their language Everest is called "Chomolunga", which was previously translated as "Mother Goddess of the World" or "Mother of the Wind" but is now interpreted as an abbreviation of the meaning "mother Miyolangsangma". The latter is a local name for the goddess of the mountain massif. All the peaks are sacred, but in the West it is only the highest point that has achieved special status. Many, many people want to climb it and almost 1,800 have so far got to the top. A couple of hundred have died.

As trekkers we have a closer relationship with the land than the climbers. We are happy to be nearby and observe. The trip to Kala Pattar is feasible for many able-bodied people, but if things go badly the little ridge in the kingdom of giants can become a private Everest. Unexpected snowstorms can make the trek extremely challenging. Altitude sickness is the biggest risk. In the Himalayas it is important to allow plenty of time. Many people suffer after climbing too quickly up to the higher levels.

The flight to Lukla is deceptive. Without the body having time to adjust, you land quite high, at over 9,840 feet (3,000m). It is far better to start trekking in the village

of Jiri, 43 miles (70km) to the west. You can get there by bus or taxi from Kathmandu. From Jiri it takes at least two weeks to trek up to Kala Pattar via Lukla. The trail crosses several passes and altogether you climb a whole Everest!

Lukla has become a busy little village. Every morning during the high season planes are constantly landing. All traffic has to be conducted during the cloud-free part of the day, usually before lunch. Delays are common and many people are forced to wait several days for their flight. Just as often, trekkers on their way to Everest get stuck in Kathmandu. This can subsequently create a lack of time that leads some people to climb far too quickly to higher levels in order to catch up with their schedule. We are lucky this time and can fly back with no problem.

In spite of the winds of change and all the devastating attention, I still consider the treks to Everest among my favourites. The landscape is captivating in a way that you don't experience anywhere else. The unique beauty is of course one explanation. And meeting the friendly Sherpas is something you never forget. But there is also something else, something deeper, a natural closeness to the eternal questions of life and death, East and West, belief and non-belief. All the destinies played out on and around Everest enhance the magic that surrounds the peak.

Catching their breath above Lobuche at 16,405 feet (5,000m) above sea level, with Mount Taboche to the left. The snow-clad heaps of gravel behind the trekkers are moraine deposits on the tongue of the Khumbu glacier.

The first rays of the sun hit the peak of Pumori, 23,440 feet (7,145m) above sea level. The dark ridge below is Kala Pattar (Black Rock), the goal of our trek. The first people to come here were Bill Tillman and company in 1950. That year Nepal began to allow expeditions to the mountains. Pumori was named in 1921 by the legendary George Mallory who saw the mountain from the Tibetan side. The name means "daughter peak" and was named after his own, Clare.

Thailand

VILLAGE TREKKING IN THE MOUNTAINS

The village of Borcraii is surrounded by the craggy limestone mountains of northern Thailand. Behind them lies the border with Myanmar (Burma). The village is inhabited by Black Lahu, one of the tribes in this area.

Panuve has drawn up the route. He is a young, go-ahead guide from Chiang Mai. Together we are to trek through northern Thailand's mountain regions where you can walk between villages and meet hospitable people from different ethnic groups. It is like a trek from one country to another but across non-existent borders. We're going to call this "village trekking". From the main town of Chiang Mai we drive northwest, past the town of Pai and approach close to the border with Myanmar (Burma), almost 125 miles (200km) west of the mythical "Golden Triangle".

With me on the trip is my 14-year-old daughter Catrin, and Panuve has also hired a porter. Our trek begins in a dense monsoon forest with teak trees that restrict our vision to a minimum, but the steep gradients tell us everything about the topography. The temperature is comfortably warm, and the path well chosen and easy to walk. Shafts of afternoon sun penetrate the jungle, which only seems wild. An abundance of bamboo indicates that people have cleared and felled for many years, which has depleted the fauna. The forests have also been scorched by the hill-folk. After just a few miles we reach a burnt-out clearing where rice is being grown.

Dusk falls quickly and we reach the first habitations as the sun goes down like a ball of fire in the humid haze. On a hill with extensive views there are a few houses and in front of them pigs and chickens are grubbing about in the earth. Two families live here. They belong to the Red Lahu tribe and Panuve says they want to live in peace. A woman ducks away shyly as we pass through the yard.

Soon it is pitch black. We pick up speed as we head for the village of Pamon, which has a couple of hundred inhabitants. There we look for a house to sleep in. They are built on stilts with floors of split bamboo and gaps for sweeping all the dirt down. In spite of an open fireplace on a stone base on the short side of the main room, the house is very clean inside, but the roof beams are sooty from the smoke that has to find its way out. Behind one of the long sides there is a room where our host family lives. We camp down by the hearth and spread out our sleeping bags.

Panuve cooks up the local staple food, rice and vegetables, and at the same time tells us about the peoples of northern Thailand. There are six mountain tribes here, who are also subdivided into smaller groups, each known for its special costumes and traditions. Almost all of them have arrived here in recent centuries at times of political unrest. They have probably been wanderers for a couple of thousand years. Time after time they have been pushed out by stronger cultures in the fertile lowlands. The real origin of the tribes is shrouded in mystery and almost all of them have no written language. On the other hand their oral traditions are highly developed. Old people can tell tales of social upheaval and long journeys.

The mountainous areas they inhabit are part of the Himalayan foothills and consist mainly of limestone. Many of the hills stretch out like long ridges, some look like round hills and a few are jagged with steep cliffs along their sides. The highest on our route are not more than 4,265 feet (1,300m) above sea level and even on the tops dense jungle grows. The landscape is splendid but not monumentally so.

Red Lahu live in the village where we are staying. The red element in their costumes is typical for them. The tribe tries to be self-sufficient, with cattle and rice plantations. The use of opium is part of their tradition and quite a few elderly men still smoke it. The next morning we walk past a little field of poppies. The lanky plants have finished flowering and a young woman is standing among the seed heads, cutting small notches into them, which allows the milky juice to ooze out. The harvest is a painstaking job. Panuve informs us that the authorities are trying to encourage the last opium growers to plant vegetables instead. They tell the villagers about the risks and survey the land by plane to find the remaining fields of the crop.

At an elephant camp further on we enter the domain of another people, the Karen, the biggest tribe in northern Thailand. They are different from the others, their lifestyle has no trace of Chinese culture and they have never been keen opium smokers. They are said to come from Thibi Kawbi, a place on the frontier between Tibet and the Gobi Desert.

Two big elephants walk down to a creek. From the high bank we place one foot on the broad forehead of the animal and swing ourselves up into the seat on its back. There we sit for the rest of the day like *pasha*s, with a firm grip on the poles as we jog through the rolling jungle terrain to the large village of Muang Paena. We spend the night with the village chieftain, Ratana Aa Rayatam, a middle-aged man with a large family. Ratana is walking with crutches and tells us that he crashed his motorbike. There are a lot of bikes in the village. The Karen people are more sociable than the other tribes and live easily in two different ages.

Ratana's 85-year-old mother is sitting by the fire when dinner is served. As guests we are served before our hosts and the old lady peers curiously at us with her limited sight as we eat. But mostly she stares in the other direction while the home's private life continues as if we weren't there. Everyone seems used to strangers. The next day as we leave the village Ratana has put on a traditional costume with a red tunic and matching pointed hat on his head. It looks splendid but the Karen people's costumes are considered less showy than those of the other tribes.

She is 85 years old and mother of the head of the household, Ratana. Everyone gathers round the hearth in the dark timber house that stands on stilts. The Karen are one of numerous tribes in northern Thailand.

After a short walk we reach a watercourse some tens of metres wide, surrounded by lofty mountains. Here our route takes a new turn. Time for rafting. We glide downstream on a bamboo raft. Water levels are low and there are long stretches of rapids. Sometimes we get out to push, but the further downstream we go the deeper the current and the trip is more comfortable than trekking. The countryside keeps changing character, from dense jungle to open grazing land and back again. Finally the water disappears into a deep limestone cave called Tham Lot, which is a well-known tourist attraction with a road leading up to it. This is where we disembark.

In the light of a paraffin lamp we are guided through the dark chambers, past stalactites as thick as bridge pillars. There is no electric light and the fact that the cave is so undeveloped means that we have to become potholers for a while. There are a few ladders erected between the galleries, which spread out on several levels. The flare of the paraffin lamp and some daylight from the cave opening allow us an impression of the imposing dimensions of the main gallery. Down on the gravel beds a new raft is waiting, and a little fairytale trip on the stream through the cavern.

After lunch we keep up a cracking pace to reach the village of Borcraii before nightfall. There are just 6 miles (10km) to go. The terrain continues to be very undulating and the jungle is matted the whole way. In the dusk we discover the village, delightfully located on a long narrow ridge. By the first houses a cheerful man offers to put us up. His name is Jayorh, he's about fifty years old and has smoked opium half his life but finally stopped. He turns out to be the village musician and we also learn that they are to hold a ceremony to celebrate an important spirit.

The people in Borcraii belong to the Black Lahu tribe, which calls itself "the blessed people". They migrated here from Burma at the end of the nineteenth century and are admired by others as skilled hunters. They are more open to modernity than their Red Lahu brethren – for example, in the village there is electricity. There is a road here but in spite of frequent contact with the outside world they devote themselves to old, indigenous, religious rites. The Black Lahu worship an all-encompassing god called Gúi Sha.

We are invited to a dance on an open square just beside the village street. In the middle of a patch of gravel stands a stone base. People move around it in a kind of stiff foxtrot. In this circle of people Jayorh struts and blows an instrument that might be a cross between bagpipes and Pan pipes. Emotive notes with a deep bass resonance can be heard over a wide area as I join the dance. The next day our delightful trek is over and we drive to the town of Mae Hong Son.

In the village of Pamon we stay with the Red Lahu. In the morning this young housewife feeds corn to the pigs. They spend the night between the stilts the house stands on.

The village of Borcraii is full of life. As trekkers, we are struck by how obliging and friendly these hill people are.

Gunung Kinabalu

THE ROCKY MOUNTAIN ROAD

Pouring rain makes the grey granite greyer still and very slippery. Occasional trees grow in cracks where there is earth, but the slabs are otherwise bare. For the Kadazan people around here the word Kinabalu means "the mountain of the dead". Legend has it that a Chinese prince was searching on the top of the mountain for a pink pearl, which was guarded by a dragon. After a dreadful fight he killed the dragon and took the pearl. He then married a Kadazan maiden but later abandoned her to return to China. The distraught wife then climbed the mountain where she was turned to stone.

We leave the Laban Lata inn in the early hours. Moonshine enables us to make out a mountain wall up ahead. Where the forest ends, 9,840 feet (3,000m) above sea level, we step into a rocky landscape that is nothing like what one expects of Borneo. The trees should really grow further up since the mountain is in the tropics, but there is simply no soil to take root in. The granite is smooth-shaven. And in spite of the latitude the air feels cold. It's only a few degrees plus. Warmly clad with gloves and hats, we climb up steep, wonderfully smooth slabs, held in place by friction. A thick and extremely long rope is stretched across the granite right up to the top.

Remarkable columns of rock form silhouettes against the rapidly lightening sky. The great height begins to make itself felt as we pull ourselves up by the rope. At half past four, just before dawn, we are standing on Low's Peak, 13,455 feet (4,101m) above sea level, and we feel as if we can see half the world. There is nothing anywhere near as high within sight. Borneo spreads its indented terrain to the south where dense banks of fog rest in the hollows. To the west, north and east we can follow the crooked coastline where the northern tip of the world's third largest island meets the sea. About 13,125 feet (4,000m) below, the lights twinkle in the town of Kota Kinabalu.

When we have regained our strength, we can orientate ourselves in the massif. The high plateau on Kinabalu is a strange world of smooth precipices and carved obelisks. Anyone who thinks Borneo just consists of jungle is deluding themselves. This is an incomparable mountain landscape, just 3 miles (5km) from east to west, and less than 3 miles (3.5km) from north to south. Not a particularly large area, but cut off from the rest of the island as a territory high in the sky.

The first person to climb it was Hugh Low in 1851. His biggest problem was getting to the foot of the mountain. It took him fifteen days from Kinabalu, something which today takes just two hours on the fast road. Dense rainforest made travel incredibly slow on the island. But Low is thought to have climbed the final slope to the top about as fast as today's trekkers. It is not difficult. We look down into a 4,920-foot (1,500-m) deep chasm, to which he has given his name, Low's Gully. It

A few guides are resting on the granite. Sometimes ice forms in the small rock basins up here and snow can fall on rare occasions, roughly every twenty years. The wind is biting cold. But as soon as the sun comes out it gets warm.

From Low's Peak we can look toward Victoria Peak. This is a wild, broken landscape, about 3 miles (5km) from east to west and just over 2 miles (3.5km) from north to south. Fifteen million years ago magma was formed underneath there. The magma cooled slowly and turned into granite, which was then pushed upwards nine million years ago; eight million years later it had forced its way through the earth's crust. Since then the mountain has simply continued to grow and is still doing so today.

cuts into the middle of the mountain and makes the massif look somewhat boomerang-shaped.

In Low's time people thought that Kinabalu was a volcano and the chasm a crater, but the mountain was actually formed by a batholith, a subterranean mass of granite pushed upward by forces in the earth's core. Unbelievably, Kinabalu gets half a centimetre longer every passing year, and in the last Ice Age the appearance of the mountain changed when glaciers ground down the hard rock. The result was a grey rocky landscape that has few, if any, counterparts in the world.

We don't spend long on the top. Almost every morning at around nine to ten o'clock thick cloud invades the massif and when the rain pours down you need to take great care. The granite becomes as slippery as ice and even lightning is a threat.

We descend the murderous slope to the foot of the mountain in one go. Almost all the trekkers on Kinabalu attest that the descent is the real achievement. Toward the end you have a gnawing pain in your knees, but the walking is bearable thanks to the vivid experience of the natural world. Tired but content, in the afternoon we can rest where we started from, at Timpochon Gate. Here there is a thought-provoking plaque with the results of a "climathon" competition.

The winner walked from here to Low's Peak and back in a time of 2 hours, 44 minutes, 22 seconds (!) – a distance of 16 miles (26km) for the round trip and a climb of 7,545 feet (2,300m) plus the same distance down. Not bad, but personally I think the two days we have spent trekking to the top and back have been far too short to boast about. I would rather have had a whole week to explore this mystical mountain landscape.

Gunung Mulu

THE CANNIBALS' HIGHWAY

The path on the Mulu mountain ridge is a real jungle march. The dense forest and undulating terrain present difficult obstacles. Here between Camps 3 and 4 there is a fixed rope past a bluff.

Next pages: The stone forest of "the Pinnacles" on Gunung Api is a unique collection of rock pillars, almost 165 feet (50m) tall and chiselled out by corrosive rainwater. These are perhaps the biggest rock needles in the world. There are similar stone forests formed from limestone on Madagascar and in a few other sites in the world.

Soaked with sweat, I balance on a knife-edge of rock and can't decide which is the most awe-inspiring, the landscape or our guide Ipoi Lawin. For three hours we have trekked through steaming rainforest in the interior of Borneo. Ipoi has shown us the way up a 3,280-foot (1000-m) high mountainside with an average gradient of more than forty-five degrees. We have grabbed hold of tree trunks and roots, climbed up metal ladders and dragged ourselves across slippery bluffs with the help of ropes fixed to the rock. And although I am sweating like an exhausted marathon runner, Ipoi is as dry as a couch potato. He smiles and shows no sign of exertion. He's a Berawan and, by the grace of God, a pathfinder.

To reach the rocks on the Gunung Api mountain like us, you have to struggle up the precipitous path. Reaching the little mountain ledge is an incomparable trial of strength, but the reward is a vision of bizarre beauty. The rocks are smooth, hard and ridged like corrugated iron with edges sharp as razor blades. They look like monstrous shark's teeth, but are also as tall as giant trees, up to almost 165 feet (50m). Altogether they form a real stone forest.

We have come here along the same route as the pioneers in the nineteenth century. After a lengthy journey in traditional longboats up a tributary of the Limbang river, we land on the border of Mulu National Park. From there we follow an old path that is now called the Head Hunters' Trail. In this rainforest in the nineteenth century, Kayan warriors stalked around hunting heads. Their targets were the coast-dwellers, whom they attacked.

After walking just over 6 miles (10km), we reach the huts of Camp 5 in pouring rain, 3,280 feet (1000m) below "the Pinnacles" as the rock needles are called. Between two high limestone mountains, Gunung Api and Gunung Benarat, the Melinau river has carved out a deep valley surrounded by steep, pale-coloured rock walls. The top is 5,250 feet (1,600m) above us.

"Only about a thousand people a year manage to get up to the rock needles," says Brian Clark when we meet him later in Mulu Resort. He is from Australia and works for the national park.

The Melinau river runs through a narrow valley it has dug out between Gunung Benarat and Gunung Api, on the right beyond the picture. Head hunters had a trail along the river in the nineteenth century. This is the location of Camp 5, which is passed by the Head Hunters Trail.

We meet a Penan couple in front of their house at the headquarters of the national park. The Penans were nomads who hunted game in the rainforest. Large-scale forestry operations have altered their living conditions, but many continue to live the traditional way. The national park provides them with a refuge.

"Many people turn back on the slope. You really need to get up there before lunch and before the clouds form. That demands a good turn of speed. How did you get on on the way down?" he wonders knowingly. "That was worse", I reply. "We didn't have enough water. On the way up I drank nearly half a gallon (1.5 litres) but I felt dizzy with dehydration on the way down and the bottle was empty. Luckily, Ipoi had left a full bottle halfway up the slope. That saved me."

Gunung Api was first climbed in 1978, when a small expedition reached the highest point: 5,610 feet (1,710m) above sea level. The stone forest is 1,640 feet (500m) lower. In 1857, Spencer St. John, the English consul to the Sultanate of Brunei, got to the mountain, which is around 60 miles (100km) from the coast, but he turned back because of the impossible terrain. These knobbly mountains in the rainforest were then virtually inaccessible. They were known as a landmark under the general name of Mulu. However, the only way to get to them was by making a dangerous river journey up the Limbang, where cannibals were a real threat.

St. John undertook three expeditions. On the first he discovered that the stream at the foot of the mountain came from under the ground and when he returned the next year he wrote that "the whole mountain is a massif with a honeycomb of limestone." Caves were also discovered. The mountain was not the highest in the region as he had thought, but was called "Api", which means "Fire Mountain". The name comes from the huge forest fires that often rage across the slopes. The ground is dry, as the rainwater runs down into all the holes in the rock and a lightning strike can start wide-ranging fires. The area's highest peak is Gunung Mulu, which stands next to the limestone mountains, even though it is made of sandstone. Movements in the earth's crust five million years ago caused these mountains of different rock to end up side by side.

Nowadays, a couple of hundred trekkers climb Gunung Mulu every year. It is a challenging trip. I make the attempt with Arne Larsson and Ipoi. Trekking through the rainforest with a heavy pack in thirty-degree heat and dripping humidity calls for different strengths from those needed on trips to European fells. The first insurance against exhaustion is fluids – you have to drink a lot. The second is to walk slowly and methodically. Leeches are an unavoidable scourge. I regularly have to pick these bloodsuckers off my legs. If they have been there a while, (which they often have, because you don't feel them bite) you bleed for some time. But if you don't let leeches bother you, you can put up with them. There is no risk from the bites, provided you keep them clean.

We cross a river, swim, and enjoy the longed-for coolness. Then the prolonged climb begins, through a tropical forest that changes character with altitude. The trees become shorter and thinner, the undergrowth more tangled and the moss on the trees thickens. We see pitcher plants, which are typical of Borneo's mountain forests. A few splendid butterflies waft by and in the background we hear the constant pulsing sound of the cicados' vibrato. A warthog suddenly appears and then just as quickly disappears. A hornbill clatters high up in a tree, but the big black bird flaps away like a fleeting shadow. And a poisonous Wagler's viper slithers cautiously away from the path. The rainforest is rich and poor at the same time. The foliage creates a roof that filters the light. The strongest impression is the smell of decay, as we walk hour after hour in strange, unbridled vegetation; it is an aroma that titillates rather than nauseates.

In Camp 3, at 3,280 feet (1000m), there is a shed where we spend the night, which turns cool. And the next day we climb a further 2,625 feet (800m) to Camp 4, on the highest part of the mountain's wooded spine. In around 1920, when there were still Sumatran rhinoceroses in the area, a hunter came here along a path the animals had trampled. That path opened up the mountain for an ascent. An expedition of young Oxford University students were the first to reach the highest point – they got through where the hunter had been. They pitched camp where we have now stopped and many of them felt the cold that night. They climbed the remaining 1,970 feet (600m) the next day and reached the top early on the morning of 18 November 1932.

The highest part of the mountain is often shrouded in cloud. When we wake up the weather does not look promising and after a while we decide not to try for the top. Without the view there is no incentive to climb right up there and the cloud continues to hold the mountain in its grip all day. But satisfied anyway, we turn back down through all the zones of the rainforest. Gravity helps us to pant less, but we get tired anyway. It takes two days to descend.

A Wagler's viper slithers away from the path on Mulu. Snakes usually do. This green male is a different colour from the females. It gets its name from a German naturalist. This species is sometimes called the "temple snake". The males can be aggressive if they are cornered. Nobody is known to have been killed by Wagler's viper, but the poison is strong.

Wilsons Promontory

FROM BEACH TO BEACH

A granite block that has been ground by the waves stands by the beach of Little Waterloo Bay. The trekking trail follows the sandy beaches and in between it crosses ridges of higher ground.

On the map Wilsons Promontory, "the Prom" as it is popularly known, forms a long peninsula sticking out into the storm-lashed Bass Sound. The southernmost two-thirds have a range of hills up to 2,300 feet (700m) above sea level, and nestling between the mountains are wonderful sandy beaches that can only be reached on foot. Here you can tramp from beach to beach and reach the southern tip of Australia. A very fine coastal walk.

When we reach our starting point in the car I immediately notice a peculiarity of the landscape. Appearing as patches on the wooded mountainsides, there are domed granite slabs. The hills are part of a formation that is 380 million years old; this formation continues under the sea to Tasmania. In the last Ice Age, when the surface of the sea was much lower, the hills formed a land bridge to the big island to the south. During other periods when the sea was higher, only the summits stuck out of the water like an archipelago. Today eucalyptus trees clothe the heights of Wilsons Promontory and in sheltered ravines and on boggy land the rainforest grows impenetrably.

The trekking trail, "the Prom Circuit", follows the coast of the peninsula. At the visitor centre in Tidal River you pay for your overnight stops. You can only camp at designated sites and the number of trekkers is controlled, so we have booked our places a month in advance. In February, the time of our trip, it is the high season.

Although Australia has a short history as a nation, this national park is one of the oldest in the world. The idea of protecting it was mooted in 1880, when the first field biology club was formed in Melbourne. At that time the British colony was expanding rapidly and new lands were being taken into cultivation. At the same time Australia's first national park had been created outside Sydney and it became a source of inspiration for John Gregory, a highly colourful member of the club. He wanted to protect "the Prom" against tree felling and received some support for that when the authorities forbade the sale of the peninsula. But it took a couple of decades before the protection measures became all-encompassing. A professor pursued the matter and in 1908 "the Prom" was declared a national park.

We trek east over the mountains from Tidal River to Sealers Cove. A long gentle slope on the other side of the summit of the peninsula leads us down to a wide bay where a sandy beach creates a golden boundary between the forest and the sea. The granite mountains curve out towards the sea like breasts, framed by the forest's luxuriant foliage. Where the sand ends we paddle across a little river, which flows out into the sea, and reach a campsite in the leafy chamber. The combination of a deserted beach, lush forest and grand topography imbues this place with an aura of both paradise and wilderness.

George Bass landed here in 1798. His crew shot seals in the bay, hence the name Sealers Cove. Fifty years later a sawmill had been set up and timber was supplied for the building boom in Melbourne. A little village grew up but after about ten years the timber ran out and the business died. In 1903 a new sawmill was established, but it burnt down after a few years. There was great pressure from the timber industry and the area was actually protected in the nick of time. Nowadays "the Prom", with its pristine landscape, is a unique place in Victoria, the most developed and densely populated state in Australia.

In the next few days we follow the path over the coastal mountains, walk up and down the hills and most of the time we are alone with far-reaching views across the sea to the east and the undulating forest landscape to the west. On the beaches we can take swims, which are unexpectedly cool. The temperature of the water is below 20°C and I have rarely experienced such pleasantly refreshing bathing in tropically warm weather.

Latrobe Range rises behind Sealers Cove. There was a whaling station here in the mid-nineteenth century, but now the beach is deserted and provides a welcome campsite for the trekker.

Sandy beaches are not the easiest terrain to walk on in the world, but walking alone across the half-mile-long (kilometre-long) beach at Waterloo Bay is a Robinson Crusoe experience.

The sun shines. However, on the third day there is a downpour – not unusual in this region, which is one of the wettest on the Australian continent. The famous lighthouse on the outermost point of the peninsula dates from 1859, but it disappears in veils of mist. When the weather clears up we walk down to Australia's southernmost tip from our campsite at Roaring Meg. Steep-sided islands are visible in the sea beyond and in the far distance lies Tasmania. Knowing that gives the horizon an extra dimension.

On the western side of the peninsula the beaches are more open, wider and more gently shelving. Powerful breakers, driven by the wind known as "the roaring forties", thunder on to the sand at Oberon Bay and there is a fresh breeze. Birds such as gulls and terns seem to prefer these exposed beaches to the more protected bays of the eastern side.

We end our trip at our starting point on Tidal River, which is something of a holiday village inside the national park. There are shops, trailer campsites and rental cottages. About 100,000 visitors come to Wilsons Promontory every year. However, in spite of that the greater part of the peninsula's large area remains a genuine wilderness.

AUSTRALIA

Overland Track

RENDEZVOUS IN THE WILDERNESS

Dove Lake lies in the shadow of Cradle Mountain, Tasmania's most famous peak, some 5,070 feet (1,545m) above sea level. In 1912 the legendary Austrian pioneer Gustav Weindorfer built a hostel nearby for walkers and called it Waldheim. It has since been rebuilt, but in the manner of the original, and forms a natural starting point for the Overland Track, which passes above the lake and below Cradle Mountain. Weindorfer had visions of a national park and today the area is classified as a World Heritage site.

The Scott Kilvert Memorial Hut was built in memory of two young men who froze to death in an unexpected snowstorm here many years ago. Tasmania's weather can be harsh even in summer, but this evening it is mild and I am waiting at the hut to meet Martin Gwynne and Gordon Sanders, a couple of friends from Australia. The two cousins turn up extremely late, in the dark, fired up by their delightful night hike.

The hut stands by a lake a few miles from Overland Track and the next day the three of us move on to the famous trail, while a gentle rain begins to fall. A path leads us through aromatic eucalyptus forest, up to curving plateaux with mountains looming in the distance. After one day the weather settles down and we stop by a fork in the path that can only be found by those who know it is there. Martin turned off it the first time he walked here – on a guided tour with accommodation in the well-appointed private cottages that lie hidden a little way off the track. The half-overgrown fork leads to one of them. "Good food that time and a light pack, but the walking was far too restricted," says Martin. "There's more freedom like this," he laughs.

The Overland Track passes through the extensive national park of Cradle Mountain–Lake St. Clair, and has become an internationally famous trekking trail. After my first trips to Tasmania, I would now really like to walk the whole trail. The island's wildernesses have made a big impression on me. In spite of a relatively low altitude above sea level, at most just 5,250 feet (1,600m), the terrain is very hilly. Stocky summits alternate with liberating plains. Lakes and streams are full of perfectly clean water the colour of tea, owing to organic substances from the peatlands. And there are many remarkable species of plants and animals. But the landscape also has an integrity that I appreciate. The weather is temperamental and presents challenges. Walking off the path is almost impossible. Deep ravines, tangled vegetation and impenetrable woods are not readily accessible features. Tasmania's beauty inspires the same sort of feelings as an old person's richly furrowed face. You feel both captivated and humble.

We rest a while below the summit of Barn Bluff, beside some big pencil pines, one of the most beautiful species of tree on the island. The mountain is an imposing

volcanic plug, 1,310 feet (400m) high from the base, with dolerite cliffs often weathered into hexagonal columns. Coal occurs sporadically in this hard rock and at the beginning of the twentieth century the pioneers tried to mine a seam near here, but it proved unprofitable, thank goodness.

The sun shines as we later pitch our tent on decking in the tangled bush around the Windermere hut, which stands by a lake surrounded by marshy land. On the next leg towards the high mountains, which have been looming for a long time in the direction we are travelling, there is more wetland, and boards have been laid across the muddiest sections to protect the ground from wear.

Beyond the edge of the wood at the Pelion hut grasslands shimmer gold in the twilight, but the mood is broken by a pair of brushtail possums. These marsupials are as big as hares and cheeky as baboons. As Martin is sitting by the spirit stove in front of the tent, one of them pinches a bag of nuts right in front of his nose. Martin gets annoyed and chases it up into a tree. The animal comes back and the same thing happens again, and again.

At the pass called Pelion Gap you can leave your pack to climb Tasmania's highest peak, Mount Ossa, 5,450 feet (1,661m) above sea level. We tackle it, but the mist comes down just as we reach the very top. We are luckier with Acropolis Mountain. This is two days later and we are camping in Pine Valley, a beautiful site beside the Overland Track. We trudge through the cool rainforest. Mighty pines with huge needles, King Billy pines, veil the sky almost like broadleaf trees. But when we climb the mountain walls surrounding the high plateau the sun is scorching hot. Within our far-reaching field of vision there is not a single building or other trace of civilization. Columns of dolerite flank the precipices like a field of tree stumps. The first cartographers decided to call several of these mountains after classical models – and of course Acropolis looks like a temple.

The most enticing place around the Overland Track is definitely "the Labyrinth", a slightly undulating plateau below Acropolis. The terrain consists of a network of tarns, narrow crests and polished slabs. Between the glens stands a sparse forest of pencil pines and eucalyptus. The landscape, not unexpectedly, forms a labyrinth.

I walk there alone in the darkness of the night to see the sunrise. The same day the cousins continue on to the end of the Overland Track at Lake St. Clair. When the dawn is over I wander for a long time in the lovely surroundings of the Labyrinth and try to avoid getting lost, which one can easily do. The dark water of the tarns lies still without a ripple, not a leaf stirs on the trees. In the background stand solid mountain-tops with big heaps of boulders at the foot of the precipices. This far from the island's towns and inhabited areas I feel I have found the essence of Tasmania's wild landscape. There is an aesthetic harmony in the interaction between the decorative trees, the carpet of green on the ground, the brown sheen of the lakes and the grey bulk of the scarred mountains. The landscape of the island looks to me like a rockery run wild, on a giant scale.

Previous pages: The dawn sun blazes on Mount Eros and highlights the eucalyptus trees by "the Labyrinth". This is one of the most prized sites in Tasmania, a short way away from the Overland Track.

You can understand why the first cartographers looked to ancient Greece when they wanted to name the land forms. Up here on Acropolis, 4,825 feet (1,470m) above sea level, the dolerite rock has thrust up temple-like columns. The view encompasses large parts of the uninhabited wilderness of southwest Tasmania. On the horizon to the right you can even make out Frenchman's Cap; the mountain straight ahead is called Mount Gould.

Frenchman's Cap

THE VIEW OF THE TITANS

Looking northwards from Pine Knob, we see the mist lying eerily in the hollows. The dry trees are remnants from the great forest fire of 1966. When aboriginal people lived in these areas they regularly burned the forest in low-lying places, but the fire damage here was the result of a wholly natural rather than man-made event.

The prisoners on Sarah Island thought Frenchman's Cap reminded them of the patriots' caps during the French Revolution, and that is how this prominent mountain got its name. From where we are, the profile is more like a tooth and it looks extra big in the early dawn. This peak is unusually sharp and dominant for Tasmania. But when the darkness begins to lift we lose sight of it. The path has taken us to the wrong place. The best angle was an hour earlier, at the Barron Pass, but we didn't know that then. When you walk a path for the first time you tend to think that there will be better views further on. We jog a little to see whether Frenchman's Cap will emerge again from behind a hill that is in the way, but in vain. Finally we give up and stop to watch the dawn without Frenchman's Cap in our sights. The light strikes a group of dry trees which bear witness to the great fire that struck the area in 1966. Behind them, under the glow of the dawn, the land stretches out with mile after mile of forest-clad ridges and steep mountain crests. Tasmania is showing us its best side.

Fires occur often on the island. The breakdown of dead material in temperate rainforests like those of Tasmania takes longer than in a tropical one. The leaves of the eucalyptus are tough and accumulate on the forest floor as combustible material, together with fallen trees and branches, giving a fire something to really get its teeth into, especially during periods of dry weather.

The rosy glow around Frenchman's Cap has faded when we see the top again from the tiny Lake Tahune, a body of water which seems to have been shoehorned into its mountain basin, so steep are the slopes around it. A team of climbers is based in the little hut here. High in the sky rises the tooth that has aroused their ambitions. Frenchman's Cap is not just a dangerous and powerful mountain but also one of Tasmania's highest at more than 4,730 feet (1,443m) above sea level. But behind that impassable mountain wall there is a convex shoulder which poses no problems for the climber.

We continue on the path up to the pass to the north of the peak. The end of it leads us across rocky slabs and shelves where we have to scramble playfully. From the highest point the island appears freshly scrubbed in the sharp morning light.

The view is boundless. The peak lies in the middle of a cluster of steep mountains. Beyond them the land is gentler, with undulating folds extending to other sharp mountain profiles in the far distance. Small banks of mist in the hollows are vanquished by the sun.

Frenchman's Cap is like a titanic watchtower in the midst of this historic wilderness. The aborigines who lived on the island for 25,000 years chiefly stayed on the coast, but sometimes came here to hunt. When Europeans came to Tasmania at the beginning of the nineteenth century the aborigines were eradicated in a horrendous way. At the same time the conquerors began charting the land. In an attempt to reach the coast from the interior in 1840, James Calder was halted by the mountains and the river gorges around here. Afterwards he noted that: "The mountain range of the Frenchman's Cap being so contiguous to the part and shooting out its branches everywhere like arms of a polypus leaves very little choice in the direction of a road." The expedition was forced to turn back.

The first to climb this dominating landmark was the surveyor James Sprent in 1853, but Thomas Moore interests me more. He was a genuine nature-lover who crossed great tracts of the Tasmanian wilderness. In 1887 he climbed Frenchman's Cap from the west and thought "that the mountain has the most majestic cliffs of overhanging rocks that I have ever seen."

Our trek to Frenchman's Cap is a return journey. The trail is ranked high among the bushwalkers on the island. The forest is beautifully cool when we come down from the Barron Pass on our way back, often using our hands for support on bluffs, ladders or fallen trees. Our tent stands beside the pretty Lake Vera, which is surrounded by steep mountainsides and dense vegetation. We have pitched it on a minimally cleared area, close to the little hut that is there for trekkers to use.

As on the way here, we now have to squelch across Loddon Plains, a marshy river plain where the path consists mainly of mud. From there we see the mountain for the last time before we pass across the brow of a hill down to Franklin river, the world-famous river that caused such uproar when the Tasmanian government wanted to expand its hydro-electric power in 1984. The project caused people from far and wide to occupy diggers driven out into the bush. About a thousand people were arrested but the project was later stopped by the country's Supreme Court. The strong tide of public opinion helped to save one of the earth's most valuable natural sites for posterity.

Where we cross the Franklin on a little suspension bridge, about 60 miles (100km) upstream of the confluence with the Gordon river, the stream is narrow and quiet. The water seems to be biding its time. You will soon be roaring more loudly, I think, as I look toward the bend where the river disappears on its journey toward narrow gorges and dangerous rapids. It is a lovely ending and feels absolutely right to dip our bodies into this cold water, which is of such great symbolic value for the progress of nature conservation. Refreshing for the body, good for the soul.

The path leads through a so-called temperate rainforest, which occurs in many different forms in Tasmania. This one is classified as mixed and has mainly southern beech trees, the same species as is found on New Zealand and in Patagonia. The tree fern *Dicksonia antarctica* covers large expanses of the forest floor.

Tongariro

ON VARIED GROUND

Volcanoes are not only colourful during an eruption, the lava they leave behind becomes nature's own artist's palette. Here we see the Red Crater, which is part of the Tongariro massif.

I don't *always* want sunny weather. Moods can be swept away by the sharp light and the landscape seems tamer, but when trekking without companions I prefer blue sky. It feels safer and makes the trip more enjoyable. During a solo trip around the Tongariro massif on New Zealand's North Island I was granted such weather – fortunately enough, since the area is usually pretty rainy.

A short walk from the village of Whakapapa leads me to the Mangatepopu hut beneath Ngauruhoe, the most symmetrical of the peaks. It is easy to understand why the Maoris have long considered these volcanoes to be holy ground. The mountains, with their looming shapes and multiple colours, seem mystical. They are symbols of the aboriginal people's identity and self-esteem, their *mana*. If a European settler climbed a peak, it aroused the Maoris' fury. After 1839, when the botanist John Bidwell became the first man to climb Ngauruhoe, conflicts between the aboriginal people and the Europeans increased, in parallel with the establishment of new farms and logging. The Maori leader Te Heuheu Tukino saw that Tongariro was threatened by land sales and grazing cattle, and he had the brilliant idea of giving the volcanoes to the New Zealand government (in other words, the British Crown) as a gift from the Maori people. It became a national park in 1895 – one of the first in the world – and this protection lifted the threat of development.

From the hut my trail takes a steep, upward route to a natural amphitheatre where a flat stony desert is encircled by scree slopes, which are like immense grandstands. Here, I take off my backpack and climb Ngauruhoe, which is no longer controversial. On the top are two craters, one inside the other. The volcano is active and for a long period last century it erupted every ninth year, but it has now quietened down. More than two decades have passed since the last eruption. Is a new one on the way? In volcanic areas you can feel that the ground is not to be trusted, but nobody needs to be uneasy here. The authorities issue warnings before potential eruptions and at present there is only the steam rising along the crater rim to remind us of the latent danger.

Down on the path again I continue on loose lava gravel and climb up to a pass 5,575 feet (1,700m) above sea level. From there you can look down into the geological

artist's palette of Red Crater, which belongs to the volcano called Tongariro. Inside the oxtail-coloured crater you can see an exploded lava seam and the slopes are decorated with rust-red, coal-black, lead-grey, ivory-white and dirty-beige patches. In the lower part there are also some sulphuric deposits where the steam billows up, and from time to time the smell of sulphur pervades the air. On the other side of the pass a couple of small lakes add new colours to the palette. Emerald Lake is an emerald-green jewel with water that contains soda. Blue Lake has different chemistry and lies in a bowl that resembles blue ink. Both are beautiful but deadly poisonous.

A long, downhill slope on the north side of the massif ends at Ketatahi Hut, close to springs still owned by the Maoris. In the dusk a few trekkers gather on the veranda of the hut to watch the sunset over the great, but distant, Taupo Lake to the north. Many people make a day trek here from Whakapapa, and finish at a road below the hut. This stretch, which is called the Tongariro Crossing, is very popular. But I want to continue around the whole massif on a route called the Tongariro Northern Circuit, which takes four to five days.

The next morning I follow the trail back a bit and then turn off over a mountain saddle and down to the lava field west of the cone of Ngauruhoe. Here, there are far fewer trekkers and, as the landscape is very desert-like, it seems more desolate. It now looks more like Iceland than it did earlier, but the sparse, thorny tussocks of plants attest to the fact that I am far from the Arctic region.

The path goes down into the Oturere valley, where it passes a little overnight hut. Continuing southwards it crosses the Rangipo desert while the contours of the massif's third volcano, Ruepehu, slowly rise up in my field of vision, the highest point in the whole massif at 9,175 feet (2,797m) above sea level. This leg ends with a walk through a dense forest to Waihohonu, the fourth tourist hut.

From here one can continue south on the trail, over fresh lava fields, and around Ruapehu, to end up back at Whakapapa village. But instead, the Northern Circuit turns to the east and climbs slowly up a shallow saddle between the volcanoes. Close to the summit I take a detour to Tama Lakes, immediately below Ngauruhoe. The weather is chilly and, with its glassy pools and dull lava slopes, contributes to a less hospitable image of this volcanic landscape, which looks so splendid in sunshine. However, the change doesn't bother me. I am approaching the end of a successful trek and the fact that the clouds are drawing in enlarges my experience of the region's variations. You can get tired of both good weather and picturesque mountains, but when my impressions have settled I realize that it is the unusual nature of the volcanoes that makes Tongariro Northern Circuit one of the world's more colourful treks.

Previous pages: From Ketatahi we can see the great Lake Taupo, which is a collapsed crater that has filled with water. Both it and Tongariro lie along the volcanic belt that cuts across North Island. Taupo exploded in AD186 in one of the world's most powerful volcanic eruptions for many thousands of years.

I look at the upper cone of Ngauruhoe and Red Crater, which can be seen below it on the left. The trail passes across the ridge there and the saddle below it.

Milford Track

THE ONE-WAY TRIP

Few trails have a more magnificent finale. By boat we glide out into Milford Sound while the rain clouds sweep across Mitre Peak, which rises 5,550 feet (1,692m) straight up from the sea. The depth of the fjord adds a further 985 feet (300m) to the height difference. This is the world's most impressive coastal mountain.

Sometimes one is lucky. Like when the sun shines uninterruptedly in an area that normally sees 26 feet (8m) of precipitation a year. The sky is already blue during the boat trip across the lake Te Anau. At Glade Wharf, the starting point for the trip, we disembark, shoulder our backpacks and then stroll off in the heat towards the first hut. A dense enchanted forest surrounds the path, and then the next day, in the continuing sunny weather, we trek over open spaces in the middle of a valley floor.

The fact that the path is deserted has nothing to do with the trail. Milford Track in New Zealand's South Island is a one-way-street – you don't meet people coming towards you. It's an ingenious arrangement. In spite of the fact that 10,000 trekkers walk here every year, you don't feel crowded at all. In order to reduce the wear and tear, the people who look after the path and the national park have established a number of rules which make Milford Track one of the world's most regulated trekking trails. People walking with a guide can be out six days and sleep in privately owned cottages, while independent trekkers must manage the 34-mile (55-km) long distance in four days and sleep in more basic huts.

The rules undeniably limit one's freedom but they also create considerable advantages. All the people walking independently and starting on the same day form a group that meets up in the huts every evening. That is fun. And the person who rambles along the path alone, behind all the others, can experience an unspoilt wilderness. The largest number of people allowed to set off on the path each day is forty, whether independently or with a guide. Milford Track is immeasurably popular and I booked this trip a long time in advance. There is another peculiarity that makes it special too – the path reaches an obvious climax and divides naturally into two halves, before and after Mackinnon's Pass.

During our walk we are in the Fiordland National Park. The area is broken up by narrow and jagged mountain crests, some up to 5,905 feet (1,800m) above sea level. Between them there is a tangle of deeply carved, sinuous valleys, clad in impenetrable rainforest. From the sea narrow fjords of the Norwegian type penetrate between the precipitous mountains, and overall the topography is a real labyrinth.

The blazing sun makes Clinton Valley a tranquil environment. The valley twists a little below almost vertical cliff walls that effectively shut out the view. Only where another valley branches off is there an opening. Feeling isolated from the outside world, we move along an enlarged alley between the mighty faces of the mountains.

The path runs parallel with the valley's crystal clear river. In this weather the landscape feels contemplative, but at the same time the constricted space urges us on. The longer you walk in this long narrow valley, the more you long to reach the famous pass, and a wider view. In the end my longing is so strong that the climb from the innermost part of Clinton Valley, where it ends in a cauldron, hardly tires me at all. What is awaiting us up there?

Finally, a view! That is the first feeling. An ascent of just 1,640 feet (500m) leads up to Mackinnnon's Pass, which sits on a mountain ridge, just a hundred-feet wide and covered with low-growing grass vegetation. Here we meet the kea, the fearless parrot of this region, which is only too happy to sink its beak into your pack to find something edible. We have actually been warned about the damage these birds can do. The view encompasses sprawling mountains with some residual snow and small glaciers. In the breathtaking chasm on the other side we can see Arthur's river disappearing behind a bend in the valley.

A cairn, the Mackinnon Memorial, set up in honour of one of the pioneers who established the route here is a reminder that the pass once represented a real obstacle. Quintin Mackinnon, together with a Donald Sutherland, had been looking for a land link to the Milford Sound fjord about 12 miles (20km) north of the pass and the goal of their trek. There, the eccentric Sutherland ran a tourist hut with his wife. Even then Milford Sound was famous for its beauty and tourists were carried there by boat. In 1888 Mackinnon and Sutherland stood on the pass and twenty years later an English newspaper designated Milford Track the world's finest trekking trail.

When we have crossed the pass we descend steeply. At one risky point there are steps that make the going easier. On the last day of the trip rain falls, causing the forest to clothe itself in rich green. The change in the weather is welcome. Now I can see this landscape in its usual state. Veils of mist hang on the mountains like curtains and the penetrating damp explains why the forest is as dense and fertile as it is.

It is a walk of almost 12 miles (20km) from Dumpling Hill to the infamous Sandfly Point. The point takes its name from the biting flies that look like gnats; they are scarcely a problem for me, however, used as I am to Scandinavian winged insects. Our walk ends an hour or so before a boat takes us to the road at the innermost end of Milford Sound.

As the boat glides out into the mighty fjord, we can see Mitre Peak, rising 5,575 feet (1,700m) straight up from the water. The vertical sheet of water at the foot of the mountain accentuates the height. Mitre Peak looks higher than most of the other mountains in the world. That view, or should we say optical illusion, makes a fitting end to this trail.

Previous pages: Seen from Mackinnon's Pass, Clinton Valley looks like a dried-up fjord, which is actually what it is. We walked down there, just as Quintin Mackinnon had done with his companion in 1888. Born on the Shetland Isles, it was Mackinnon who cleared a path through this valley. On the other side of the pass Donald Sutherland had already set up a path through Arthur's Valley. Mackinnon found the link between the two valleys and is commemorated with a cairn on the pass.

A lovely dip under the bride's veil. Sutherland Falls are reckoned to be the world's fifth highest waterfall, dropping 1,905 feet (580m) in three stages. They are just over half a mile's (1km) detour from the Milford Track.

Waimea

THE GIANT GORGE OF THE PACIFIC

The Polynesians call the mountain ridges Poó Kaeha. The inhabitants of Hawaii greeted James Cook as a god in 1778. Waimea was the first place he landed among the Hawaiian islands. Before that nobody had suspected that there were islands in the middle of the Pacific Ocean.

Cock-a-doodle-doo! A familiar but surprising sound wakes us. Time after time the cock crows and the sound confuses us. Is the tent in a farmyard? No, not at all. Yesterday we walked through a dense forest down into a narrow canyon on an island in the middle of the Pacific Ocean. The landscape is wild and surely no place for farm animals. The environment felt exotic in every way – the forest with its unusual vegetation, the landscape with its multifarious rocks, and even the trek itself in the hot humid air. The idea that the cock we can hear has run wild is the only explanation we can come up with. But he's not alone! We can hear "cock-a-doodle-doo" from several different directions. It is quite an amusing experience in this strange wilderness.

Even more amazing is the fact that we are walking in an immense canyon on a little subtropical island as far from the continents as one can get on earth. This place is the opposite of the Altai Mountains, where you are the greatest possible distance from the sea. Geographical outposts lure persistent trekkers, and our trek this time is on Kauai, the northernmost of the five big islands in the Hawaii archipelago. It has taken us two days to get deep into this canyon, but the distance we have walked is not more than 9 miles (15km) from the starting point. This system of ravines is called Waimea, often also called the "Grand Canyon of the Pacific". The crack is about 12 miles (20km) long and 2,625 feet (800m) deep. The rocks exhibit a fantastic range of colours: red, yellow, black, violet, brown and orange. A wonderful landscape for a few days' trekking.

The geology is unique because the canyons have been carved out in hardened lava. All the islands in the archipelago are of volcanic origin. The Waimea river breaks down the rock and carries an earthy brown plume of weathered rock flour into the navy blue ocean beyond the estuary. Above the canyon lies one of the earth's wettest places, the extinct volcano Waialeale, which with its summit at 5,250 feet (1,600m) above sea level reaches altitudes where the clouds of the trade winds drop most of their rainfall. That is why it rains nearly all the time up there and the river has a guaranteed supply of water. But all this we shall soon learn first hand.

Up on Waialeale there is a huge marsh that collects the rain and sends gushing waterfalls down into the ravine system. The everlasting moisture keeps the vegetation constantly green. The rainforest is singular, and up on the mountain it is dominated by a low-growing tree called *ohi'a*. On the lower slopes creeping bushes decorate the ochre-coloured lava rock with verdigris-coloured patches. At the bottom of the ravine, around the river, the forest grows dense again but with different types of trees from those higher up on the mountain. Thanks to this interplay between different kinds of vegetation and the bare rock, the landscape has an unusually variegated colour range.

Car-drivers flock to the edge of the canyon to admire this breathtaking view. There is a busy road there with several viewing points. From one of these a steep path leads right down, on slippery ground, via unruly loops, to the Waimea river in the bottom of the canyon. When we have started to walk and are a little way along the path, there are suddenly no more people around and the dramatic landscape immediately becomes a wilderness. A couple of hours later, after a steep descent, we are standing by the river and we set up camp under the trees.

Our trek continues upstream. Further on we have to wade through the river, up to our waists in tepid water. A small path then leads into the side ravine of Koaie, where tall sisal plants have laid bayonet-like leaves over the ground. These large, grotesque rosette plants, like the cockerels, goats and wild pigs, were introduced to the island. This has upset the natural ecosystem, but the sisal fascinates us with its majestic height and the exotic atmosphere created by its leaves. The ravine is narrow. When you look for blue sky you have to crane your neck hard. With binoculars we can see the crowds up on the viewpoints along the edge of the ravine. They look like dwarves in silhouette, unaware that we are walking down here in the abyss.

The weather is sunny for a long time but rain falls in the evening, and when the cock has finished crowing the next morning a tropical cloudburst pours down on us. Above the ravine's cliffs, behind small, fleeting banks of mist that appear and disappear, parallel stripes are embroidered with slim silver threads. The mountains are weeping and we sense their displeasure. The stream in Koaie sounds more aggressive now. And the side ravine where we are standing is an uncompromising return route. A few miles further on the path ends in a blind alley. The vertical cliffs form an insurmountable obstacle. The only way out of the campsite is the path we took to get here, and when we once again stand by the ford, the river has risen by several feet. We have fallen into a trap. The only thing we can do is wait, put up the tent and listen to the music of the water. Later in the afternoon the rain stops and the next morning the river has returned to normal. We can cross the stream and then get up out of Waimea, taking with us an experience that has taught us something fundamental about this landscape.

Previous pages: From the edge of the canyon Waimea really is the "Grand Canyon of the Pacific". We look down into the Koaie ravine, which abuts the slopes of the Waialeale volcano. It was formed about five million years ago and the canyon began as a crack when the volcano collapsed one million years later. Rust from the ferrous basalt colours the earth.

We camp beside this little stream that runs through the rainforest and out into the Koaie ravine. The forest is dominated by the kukui tree, from whose oleaginous fruits the Polynesians used to extract lamp oil. The pointed leaves belong to sisal, a plant of the agave family.

Torres del Paine

A JAGGED ROUTE

Torres del Paine is one of the world's most spectacular mountain scenes. In the middle of the massif is Paine Grande, the highest point, at 10,010 feet (3,050m) above sea level. Its smooth granite walls are 3,280 feet (1,000m) high. The writer Florence Dixie wrote in a travel book in 1879 that the nearby rock pinnacles reminded her of Cleopatra's needles, the famous Egyptian obelisks.

In the darkness of the dawn, we are three trekkers walking up to a little mountain lake, below the famous rock pinnacles of Torres del Paine. The ascent takes just half an hour from our campsite in the Rio Ascensio valley. Up by the enigmatic lake we stop and wait for the sunlight in the cool of the morning. We warm ourselves a little by slapping our sides as the darkness slides away from the mountains and the sky lightens up. Soon the cliffs begin to glow, first faintly and then like molten metal. The pinnacles are incredibly tall and slender. Their granite walls drop smooth as concrete straight down into the water. Only by the sea of boulders where we stand shivering is there an opening in the huge bowl.

This memorable scene lasts half an hour, then the granite cools and the cliffs become grey. A cloud front swirls in over the mountains and the curtain comes down, while snow begins to fall and the wind gets up. Our trek around Torres del Paine has begun with a magnificent overture, which ends as quickly as it began.

We are all mentally prepared for the change of scene. You should be when you come here. Patagonia's welcome to its guests is often rather backhanded. During our trek it is raining more often than not, and so much so that several places receive a whole year's rainfall in twenty-four hours. There is an east wind, which is abnormal here where the Pacific's "roaring forties" usually howl across the mountains. Where these storms meet the mountains the rain falls, while the steppe east of the mountain range is as dry as it is windy. Torres del Paine is first in line but in March the weather is usually good. We are unlucky. Now the bad weather is coming from Argentina and that means it's going to get worse.

After two rainy days at least the sun is shining at the same time as we reach Lago Dickson. Beyond the meadow where we are camping there is a beached iceberg and steep, snowy mountains form a monumental, picture-postcard backdrop. Here we are reminded of more northern tracts. The lake actually got its name from the old timber merchant and patron of the arts, Oscar Dickson of Gothenburg. The Swede Otto Nordenskjöld came here in 1896 on his second expedition to the southernmost part of South America.

Torres del Paine was a focal point and Otto Nordenskjöld was the first to map the area. When he had walked round the massif, he saw the same wonderful view as us. "The pearl in the landscape was the lake," he wrote later. "The innermost creek was full of pack ice and out on its tranquil surface huge, fantastic icebergs floated, like giant swans, while the tall, snow-covered mountain chain was reflected in its water (...) At that very moment I decided that this lake should be called after Baron Oscar Dickson, who had taken so much interest in our expedition."

Just ten years later another Swedish expedition came to these parts, this time under the leadership of the botanist Carl Skottsberg. When one of the three participants rode past a hitherto unknown lake south of Paine, he gave it the name Lago Skottsberg. Together with Lago Nordenskjöld and Lago Dickson, this means that the three big lakes in the Chilean national park are all called after Swedes.

It's surprising that the three foreign names live on, I think, as the path takes us close to Lago Skottsberg on the second-to-last day of our trek around the massif. The sun is shining from a pale sky and it is warm. In this part of Torres del Paine there are considerably more walkers out and about than on the path north of the peaks, and we meet some who are following the "W", as the most popular route is called. On that trip you only travel along the southern side of the massif and walk up the two valleys that cut up between the peaks. It can be completed in two or three days. The Paine Circuit, which we are walking, includes the "W" but also goes around the massif to the north and takes longer – at least a week – although preferably nine days if you don't want to overexert yourself. It is quite demanding and many connoisseurs reckon it to be one of the world's major trekking trails. The landscape is extremely varied.

We are walking anti-clockwise, which takes us to the hardest section on the fourth and fifth legs where we have to cross the John Garner Pass – yet another example of the area's strange place names. The authorities in Chile have evidently not felt prompted to replace these names with local names. In most cases there are no Indian names for the terrain, but Paine is supposed to originate from an Indian language and means blue, probably referring to the colourful glacial lakes.

It is raining and thundering as we leave Campamento Los Perros, our campsite in the thick forest. The path climbs up 2,295 feet (700m) over trampled bogs to austere, alpine heathlands, and finally we stand on the exposed and stony pass in a biting wind and with no view. Here the national park's most magnificent view should unfold. In fine weather you can see the dazzling white expanse of the Campo de Hielo Sur glacier, a real inland icefield, 200 miles (320km) long. From the ice plateau its tongues extend down to the narrow, Argentinian mountain lakes in the east and the Chilean fjords in the west.

For a brief moment we glimpse the view under a blue sky. We battle rapidly over the pass and straight on down toward the ice. The gradient is very steep and soon we enter the forest, where the path becomes an obstacle course of fallen trees and roots.

North of the Torres del Paine massif the path leads through a valley with the Paine river. The lofty mountain, Cerro Ohnet, in the background rises "only" 6,330 feet (1,929m) above sea level.

Next pages: The Grey glacier discharges into the lake of the same name. The glacier constitutes a tongue of the Patagonian icefield Campo de Hielo Sur, which from here extends 200 miles (320km) northward. The front splits into icebergs that float around in the water.

The next day, in constantly improving weather, we keep the same elevation through this sharply sloping ancient forest of deciduous trees. Between the foliage we see the immense expanse of the glacier on our right and the high mountain tops on our left. After a strenuous hike we reach Lago Grey, where the glacier cracks and deposits icebergs in the lake. Here, the contrasts are stunning. We walk in a leafy beechwood grove where the path meanders along delightfully under the trees. Then, we walk out on to the cliffs beside the wood, where bare rocks and chaotic ice masses extend westward as far as the eye can see. It could be Antarctica.

The glacier tempts us to go on an ice walk. Our starting point is the hut, the refuge where we are camping. In several places along the Paine Circuit there are similar mountain huts offering board and lodging. The bunks are narrow, but in the main room where you eat there is often a lively atmosphere. There are guides stationed at this one. After a splashy trip on a rubber dinghy across the icy lake, we step ashore beside the awesome glacier, put on our crampons and rope ourselves together. The brilliant weather allows us to plod around among the cracks and ice grottoes. The glacier offers us new perspectives on the landscape.

A new and wonderfully beautiful stretch awaits us. We walk along Lago Grey to the Pehoe refuge, from where one can go by boat across Lake Pehoe to reach the

We walk for long stretches in a temperate rainforest with the southern beech of the genus *Nothofagus*. The forest reminds us of Tasmania and New Zealand. The fact that this genus of tree is found only in these regions reveals that they were part of the giant continent of Gondwanaland about 150 million years ago.

East of the massif a couple of cowboys pass by. They have different names in the different countries of South America. In Chile they are called "huaso".

main road to the town of Puerto Natales, 124 miles (200km) further south. But we intend to complete "the Circuit" and walk past Lake Skottsberg, on up Valle Frances, below the sensational peaks of Cuernos del Paine, "the horns". From the foot of the mountain their pink granite rocks are as vertical as anything can be, and absolutely smooth. And right at the top we can see a thick layer of clay shale, giving the summit a liquorice-coloured cap.

The boundaries between the different types of rock are razor-sharp and one ponders the reason for this peculiar geology. Granite is formed by magma from deep inside the earth, while shale is clay that has become petrified close to the surface. The granite was probably forced up from below and pushed the shale upward.

Valle Frances leads into a huge cauldron crowned with slender granite towers. Looking back along the length of this valley, we can see far beyond the great lake systems. Menacing avalanches thunder now and again on the slopes, while the dusk sets the heavens alight. On the last day we close the circle in pouring rain. The east wind is more biting than ever as we walk south of Torres del Paine, and we return soaking wet to our starting point , where a long-awaited dinner in one of the hotels is our reward.

Fitz Roy

UNLUCKY DREAM TRIP

The sub-Antarctic storms rarely leave Fitz Roy in peace. When the mountain is revealed, it proves to be one of the world's most impressive. The vertical rock wall is 5,905 feet (1,800m) high!

A constant wind is blowing. Patagonia's infamous squalls push us toward the slope, yet the weather is the best it has been so far, with the sun peeping out. There is nothing like wind for dampening one's enthusiasm, yet at the same time it enhances the feeling of the wild. The clouds swirl over Saint Exupery and Poicenot and in short "film clips" we can make out the razor-sharp pinnacles. For a moment we see the whole landscape – how rugged it is – and it makes up for the wind's torments. The vision is a delight for anyone who loves spectacular mountain landscapes.

This morning even Fitz Roy emerged for a short while, with a physical presence like no other mountain I have seen. Yet the height is "only" 11,170 feet (3,405m) above sea level. The sun made the polished granite spire shine like a glass wall as it reached straight up to the sky. The other mountains were dwarfed by comparison. We were allowed ten minutes "audience" before the clouds swept over Fitz Roy again, and that was that. From the steppe, on our way here, the spire also emerged when the cloud mass lightened up on the horizon. Such an "exclamatory" landmark is not found in many places. Other mountains in the world which dominate their surroundings, are chunkier than Fitz Roy.

Now we have reached the windswept viewpoint, Laguna de los Tres, a domed mountain ridge above an ice-cold lake that fills its little basin close against the summits. Most people trekking in the area come here, but Robert Fitz Roy, Captain of the Beagle, never made it. During Charles Darwin's famous expedition in 1834 Captain Roy only came within 75 miles (125km) of the mountain that was later given his name. In spite of that, the explorer Francisco Moreno wanted to honour Darwin's skipper when, much later, he christened the peak, unaware that the Tehuelche Indians had their own name for it – Chaltén – which means "smoking mountain". They thought that the clouds, which almost never disappeared, were the smoke from a volcanic eruption.

The area around Fitz Roy is popular with trekkers in Patagonia. It is part of Los Glaciares National Park. Behind Fitz Roy lies the great inland icefield, Campo de Hielo Sur. Long glacial tongues slide down between the summits of the Andes to the big lakes east of the mountain range. The Perito Moreno glacier further south is the most well-known.

The trekking trails keep to the east of the icefield. They are relatively short but you don't need to go far to find variation in the scenery. We start our trip in the young tourist resort of El Chaltén and climb up the slopes to Laguna Capri. There it is possible to camp in the autumnal beech forest. The path is easy to follow and we reach the next campsite unexpectedly quickly. We endure half a day here in poor visibility before trekking up to Laguna de los Tres.

At any rate, we can be grateful to the weather for one thing – we get the proper image of the landscape. Like almost no other place name, Patagonia resonates adventure. The name originates from Ferdinand Magellan, who landed in southernmost South America in 1520 and called the people he saw Patagoni. These people were tall and bound their feet in animal skins. Perhaps Magellan was thinking of a Spanish word that means "animals with big feet" or possibly he knew the Spanish story of a huge giant called Patagon. Nobody knows. For whatever reason, this wind-lashed part of the continent came to be called Patagonia. But the name has no administrative significance and comprises both Chile and Argentina south of the 40th parallel.

In the sand near Rio Blanco this nirre tree battles against the wind. The species is a low-growing southern beech. The forests of Patagonia display intense autumn colours.

"But we viewed in these grand mountains with regret, for we were obliged to imagine about their form and nature, instead of standing, as we had hoped, on their crest ." Charles Darwin's words in his classic book about the voyage of the Beagle, 1828–36, indicates that he never got to see Fitz Roy, not even from a distance. If the peak had been visible, Darwin could scarcely have dreamed of an ascent. There is no such pointed landmark anywhere else.

The Indians of this mountain had their own version of the story of the Flood. The evil snake Cai Cai wanted to drown the world. A kinder-hearted snake popped up and led the people to the tops of the mountains, but many warriors drowned. When the waters receded Cai Cai turned the dead warriors into another petrified warrior, Cerro Torre, almost as high as, but far slenderer than Fitz Roy. Since my teenage years I have wanted to see this, the world's highest "needle mountain", but hope is fading. During our trek the clouds hang low all the time and the colourful forest is veiled in mist. The odds don't look good.

The trail is hard to follow in places. It disappears from view as we walk along the shore of Laguna Madre, which is bounded on the other side by a high precipice where the clouds just glide down. On the other side of a saddle in the landscape we stroll down the broad, wooded valley with the Fitz Roy river. Its water comes from Laguna Torre. Below a moraine ridge is a campsite, our goal for today.

When the tent is up we walk to the glacial lake to look at the view. A bank of cloud refuses to slacken its grip on the mountains behind the icefield. Cerro Torre, this needle of absolutely vertical granite diorite, 4,920 feet (1,500m) tall from top to toe, is wrapped up inside that cotton-wool. We know that and yearn to be able to see it. That is why we have come here, but we have to give up after a while. The next day the weather is still heavy as we return to El Chaltén. So much for my teenage dream ... but Cerro Torre still calls to me.

Inca Trail

A SINGULAR DESTINATION

The goal of the Inca Trail, Machu Picchu, emanates a wonderful harmony between the architecture and the landscape. Even high on the sugar-loaf summit of Huayna Picchu there is a ruin. The fortress was built in the mid-fifteenth century and was probably inhabited by 10,000 people, mainly women. It was abruptly abandoned a century later, but the reason is unclear. On 24 July 1911 the archaeologist Hiram Bingham found the ruins overgrown by jungle. In the classic *The Lost City of the Incas*, he writes: "Would anyone believe what I had found? Luckily enough (…) I had a camera and the sun shone."

Wilbur Aparicio is the best guide we could have. He is a Quechua Indian, worldly-wise and a fluent English speaker. In addition, he is highly knowledgeable about the history of the Inca people. Our group consists of six people and the time is mid-October, it is the rainy season and the number of trekkers has diminished considerably. A period of more uncertain weather, but more peace and quiet.

During the 1990s there were claims that the Inca Trail was worn, dirty, vandalized and exposed to low-level criminal activity. Large numbers of trekkers walked the legendary trail that climbs over three passes in the mountain chain of the Cordillera Vilcabamba and ends at the ruined city of Machu Picchu. The reputation of the trail slumped and the authorities in Peru decided to repair the damage. Results were not long in coming. It is now well cared for and the wardens who patrol it regularly make sure that security is high.

By train we travel from Cuzco to a stop called "Kilometre 88" in the Urubamba valley. To test the participants' fitness, Wilbur leads us on a short tour when we get off the train. In the group there is one very overweight lady and her two well-toned sons. The rest of us shake our heads and wonder how this is going to go. During the climb up to the ruins of Wayna Oénta we find out, and with impressive tact, Wilbur persuades the mother to take the train to Aguas Calientes, a tourist destination below Machu Picchu, where we can meet her three days later.

The next day the reduced group walks out on the first leg of the Inca Trail. Already after just a few miles, we pass the first historic place, Llaqtapata, a ceremonial centre from the heyday of the Inca people in the fifteenth century. There, the trail turns into another valley, leads through dense forest and climbs a little. We pass through a few small settlements, and in the village of Huaylabamba the park wardens check our permits.

Here, the path changes direction again and leads us into a new valley pointing toward the west. We have to trudge up a long, demanding slope to Abra Warmiwanusqa, "Dead Woman's Pass". Two-thirds of the way up the slope there is a campsite where most trekkers stay the night. On the way up the clouds come

On the second day we reach Abra Warmiwanusqa, the "Dead Woman's Pass". A long, exhausting slope leads up to the top of the pass at 13,880 feet (4,230m) above sea level.

The clouds break up as we start the long descent toward Machu Picchu. The mountain that has given its name to the ruined city is the conical elevation immediately behind the citadel of Phuyupatamarka or "Cloud City", where we spend the night at 11,745 feet (3,580m) above sea level. These ruins were also discovered by Bingham in 1915.

down and the rest of the journey becomes a trek through cloud forests – in the literal meaning of the word.

In the mist we continue the next day by climbing to the top of the pass, which is a narrow ridge with a grassy heath, 13,780 feet (4,200m) above sea level. We walk slowly, without the spring in our step of the previous day. One woman in the group is 68 years old and Wilbur says she is the oldest woman to have walked the trail. We congratulate her; in relation to the conditions, hers is the greatest achievement. I chew coca leaves like the Indians, to improve my resistance and cope better with the altitude. It's more innocent than it sounds. The hill-dwellers have chewed these leaves since time immemorial and it's completely legal in Peru. I do feel some effect, but it's like chewing the cud and the others make do with drinking coca tea.

"Dead Woman's Pass" is the highest point on the Inca Trail – a test that causes many trekkers to give up. For a short while we can look back and see down into the valley where the path started. Looking forward we glimpse other chasms between the veils of cloud. The name of the pass, Abra Warmiwanusqa, originates from a legend about a young Inca princess who was sacrificed and buried here, and in the 1990s they found her remains. In the mist that comes and goes, it seems a mysterious and daunting place. To keep warm we continue at a good pace down into the next valley, lose a hard-won height of about 1,320 feet (400m) and enter the cloud forest again. We then climb toward the next pass and walk past yet another ruin, Runkuray, a little, circular lookout-post made of stone, clinging like an eyrie to the slope.

From pass number two, Abra Runkuray, the land slopes steeply down into the forest on the other side. The area we are travelling through is a borderland between

the mountains of the Andes and the Amazonian rainforest. The forest is stratified into different types that change with the altitude, making the biodiversity unusually rich, but owing to the weather we see very little wildlife. The mist is no drawback for the ruins, it makes them seem even more mysterious as they emerge. At a height of 11,810 feet (3,600m) lies Sayaqmarka, the most impressive settlement so far. Ruined foundations cling to a narrow ridge, and here, if not before, we are filled with admiration for the Indians' engineering skills.

From here the path runs level for a long stretch. We trudge on worn stone steps and pass through a short tunnel that has been carved through a cliff. So much work has gone into this trail; so many people have trodden it over the centuries. How big were they, these Indians who toiled with all these blocks of stone? The steps are not particularly ergonomic, they are wearing on the knees, but they have protected the ground against centuries of erosion, and contribute to our respect for the area's history, built up by the other relics. All this makes the Inca Trail a unique trek.

The path we are following is only a fragment of the extensive network of trails that connected the old empire together. The Incas reigned over an enormous territory, from southern Colombia to northern Chile. Information was transmitted by messengers who ran backwards and forwards on the paved trails. The Incas had neither money nor a written language, but they did have an efficient administrative system. The empire grew up when a strong chieftain in the fifteenth century expanded his core area around the town of Cuzco. In the space of a hundred years they built a powerful empire, and by the time the Spaniard Francisco Pizarro arrived in the area in 1532 with 168 soldiers in his train, the autocrat Huayna Capac and his two sons had divided the empire. The sons had fallen out with each other and the victor was tricked into entering Pizarro's headquarters, where he was subsequently killed. The other brother took over as king, but rebelled, which led the invaders to carry out a bloodbath. The last Inca king fled up into the mountains to the hidden city of Vilcapampa, mentioned in the Spanish chronicles of that time. That may have been Machu Picchu.

In the nineteenth century many adventurers searched for the hiding place of the last Inca king. The American Hiram Bingham found Machu Picchu in 1911 and named the ruins after the adjacent mountain. Wilbur tells us, however, that the famous ruined city was not the refuge of the fleeing Inca king as was previously thought. Where that lies is still not known.

On the last night we camp on the trail's third pass above the ruins at Phuyupatamarka. We can see nothing of the magnificent views, but the next morning the cloud lifts and the weather provides us with a splendid finale. Far below our feet lies the Urubamba Valley. Wooded mountainsides drop headlong to the river, and beside the stream we can make out the railway from Cuzco, the only fixed connection to this site. We can also see the mountain of Machu Picchu, a tree-covered hump on the long, high ridge below us.

Previous pages: From Huayna Picchu one can make out the railway along the Urubamba river, 2,295 feet (700m) below in this ravine. Hiram Bingham struggled through the rainforest down there. He was born on Hawaii, learned to love mountain climbing and exploring at an early age, and ended his working life as a senator. During his legendary expedition he met an Indian in a clearing near Mandor, where the river disappears from the picture, on the left. The Indian knew that there were ruins up here on Huayna Picchu and along the narrow ridge from here to the mountain of Machu Picchu. The Indian later led him to a worldwide sensation.

Along the path we meet the hill-dwellers – here a woman is doing crochet. They are called the Quechua after the most widespread Indian language in South America. It was also spoken by the Inca people.

Countless steps further down, the path passes stone-bound terraces for cultivation, which were only discovered in 1985. Not long after that we reach Winaywayna, another old settlement where there is a guest-house and even more imposing ruins to visit.

We reach the sun gate of Intipunku at midday. For some time we are walking in the shadow of the mountain of Machu Picchu. A ridge, on which the gate stands, runs from the mountain. After a steep climb we reach the archway and see the mythical Inca city. At the same time the sky clears and spills its light over the ruins.

Seeing Machu Picchu for the first time is a great moment. You are almost paralyzed by all the energy radiated by the place. The size of the city, its position in the landscape, its beauty – everything makes a huge impression. The Inca people must have enjoyed a holy alliance with nature.

We stay at Intipunku for an hour or so and then go down to the crowds between the remains of the houses. And there I experience something I had not expected – a feeling of obliviousness to all the tourists moving between the stone houses. The impressions are so overwhelming that you don't think about other people being there too, with their own thoughts. I take this as a sign of the greatness of the ruins. Machu Picchu is definitely a unique place and a wonderful end to the Inca Trail.

Cordillera Blanca

THE WHITE MOUNTAINS' SURPRISE

Like a symbol of the famous film company, Paramount Pictures, Artesonraju raises its pyramid toward the heavens. Only the trademark stars are missing. The peak is 19,765 feet (6,025m) above sea level. Many people consider its beauty to be as pure as that of the more famous mountain, Alpamayo.

You need to reach the Punta Union pass when the sun is rising. So we start early, the young Indian Agripino and I. In the light of our head torches we follow a path through the vale of Hauripampa. The silence is overwhelming and the forest pitch black. You can't make out the silhouettes of the mighty mountains even against the sky. We exchange few words in these three hours. The stillness of the night and the fast pace keep us quiet. I feel as if I were enveloped in a drowsy state of expectation. The thin air plays its part.

When the darkness begins to lighten, the shadowy outline of Mount Taulliraju (pronounced "taudirasju") looms. The map is full of names that are hard to pronounce. They often describe the landscape. Taulliraju means "the lupin's snowy summit" says Agripino. He works as a guide and was born in the area. Dense clumps of stately lupins grow in the valleys around here, but where we are walking the landscape is barren. The mountain is turning into an increasingly bright star, gradually changing colour: first pale peachy yellow then a richer shade like amber. When we get even closer to the pass, a thin cloud that looks as if it is made of pink tulle floats across the rock face. The high altitude, 15,420 feet (4,700m) above sea level, forces us to slow down, and in the end we stop to watch the spectacle without panting.

Dawn on tropical mountains is not very drawn-out. The light comes as decisively as if you were lighting a lamp. In just a few minutes the delicate atmosphere is erased and the landscape becomes a sparkling blue and white room. Suddenly we have to squint to see the newly awakened peaks. With these in front of my eyes I try to understand what it is that distinguishes this mountain chain from others I have trekked in. Perhaps the temperature. The air feels pleasantly mild even though the altitude is high. We are only eight degrees south of the Equator. Further away from the tropics this sort of altitude is rarely so comfortable. These mountains are by far the highest so close to the Equator. Here, there are also the highest forests in the world, and so much sticky wet snow falls that glaciers have formed on steeper rock walls than anywhere else. Their gradient causes loads of cracks in the ice and the

High up close to the snowy mountain slopes, like here in the Quebrada Santa Cruz valley, there is excellent grazing and the *vaqueros* (cowboys) drive their cattle there. They come from the villages around the Cordillera Blanca. The central parts of this mountain range are largely uninhabited.

A mule grazes peacefully by marshy ground in the Quebrada Paria valley, which lies beside the Santa Cruz Trail. The Navada Paron mountain is reflected in the water.

snow makes the peaks as pale as marble. A more dazzling landscape than the Cordillera Blanca is scarcely to be found anywhere on earth.

Just thirty mountains in this part of the Andes exceed the magical height of 19,685 feet (6,000m) above sea level. Their most striking feature is the hanging snow suspended on the summits' west-facing leeward sides, like gigantic stucco moulding. The name Cordillera Blanca – the white mountain chain – could not be more apt. Even the rocks that create the contours are uniformly pale and consist mainly of granite.

We are following the Santa Cruz Trail, which crosses the mountains from east to west. On the last slope up to the pass the path is paved with ancient steps and Agripino says that they are probably from a period dating from before the Incas' rule. People in the Andes were not afraid of climbing mountains many centuries before mountaineering took off in Europe. Some of the oldest traces of South American culture are found in these tracts. The Chavin Indians lived here a thousand years before Christ. They spread to large parts of the central Andes. But even two thousand years before that there was a culture, which has left its mark in the town of Yungay, not far from the pass. Perhaps the stones we are walking on were laid at that time.

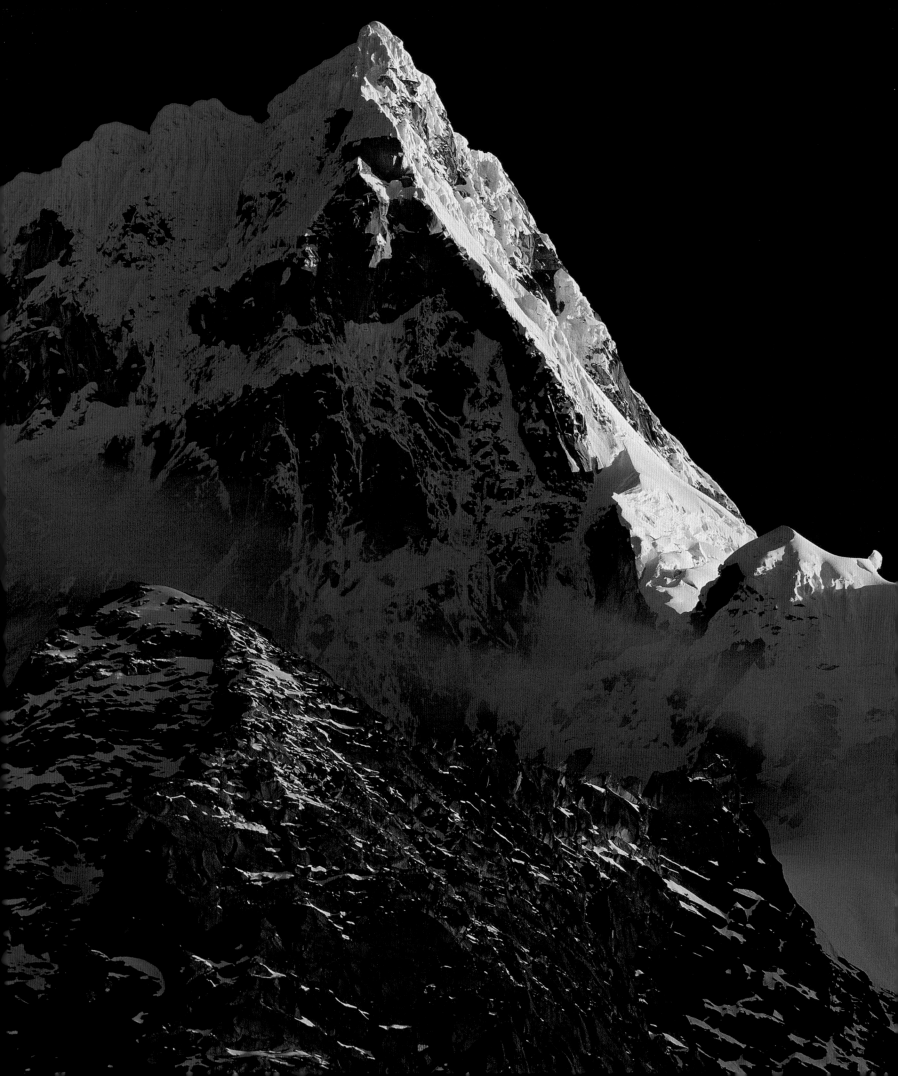

Punta Union has a cleft carved out of the narrow rocky ridge. It is a few metres wide, just as deep and about 33 feet (10m) long. We have just entered into this artificial crevice and I have this minute pointed my camera toward the landscape on the other side when Agripino yells "Condor!" With a quick reflex action I fling myself at my backpack to grab my telephoto lens at the same time as the giant bird of prey sweeps by a few metres above our heads. With its 10-foot (3-m) wide black wingspan, it literally extinguishes the light for one magical moment. Caught by surprise, it swoops across and then quickly glides out of sight. I get no photo, but a shaggy image of a flying monster is imprinted on my mind. The condor, which lives mainly on carrion, is quite common in the Cordillera Blanca, but you rarely get as close to it as we did.

A few days later we enter the hanging valley of Quebrada Arhueycocha, where I walk alone up on to a moraine ridge to look at the Alpamayo mountain. The name means "source of the muddy river". In the 1960s this peak was designated the world's most beautiful in a survey carried out by an alpine journal. Alpamayo even beat K2 in Karakoram and they were followed by a series of other well-known mountains, such as the Matterhorn and Mont Blanc in the Alps, Ama Dablam and Machapuchare in the Himalayas. One might question the value of such a league table – nonetheless it says a lot about the mountain's qualities and is still referred to today, not least in tourist brochures.

The most beautiful view of Alpamayo is from the north. Where I am standing, to the south, the peak looks more like an average mountain of the Cordillera Blanca and my interest is soon won over by other peaks, such as Artesonraju, which is more symmetrical in shape and one of the most stylish mountains I have ever seen, or Piramide, an exciting spearhead of snow-frosted granite.

During quite a long wait for the sunset, I sit still and watch the light play on the mountains. My thoughts turn to an unexpected observation at the Arhueycocha lake. The turquoise-coloured pool lies in a basin below where I am sitting. The glacier on Pucajirca tumbles toward the lake and discharges small ice floes, which have sailed out across the surface of the water, at first seemingly unmoving, then thrown together into a white jigsaw puzzle by a squally wind.

The landscape is enormously impressive, but by the lake the wilderness is unexpectedly tame. The moraine ridge, which dams the water, is cut through by a dug-out ditch. This is reinforced with concrete on the sides and equipped with sluice-gates. The outflow from the lake is regulated, and Agripino tells me later that this was done to draw off water if the lake is filling up too fast. That way they can prevent it overflowing and seriously flooding the densely populated river valley below the mountain chain.

This little intervention is, of course, easy to accept but nonetheless it takes the edge off the virgin image that the landscape otherwise emits. Along the paths in the Cordillera Blanca there are various traces, both old and new, that have been left by

Previous pages: From the Punta Union Pass we can see Taulliraju on our left, 19,125 feet (5,830m) above sea level, usually considered one of the world's hardest mountains to climb. The first to conquer it was one of the greatest mountaineers in history, the Frenchman, Lionel Terray. In his famous autobiography *Conquistadors of the Useless* he writes "Never was there a more laborious mountain to conquer."

human beings. The modest installation by the lake is not the only one of its kind and it tells me that inaccessible places in monumental mountain chains are not necessarily untouched. We are actually trekking in an old cultivated landscape with wild contours.

Our journey through the Santa Cruz valley also brings another surprise. Trapped between the valley sides lie tussocky bogs, and the greeny-blue lakes skirted by the path are bordered by dense, tall grass. Nutritious lakes such as these are not often found so high, almost 13,125 feet (4,000m) above sea level. The feeder streams bring in glacial mud that evidently fertilizes the vegetation. This makes for rich birdlife, and we see many different kinds of ducks. The distinctive Andean geese with their stubby beaks look for food in the rivulets in the bog.

Further west the valley narrows to a canyon. Our trip ends where this opens on to the wide and densely populated valley along the Santas river. But before that we pass fertile grazing lands where flocks of farm animals graze tranquilly. *Vaqueros*, shepherd boys and drovers walk along the path, some wearing traditional ponchos. They are leading their horses and cows to the sought-after meadows higher up. The animals and people make up an image as timeless as the jagged snowy mountains.

Roraima

AN ISLAND IN TIME

Dawn lighting the edge of Roraima's rock face is a magnificent sight viewed from within the national park and world heritage site of Canaima. In 1838 Robert Schomburg wrote: "Those stupendous walls rise to a height of 1500 feet. They are perpendicular as if erected with a plumb-line, nevertheless in some parts they are overhung with low shrubs which, seen from a distance, give a dark hue to the reddish rock." He was probably referring to the almost black lichen that clothes the mountain. He added: "I can imperfectly describe the appearance of these mountains. They convey the idea of vast buildings, and might be called nature's forum."

The mist lifts and a strange landscape emerges. We see undulating cliffs and water-filled vats ornamented with thorny plants. On the sweeping rocks strange-shaped boulders rise up. In the haze some of them look like petrified dinosaurs.

Kendall, a Pemon Indian, is showing us the way past the system of cracks in the rock. The surface we are treading on reminds us a little of glacier ice, it's just as uneven, but dark. A few metres from the abyss we instinctively stop. You can feel the gaping void even though cloud hides the view. We creep over the last bit, toward a "table edge", at the same time as veils of cloud swirl past, driven by powerful upwinds. When that has eased off, we peer cautiously over like terrified Lilliputian figures.

What we see is not exactly for anyone with a tendency to vertigo. An absolutely vertical rock wall drops straight down, several hundred metres, to the Amazon rainforest, which in turn slopes towards a flat valley floor. At the bottom of the dense jungle, some 4,920 feet (1500m) below us, shimmers a winding river and on the other side of the valley rises another table mountain, just as majestic as the one we are on. Where are we? On a *tepui* in southern Venezuela. It is called Roraima.

Tepui means "mountain" in the Indian language, and there are about a hundred such table mountains spread over an enormous area in southern Venezuela and Guyana. Roraima stands in some of the world's most magnificent countryside, known locally as La Gran Sabana (the Great Savannah). Wide grassy plains extend between large islands of rainforest, but it is the *tepui*s that make the landscape so special. With their flat tops and monstrously steep mountainsides, they pop up out of the plains like impregnable fortresses – gigantic building blocks or islands in the sky.

On the plateaus, flora and fauna have developed in isolation over millions of years. Roraima caused Arthur Conan Doyle to write *The Lost World*, published in 1912, about a kind of real-life Jurassic Park, with dinosaurs living on one of the mountains. We don't see any – apart from the strange rock forms! Instead it is the landscape that excites us and we understand how Conan Doyle, like so many other Britons of his time, was fascinated by Roraima, even though he never came here. The mountain is inaccessible, located where the borders of Venezuela, Brazil and Guyana meet.

The slightly undulating surface of the top of Roraima enables there to be campsites beneath some bluffs, called "the hotels". In 1884 Everard im Thurn and his companion found a way up here that even the Pemon Indians did not know about.

"South America is a place I love and I think (…) it is the grandest, richest, most wonderful bit of earth upon this planet (…)." Sir Arthur Conan Doyle waxes lyrical in his book on *tepuis*, *The Lost World*, published in 1912. The leaves in the fissure belong to the endemic genus of Stegolepis, which has thirty-two species throughout the different table mountains. The red bush is a *Bonnetia roraimae*, also a plant unique to Roraima.

The first time it attracted attention was in an engraving in the 1841 book *Twelve Views in the Interior of Guyana*, by the Prussian botanist Robert Schomburg, who charted the topography of Guyana, a British colony. His picture turned the mountain into an icon. "Is there no-one who can explore Roraima?" asked an English newspaper forty years later, and the adventurer John Bodham promptly set off, but never conquered it. His book whipped up even more interest and in December 1884 Everard im Thurn, Director of Music in Georgetown, Guyana, succeeded in finding a route to the top. Subsequently, he told of his exploits in a lecture in London. Conan Doyle was there and that is how the idea of a fabled "lost world" came into being.

The broad ramp used by Thurn runs diagonally up the vertical rockface and is the only possible way to ascend Roraima without some very difficult climbing. The plateau is surrounded by an impressively high rock wall that is several miles long and consistently perpendicular. Seen from the sky, the flat top of the mountain is shaped like a spearhead. We are exploring this cut-off world for a few intense days.

With Kendall, our group of five drives by jeep from Santa Elena de Urien, close to the border with Brazil, to Parai. From there we trek across the undulating grassy plain towards two *tepuis*. One is Kukenan, the other is Roraima, which at 9,220 feet (2,810m) above sea level, is the highest table mountain in the Gran Sabana.

Previous pages: From Roraima we can watch as Kukenan, another table mountain, is gradually swallowed up by the clouds and turned into a "lost world". Sherlock Holmes' literary creator, Conan Doyle, wrote an adventure story of that name. It tells the story of some dinosaurs surviving on a mountain like Roraima. The following quotation shows what a great yarn the story Is: "The summit showed every sign of luxuriant vegetation (…) and farther back many high trees." In real life, Conan Doyle didn't know how barren it actually is up here because he had never been here.

We meet a few Pemon Indians near Kukenan. The tribe settled in Gran Sabana 200 years ago and burned the land to keep the savannahs open. For them, the *tepui*s or table mountains are sacred and act as the guardians of the savannah. The Pemon say that on the peaks, where no one is allowed to live, there are *mawari*, people who steal souls from the living. The Indians once lived in small, scattered villages along the rivers, but increasingly they are congregating in bigger settlements.

After two days we set up camp beneath the mountain wall and wonder whether it really is possible to get up to the plateau. It seems to stick straight up into the sky, but the next day we continue upwards through the dense rainforest to the foot of the precipice. After a strenuous but nonetheless straightforward climb up the ramp we finally step over the rim of the plateau, into the mist and another realm. The path leads us to one of the "hotels", as three bluffs on the plateau are called, where you can camp on narrow, sandy strips beside the cliffs. The first one becomes our base camp.

The surface of the plateau is very undulating. We walk down into the "crystal valley" where there are rock crystals. Unfortunately, many of them have been crushed by visitors and we suddenly become aware of the effects of trekking in this sensitive environment. At the same time as us there are about fifty other trekkers on Roraima. A few thousand people climb the mountain every year.

Until modern times all the *tepui*s were unclimbed, worshipped by the Indians of the plains as the home of the gods. Naturally isolated environments, the plateaus enabled unique flora and fauna to evolve undisturbed. Many plants and animals are endemic and some species exist only on a single table mountain.

A geological breakdown has created these *tepui*s. The mountains have been weathered from a 4-mile (6-km) thick layer of sand that was packed beneath a prehistoric ocean. The sand solidified slowly as sandstone, and when South America and Africa glided apart due to continental drift, the sandstone split and most of it was broken down. The Amazon and Orinoco rivers, which drained the area, carried away the gravel from the weathering and left behind a number of *tepui*s, which today are covered in black lichen. In the chasm, where the lichen does not thrive, the sandstone displays its normal yellow colour.

In the dawn light Kendall and I walk to the edge of the abyss to see the sun rise. The plateau ends abruptly and the winds can sweep a trekker over the edge – and have done. But today there is a calm and I dare to stand on the brink to look at a fascinating spectacle. Way down in Amazonas a bank of cloud is growing. It rises, or rather floats upwards, and gradually swallows up the other table mountain, Kukenan. To the north and east, in the interior of Guyana, lies mile upon mile of rainforest, and the precipice on which we stand continues uninterrupted in a massive bay that frames the carpet of forest. Across the bay we can see the northern parts of Roraima. The enormous rock walls and wide plateaus, the stomach-churning chasms and the strange dynamics of the clouds make the *tepui*s the most extraordinary landscape I have ever seen.

Half a day goes by with no mist and then the landscape becomes ghostly again. The view disappears into nothingness. Roraima means "the mother of all water", and we come to understand how the name arose during our time on the plateau. It takes us two days to get back to the starting point for this unusual trek in a "lost world". The mountains, these "islands in time" as a writer from Venezuela called them, are already calling us back, .

Sierra Nevada

THE MOUNTAINS OF LIGHT

The dawn light is whitened by smoke from a fire, enveloping the naked granite domes of Half Dome, on the left, and Liberty Cap, on the right. Here the John Muir Trail passes the Nevada Falls. Local Indians call Half Dome "Tis-sa-ack", after a maiden whose tears for the disappearance of her beloved turned into the black streaks on the mountain. During the gold rush of the mid-nineteenth century, Europeans entered the Sierra Nevada for the first time. In 1865 Yosemite became the modern world's first nature conservation area when it was declared a protected site by President Abraham Lincoln. A few years later, in 1868, the legendary John Muir came here. Fascinated by the landscape, thereafter he worked to have the national park created, which it was in 1890.

Of all the chasms I have looked into, Half Dome takes the prize for thrills. Far below my feet I can see tiny cars and houses, which illustrate the scale of the thing. The free drop is far worse than a terrifying, gigantic bungee jump. You feel the size of the mountain in the pit of your stomach and you tense up. You need real willpower to approach the edge.

The mountain walls in the legendary Yosemite Valley in California are among the steepest and smoothest in the world. Every year millions of tourists admire the precipices; most of them stand on the civilized valley floor where the vegetation is as leafy as a municipal park and the national park has its popular visitors' centre. Up on Half Dome the view is wilder, but wherever you are there are no words to do full justice to this awesome landscape. Few places have been described with so many superlatives as Yosemite. Since the valley became generally known in the 1860s, writers and artists have tried to depict their impressions. "The only place which comes up to the brag about it, and exceeds it," thought Ralph Waldo Emerson in his time. So much has been written, painted and photographed in Yosemite, and over the years there has been such a multitude of people, that the valley has not only lost its virginity but also a little of its charm – one has to concede that in all honesty. So it is liberating to shoulder your backpack and walk away from the well-known scenery, out into the backyard of the national park where there is still wilderness, the views are less well known and there are no more people than you can greet as you come across them. On Half Dome we are admittedly not on our own on this beautiful summer's day, but up here our feelings are heightened by the achievement of getting here. You don't have to be a climber – two wires have been fixed to the steep north face of the mountain, but nobody inclined to vertigo should even attempt it.

The mountains around Yosemite are part of the Sierra Nevada, which is called the "range of light". The man behind the name is the most prominent pioneer and prophet of the area, John Muir. For many people he is still a god, a century after his death. His writings about the value of pristine nature are timeless and absorbing. The long-distance trail through the mountains is therefore quite naturally called the

John Muir Trail and it begins in Yosemite, where he himself lived at times. The trail follows the backbone of the Sierra Nevada, 224 miles (360km) up and down, and ends by crossing the highest mountain in the United States outside Alaska, Mount Whitney, some 14,495 feet (4,418m) above sea level.

Today we are walking along the John Muir Trail from the busy valley to a campsite in the Little Yosemite Valley. The path is flanked by tall forest, and behind the trees we can glimpse smooth cliffs. The sides of the valley are terribly steep and the "incomparable valley", as Yosemite is often called, is actually a glacier-carved canyon with several high waterfalls which drop from the precipices. Since the Sierra Nevada is largely made up of pale granite, the mountain walls have been polished by the ice and this contributes to the unique appearance of the landscape. We get to know this dazzling surface during our climb on Half Dome, which is a monolithic and strangely shaped mountain – "... the loftiest, most sublime and the most beautiful of all the rocks that guard this glorious temple ... finely sculptured and poised in calm, deliberate majesty". John Muir had the advantage of being able to describe this landscape before anyone else. He has had many followers and one of the most eminent was the photographer Galen Rowell. "Half Dome is not really a half dome," he said, and thought that "it actually is a whole dome with a character unlike any other dome in America." I would say in the whole world.

Many American national parks have a sharp dividing line between the touristy places and the pristine landscape. Where there are roads, hordes of people will drive. If you walk along the paths the isolation is striking. When a few days later we trek through King's Canyon, another national park in this long mountain range, the desertedness is palpable. Our packs are now weighed down with food for several days. Here, we are in an uninhabited area where black bears have residential rights, so every night we have to hang our supplies in a tree. Our destination is the Granite Basin, where we want to take a closer look at the features that make the Sierra Nevada the individual mountain range described so poetically by John Muir. Up at an altitude of 11,485 feet (3,500m) the pine forest is sparser, and only lone pines grow in soil-filled pockets between the barren surfaces of the rocky slabs. All around us there are mountain ridges, quite long and not so steep. Jagged peaks stand like a distant backdrop. There are many bare mountains in the Sierra Nevada and I see some similarities with certain areas of the Pyrenees and Tasmania. These natural rockeries with their bare heights, knobbly trees and tightly ensconced small pools do not just create a picture of a romantic wilderness but also provide great inspiration for anyone who wants to design their own rockery. As John Muir wrote: "From one natural garden to another, ridge to ridge, I drifted enchanted ... gazing afar over domes and peaks, lakes and woods, and the billowy glaciated fields ... In the midst of such a beauty ... one's body is all tingling palate. Who wouldn't be a mountaineer!"

The Granite Lake in the national park of King's Canyon. John Muir declared of this beautiful region: "And after ten years of wandering and wondering in the heart of it, rejoicing in the glorious floods of light, the white beam of the morning streaming through the passes, the noonday radiance on crystal rocks, the flush of the alpenglow, and the irised spray of countless waterfalls, it still seems above all others the Range of Light."

Grand Canyon

THE TREKKER'S DESCENT

At 280 miles (450km) long and an average of 3,935 feet (1,200m) deep, the Grand Canyon is nothing less than nature's biggest wonderland. Broad terraces and precipitous drops alternate, and they bear witness to the enormous explosive power of water. In this aerial photograph we can see Tonto Platform and the inner granite ravine with the oldest rocks. Since the Colorado river was dammed upstream, the volume of sediment has diminished and the water has become greener. The name Colorado comes from Spanish and means "red-coloured".

The Spaniard Garcia Lopez de Cárdenas drew the wrong conclusion when in 1540 he "discovered" the Grand Canyon. He thought the precipitous ravine was of no interest to humankind. Lieutenant Joseph Ives made the same mistake in 1858, as the first pioneer to stand beside the Colorado river in the depths of the canyon. Neither of these early explorers suspected that millions and more millions would come here much later just to look at this wonder. The view is a staggering experience of wild beauty, monumental scale and primitive geological forces. The cleft is 280 miles (450km) long, at most 5,250 feet (1,600m) deep and its width ranges from 6 miles (10km) to 19 miles (30km).

As a trekker, on the brink of the canyon you feel an irresistible urge to explore this "underworld" – a sweaty ordeal – but you don't have to do what the legendary long-distance walker Colin Fletcher did in the mid 1960s. He became the first to walk the length of the Grand Canyon. The trip took two months. A trip straight across, from the southern edge of the ravine to the north, is considerably shorter and very popular. It turns into a kind of upside-down mountain climb. You start at the top, walk down to the foot of the "mountain" and then up the other side.

The walk is a journey to the inside of the earth. Geology is rarely so fascinating as it is here. The top limestone rock is 250 million years old and the granites down by the river are 2,000 million years old. Between these ages a great part of the earth's development was played out: life was born and continents moved. At the start we are just 7,220 feet (2,200m) above sea level. Pine forest grows there and the climate is temperate with snowy winters, down by the bridge the altitude is 2,300 feet (700m), the terrain is open and the climate like a desert.

The span is difficult enough to comprehend, but what fascinates me most is the young age of the Grand Canyon. Only six million years of river erosion have hollowed out this gigantic peephole into remote prehistoric times. Where the rock is hard, tall precipices have formed and the path leads in a zigzag. Where the rock is softer, easy terraces extend at different levels. You can walk along these on quite flat ground, absorbed, with no eye contact with the world above.

One of the terraces, Tonto Platform, 3,280 feet (1,000m) below the much-visited canyon's rim, houses Indian Garden, a popular tourist destination. Several streams water the luxuriant vegetation and we stop to fill our bottles before the last, strenuous slope. People lived in this place in prehistoric times. During the sixth century the Anasazi people moved here to live in this naturally protected environment. A worsening climate in the thirteenth century caused them to abandon their settlements, but 150 years later another people appeared. They were the predecessors of the Havasupai, one of the two tribes living in the Grand Canyon today.

The Indians' own canyon draws me to a trek many years later. The Havasu river, which runs out into the main canyon, flows through a beautiful and secluded corner of the canyon complex. It is famous for its beautiful waterfalls. The trail is managed by the Indian tribe Havasu Baaja, in the isolated Supai village, where you have to ring and ask for a permit for a trip.

From the Hualapai hill where the road ends, we walk down into an increasingly deep and narrow canyon. After a day of walking you reach the Indian village, halfway between the starting point and the Colorado river. The houses stand in a large depression, surrounded by precipitous slopes and a few slender pinnacles. Almost five hundred people live here, with no road link; nonetheless the blessings and

Previous pages: Few places in the world evoke the term "Garden of Eden" as strongly as Havasu Canyon. When we get down to the middle waterfall the landscape becomes biblically beautiful. The Havasu Falls drop 100 feet (30m) into a basin in which the mineral content causes the deep blue water to deposit limestone sediment, so-called travertines.

Cecil Watahomigie leads the caravan of horses, carrying our supplies, to the village of Supai in Havasu Canyon, where there are no roads. He is a member of the Havasu Baaja tribe, which means "the people of the blue water".

curses of modern living have affected their traditional lifestyle. Most of them now live on tourism. We register at the house pointed out to us, pay the fee and quickly leave the village, which oscillates between moments of old-time tranquillity and busy times when helicopters and animal caravans arrive with goods.

When you get closer to the Colorado river, camping is permitted. We set up camp beside the stream with its warm, blue-green water. The first waterfall is called the Navajo Falls and is hidden from the path. We continue to the most well-known one, Havasu Falls. At the third and highest waterfall the path becomes challenging. Mooney Falls is 295 feet (90m) high and got its name from a gold-digger who fell to his death there. The path climbs steeply up the cliff and then we creep through a manmade tunnel down to the pool beneath the fall. Since we are out on a day trip, our packs are light, which makes the going easier. From here the path continues the length of the ravine to the Colorado river. Our trek in the Grand Canyon, this upside-down mountain landscape, takes three days in all.

Canyonlands

THE SLICKROCK COUNTRY

From "the Needles" we can look north to the Sals Mountains in the twilight. The shadow is creeping up on Squaw Butte, which stands like a fortress. In 1836 one Dennis Julien was staying around here and carved his name and the date on several rocks. That is all we know of him. Perhaps he was inspired by the many Indian rock paintings in Canyonlands.

The Colorado plateau in the western United States is one of the most remarkable landscapes on earth. The best known sight is of course the Grand Canyon, but there are many other formations that are even more surreal, such as hyper-narrow clefts, natural stone bridges and fantastically moulded rocks. A desert climate combined with extensive sedimentary rock has laid the foundations for this fairytale land, which Americans often call "the slickrock country".

The author Edward Abby knew the Colorado plateau better than most: "Canyon country does not always inspire love. To many it appears barren, hostile, repellent – a fearsome land of rock and heat, sand dunes and quicksand, cacti, thornbushes, scorpions, rattlesnakes and agrophobic distances. To those who see our land in that manner, the best reply is, yes, you are right ... " But then he continues: "For more and more of those who now live here, however, the great plateau and its canyon wilderness is a treasure best enjoyed through the body and spirit."

If you like trekking, it is natural to direct your steps this way. Among infinite options, we choose a trip to the Needles in the Canyonlands National Park. This is a richly varied area in the southeastern corner of the national park. The name comes from the fact that the sandstone has sprung up in narrow rounded "needles", which stand close together, coloured red and white. At a distance it looks like a big pincushion, but there are also other strange-looking, sculpted stone formations, some of which remind me of fungi.

In a visitors' centre, we work out our route. The park wardens suggest we walk to campsite BS2 in Big Spring Canyon, which is free. This is how it works in a lot of the American national parks. The system of having appointed places for camping seems a bit disappointing and restrictive to begin with – who could find "BS2" attractive? But on the other hand we are guaranteed to have the place to ourselves, right in the middle of unspoilt country.

Not far from where the road ends at Squaw Flat we take our first steps on the "sliprocks". The sandstone has rough slabs that give the soles of your feet a good grip when they are dry, but are slippery as ice when wet. The sun is shining brightly and

UNITED STATES

When the rock is dry you can easily stroll across this so-called "sliprock country". When it rains the slabs are treacherously slippery.

The massive, almost 330-foot (100-m) high sandstone pinnacles in "the Needles" were once a sandy desert. Through geological developments a fascinating labyrinth of rocks has formed. The first pioneer, Captain J N Macomb, described the area as worthless in 1859. Just a hundred years later the Canyonlands National Park was formed, a highly valued landscape among trekkers.

at this moment thirst is a bigger problem than the risk of losing your footing. The waterholes in the area are not always safe and we don't have a filter. Instead, we have stocked up on bottles filled to the brim, which we carry in our backpacks. It means extra weight, but it's not a long distance. BS2 is only 3 miles (5km) away.

This trek is turning into an interesting trip. In the Needles you don't have to go far to find major changes in the landscape. Our boots grip well even in steep places, and crunch along on the path. We cross bare ridges that are not particularly high, and come down to a valley with dense bushes beneath contorted and polished sandstone formations. The needles stand like a prickly backdrop not far away.

There are imaginative land formations in every direction. You have to remember that these needles were once a flat surface – that is what was here before the earthquakes broke down the layers of sandstone, and water penetrated the cracks and subsequently carved out the needles. The long period all this work took is hard to grasp, and wonderful things also took place under the ground, which make the conditions in Canyonlands all the more complex. A long time ago, evaporated seawater produced thick layers of salt that gradually began to move under the pressure of all the sandstone on top. The result was that the sandstone layers either collapsed into a valley or bulged up to form a dome.

In the evening I leave BS2 to wander around by myself on the warm slabs. An absolutely fabulous sunset takes shape and far to the north the blue light fades over the Sals mountains. To the west the distances to remote highlands are enormous. The heart of Canyonlands lies in that direction and there, far below all the cliffs and table mountains and out of sight from where I am standing, the two rivers, the Green river and the Colorado river unite to form an even bigger watercourse flowing on through the Grand Canyon. What a grand country this is.

Rocky Mountains

A MASSIVE WILDERNESS

The clouds pile up as we trek along Yukness Ledge toward the Opabin plateau. In the pine forest in the valley, American species of pine, fir and larch alternate. High above Lake O'Hara stands Cathedral Mountain, 10,460 feet (3,189m) above sea level. The artists who were drawn to the area rated this mountain very highly.

Eyeball to eyeball with a little, crystal-clear lake, I can see why the Cree Indians called this area "Yoho". The word means "respect" and since 1886 has been the official name of one of the four national parks within the great World Heritage site of the Canadian Rockies. And respect, or perhaps rather reverence, is what this clear lake arouses in me as it lies there beneath the giant mountains. The Rockies are a wilderness beyond humankind and a country of high peaks, great forests and animals such as the grizzly and the puma. But in spite of the wild terrain, one has to say that Canada has created a trekking country that is as easily accessible as it is magnificent. As early as 1885 the mountain chain was crossed by a railway, which ignited tourism. Several national parks were formed soon after. Banff was the first in the country and the third in the world, and it is also the most well known.

While Banff belongs to the province of Alberta, Yoho lies in British Columbia. The border runs along the backbone of the mountain chain, which also forms a continental watershed. Some of the rivers run east to the Atlantic and some west to the Pacific. There are a few of us walking the paths in the area around the famous Lake O'Hara, which is half a mile (one-kilometre) long and so intensely turquoise that it seems to have been created by some wilful artist trying to brighten up the darkness of the pine forests. Several lakes in the Rockies are among the most colourful natural phenomena to be seen in the world, and this is because of all the glacial mud carried into them by streams and rivers. The volume of mud and the depth of the lake cause the blue-green colour to vary considerably in intensity.

Lake O'Hara is guarded like a jewel by Parks Canada. Private road traffic is banned on the 9-mile (15-km) long link road from the Trans Canada Highway. Anyone trekking around the lake must book their place on a transfer bus, which limits the influx. Alternatively, you can walk along the road, but groups of more than six people are not allowed, and you can spend a maximum of three nights here. The rules keep the area more unspoilt than it would be otherwise.

We arrive on the bus and start our trek by the legendary Lake O'Hara Hotel. The path follows the lakeshore and climbs steeply, and then, when we have passed a little lake, we turn in across Yukness Ledge and walk along a narrow, steep stretch close to a tall mountainside. In the direction we are going we can see two sky-high mountains, whose appearance borders on the arrogant. Mount Biddle, 10,890 feet (3,319m) above sea level, is imposing and one of the many grandiose peaks in the Rockies. In spite of the large number of them, almost none has achieved the same international reputation as the most celebrated mountains in the Alps, the Andes and the Himalayas. Perhaps the best known in the Rockies is a challenging creation called Mount Robson, 12,970 feet (3,954m) high and garnished with lines of horizontally-layered rocks that are typical of this mountain range. It is 186 miles (300km) north of us.

The area around Lake O'Hara has several rugged mountains that have largely escaped international attention. The area was charted for the first time in 1887 by a surveyor working for the railway company. Soon afterwards, officer Robert O'Hara heard of the lake and began his explorations; he was subsequently honoured by having the lake of the same name called after him. Canada's Alpine Club had a members' camp here at the beginning of the twentieth century and that focused attention on the area's unique beauty. The club also built an overnight hut. Several paths were then created by three respected pioneers with a great love of their work. Thanks to their efforts Lake O'Hara became a magnet for Canada's leading landscape painters. The famous watercolour painter Walter J. Phillips wrote in his diary in 1926:

"From this plateau, which is immediately below Opabin Pass, delightful views are without number. The mountains and the meadow serve as a foil one to the other – the latter indescribably warm in tone, golden, and dappled with flowers – the mountains invariably cool."

The path leads us on to Phillips' picturesque plateau, and we then continue back to the improbably coloured Lake O'Hara. The path goes right under Mount Schaffer, which got its name from the first pioneer in this part of the Rockies. Several summers in a row and often with a girlfriend and two guides, Mary Schaffer from Pennsylvania trekked through the wilderness. It was the beginning of the 1890s and she was walking where only Indians had gone before. Her travels cause me to raise an eyebrow. It's always interesting to read about the pioneers in a mountainous area and in the case of an independent lady from the Victorian age, you can't help but be extra curious. Mary Schaffer wrote a classic book about old Indian trails in the Rockies and her attitude to travelling invites admiration: "Our real objective was to delve into the heart of an untouched land, to turn the unthumbed pages of an unread book, and to learn daily those secrets which Mother Nature is so willing to tell to those who seek."

Since her time, the Rockies have been thoroughly mapped and nobody is a pioneer any more, but we can still travel in a wilderness that inspires huge respect.

In front of Yukness Ledge Mount Biddle rises 10,890 feet (3,319m) above sea level. Like many other peaks in the Rockies, it is called after a person. Anthony Biddle from Philadelphia was an enthusiastic traveller, according to Samuel Allen, who registered the name. That is all that is recorded about Mount Biddle.

Chilkoot Trail

GOLD-DIGGERS AND SCRAP

The thorny bush Devil's Club (*Echinopanax horridum*) was a scourge to the gold-diggers when they fought their way through the forest in what is now coastal Alaska. The bush forms dense thickets and is a characteristic plant in the island and coastal area of southern Alaska known as Tongass, the world's largest non-tropical rainforest area and one of the most productive ecosystems on earth.

The rubbish along the path must not be touched. Scrap iron and mouldering bundles left over from the Klondike rush are protected! On the ground there are battered frying pans, rusty tins, odd boots and worn cog wheels, big and small, and everything has been listed as historic monuments in this wilderness. In other places in the world we would no doubt have called out the litter patrol, but not here. This is an original aspect of the Chilkoot Trail, which follows in the footsteps of the gold-diggers.

In 1897 hordes of people seeking to make their fortunes came to a fjord in Alaska. A difficult ordeal lay ahead of them: the 31-mile (50-km) trek across the Chilkoot Pass, the only overland section of the 1,555 miles (2,500 km) between Seattle and the tempting gold fields in the north. Overcrowded steamers had carried them up to the innermost reaches of the fjord and on the other side of the mountains they would travel on down the Yukon river in small homemade craft.

More than a hundred years later we are walking over the Chilkoot Pass too, like those hopeful men and women, but now it is a famous trekking trail that attracts several thousand people every year. The trek begins in Dyea, a town soon wiped out when the gold rush was over. In May 1898, 8,000 people lived here and there were 48 hotels, 47 restaurants, 39 saloons and 19 transport companies. A few years later the place was abandoned, and today it is deserted, not a log cabin left, but there is a road here and an unmanned campsite.

The gold rush started after a find on 15 August 1896 in Bonanza Creek, a tributary of the Klondike River in the Canadian Yukon Territory. Word spread fast and a year later the rush was underway. At the time there was an economic depression in the West and unemployment was widespread. A million people soon cherished plans of coming here – 100,000 hopefuls set out and 30,000 got far enough to encounter the harsh reality of the Chilkoot Pass. These fortune-hunters were called "stampeders".

To cross the rugged mountain range between Lynns Channel fjord and Lake Bennet there were only two glacier-free routes. White Pass was the most demanding

Up on the Chilkoot Pass we come across this rusty machine from the cableway set up to carry the gold-diggers' cargo.

On the Canadian side the landscape changes character. The valleys become shallower and there are lakes and wide heaths framed by high mountains. Here a meadow of American willowherb stretches into the distance.

with all its mud, and an option for anyone who could afford a horse, but it was soon christened "Dead Horse Trail". Most people crossed by the Chilkoot Pass, "the poor man's way", which was higher and steeper, but at the same time somewhat shorter. The last slope up to the pass was called "the Golden Stairs".

The path from Dyea by the fjord leads us into a narrow mountain valley with incredibly dense arctic rainforest. Alpine brushwood heaths and meadows begin at about 2,955 feet (900m) above sea level, rocks and snowfields take over higher up, and on the Canadian side there are pine forests like those of northern Europe. The pass is a continental watershed extremely close to an ocean. Few trails in this latitude and of this length offer such a great variety of natural species as the Chilkoot Trail.

At Canyon City the Taiya river runs through a narrow ravine. This place was the first stop for the fortune-hunters. Hundreds of tents filled this valley in the autumn of 1897. The following spring, two companies had built cable railways for the freight. These operated with steam machines. The cable cars were popular because the slope up from Canyon City is steep and debilitating.

Via a bridge over the river we reach the site of the tent city, today a dense forest, at that time a cleared area. Between the trees we suddenly see an ugly, rusty old boiler that belonged to the cableway. Now it is an historic monument, which we

respect. The next night's campsite is Sheep Camp. Here, and at the other campsites, there is now a simple hut for trekkers, but most people prefer to camp. A park warden is staying in a little cottage not far away. In the evening he talks to those who are staying overnight. "Walk slowly and drink regularly when you cross the pass tomorrow," he recites, like a mantra.

Thick cloud obscures the peaks as we walk toward the high point of our trek. The weather lets us feel the hardships of the gold-diggers in our very bones. By the Scales there is a mass of protected lumber. Here all the fortune-hunters' packs were weighed. The professional porters were very particular about the weight, some of them were Indians, but most of the stampeders carried their own load, which often weighed up to 55 pounds (25kg). It could take forty to fifty laps up to the Scales and back before it was all carried up there. Canada's police authority placed a customs post on the Chilkoot Pass and demanded that every fortune-hunter brought with him a ton of provisions. The customs also provided a way for Canada to mark the national frontier. In spite of an agreement in 1825 between Russia, which then owned Alaska, and the Canadian Hudson Bay Company, the frontier had never been marked out. Now Canada wanted a definitive line.

Of a group of about forty who spent the night in Sheep Camp, we are the first to set out. The mist is lifting a little and allows us to make out the "Golden Stairs". But the mist closes in quickly again and we thoroughly appreciate the mixture of hope and fear that this place generated among the fortune-hunters. Most of the stampeders came here when winter snow covered the boulders. That made the slope a little easier to climb, but there were several avalanches, which led to fatalities. In a short space of time entrepreneurs built a cable railway, while others dug out a path, for which they charged a toll.

In summertime with no snow and in poor weather, the "Golden Stairs" comprise a steep, forbidding sea of boulders. Debris, rusty wires and mouldering shoe soles lie strewn around where we are climbing over the boulders, without being able to see anything of the views. On the pass, just 3,280 feet (1,000m) above sea level, Parks Canada have a house with a resident warden, but we can't find anyone. After a short rest we descend on steep snow to Crater Lake on the Canadian side, and when we are below the cloud a Scandinavian-type mountain landscape opens up.

At a stroke, the country feels more familiar to us. The path follows a mountainside with flowering meadows and plants we recognize. Happy Camp lies where the valley narrows. After another night in the tent we continue past a couple of lakes, Long Lake and Deep Lake. Here the pine forest begins and the trail follows Moose Creek, which runs through a deep ravine. We can look out from the edge of the ravine over an expanse of forest with a big lake in the middle, Lindeman Lake, our destination for today.

The campsite of Lindeman City has a tent that houses an interesting exhibition. The photos provide a living image of the tough characters who toiled here for their

This view over the northern wilderness must have been a sight for sore eyes to the gold-diggers. The lake system with Lindeman and Bennet lakes meant that they could travel on by boat. A huge tent city grew up between the lakes and that is where the Chilkoot Trail ends. A few years after the rush the railway was built linking Skagway, by the sea, with Whitehorse on the Yukon river. There is a station on Lake Bennet.

future. Their struggle with the equipment and the harsh climate took its toll, and the landscape they traversed was ravaged. Lindeman City was a huge, clear-felled area and a shanty town of canvas "houses". To walk in the footsteps of these fighters and enter into the destinies played out here during the gold rush is to walk in living history. In sunnier weather than we have had, the impressive landscape is also a great attraction in itself.

The last leg is entirely in the depths of the forest, and the Chilkoot Trail ends by Lake Bennet. On the shore the fortune-hunters built their floating craft – rafts, canoes, sailing boats – to continue another 311 miles (500km) down the Yukon river to Klondike. A few years after the climax of the rush the "White Pass and Yukon Route" railway came to the lake, but by then the place was deserted. The train continued to Whitehorse, the principal town in the Yukon Territory. Today, tours depart from Skagway to Lake Bennet but no further – the rest of the line has fallen into disrepair. Most trekkers take the train back to the coast.

UNITED STATES / CANADA

Yukon

WALKING WITH GHOSTS

In the glow of the evening sun the straggly shadows of fir trees point toward Slim's River and Vulcan Mountain, some 7,000 feet (2,133m) above sea level.

"Sorry but Parks Canada have closed Observation Mountain to climbers," says park warden Brian Buck, standing outside our tent. Yesterday they had a serious incident on the trail. A four-year-old grizzly bear attacked two trekkers who fled up a rock face. That is the second time in a short period that the same bear has gone on the attack.

At that moment our chance of seeing the mighty glacier landscape of Kluane Range in the Yukon Territory vanishes. Our tent stands a long way up a splendid valley. Yesterday we took Slim's West Trail which begins at the Alaska Highway. In the visitors' centre where you have to register your tour, the park warden told us that the valley, which is just under twenty miles (32km) long, is home to about fifty grizzly bears. That is an extremely high number for such a limited area.

The bear is now blocking our plans to investigate this magnificent wilderness. Instead we shall have an involuntary rest after yesterday's long walk. At the start there was a memorial plaque that made us quake in our boots. On it we read of a grizzly that had killed a woman nearby. As we started to walk through the forest it was with heightened awareness, but the tension ebbed away toward the end when no bear appeared.

Around the campsite where we now are, there are eight people from Parks Canada. Their job is to clear away any rubbish in the vegetation around the campsite. An hour later we hear four bangs and from our tent opening we see smoke trails. A few hundred metres away the male bear had crept up on them. They are all shaken.

"We fired a starter's gun to frighten the grizzly," says Brian Buck, who is the leader of the gang. "I suggest you move your tent to our camp behind the hill. We're going to put up an electric fence."

For a long while we sit on the bare top of the hill with Brian and the others. Everyone is on the lookout over the wide gravel beds where Slim's River runs in many interlocking streams, weaving in and out of one another, but no bear appears. Our interest in walking here was aroused by this unique landscape. The river in front of the hill rises in Kaskawulsch, a long tongue of ice which protrudes from a mighty glacier. The Kluane National Park here on the Canadian side and St Ellias in Alaska

together form a gigantic wilderness, which houses the biggest continuous ice mass in the northern hemisphere outside Greenland. The many peaks of this mountain chain have their feet in a snow-white bed. Ninety-three miles (150km) across the glacier to the west of us, without a single road in between, lies Mount Logan, Canada's highest mountain, almost 19,685 feet (6,000m) above sea level.

Beneath our hill the meltwater from the glacier has laid out a flat delta landscape with extensive gravel beds. On the other side of the delta we can make out the ice, like a pale-coloured wall. In all directions stately alpine peaks stand clad in dark green skirts of pine forest beneath the topmost rocks. The feeling of wilderness is stupefying, almost numbing, when we think of all the grizzlies that must be within our field of vision, but have not yet shown themselves.

Late in the afternoon the bear specialist Terry Schoenberg comes in by helicopter. His job is to shoot rubber bullets at the young bear. The idea is to teach it to associate people with something dangerous. Parks Canada do their utmost to avoid killing a threatening grizzly. When the helicopter has landed my traveling companion suggests we fly out. I hesitate and in the end we agree that the price is too high. And Terry reckons that we can easily go back tomorrow.

"The bears will avoid you, they usually do," he laughs. But the mood in camp is scarcely relaxed. Nobody goes very far from the tents.

Early the next day we are on our own on the path again, after some good advice from Terry. An uneasy feeling is creeping up on us. Imagine if the grizzly went past the camp last night and is now going the same way as us along the valley. We sing and shout at every twist of the path and after just half a mile (1km) we can see that bear paws have trodden in our tracks from the day before yesterday. They lead in the direction of the path and after a few more kilometres we reach a heap of fresh bear droppings. With just a little can of pepper spray to defend ourselves and an aggressive grizzly male nearby, we are decidedly jittery, but at the same time it is fantastic to be walking here in this enormous wilderness, in bear country, and to have these animals around us.

These 3 miles (5km) in the footsteps of the grizzly feel like a long trek in the company of a ghost, and although we are still in bear territory we are hugely relieved when the tracks disappear from the path. Our field of vision expands by the marshes on Slim's River, the clouds lift and we walk towards safer terrain – we hope.

However, on our way out to a bank in the river bed, another danger reveals itself. Intuitively I feel that the gravel bed looks suspect and poke it with my trekking staff. I can't touch the bottom. This kind of quicksand consists of glacial mud which could have drowned me. Afterwards we find out why the valley is so-called. A rookie gold-digger on a horse named Slim tried to take a short-cut across the river. Horse and rider got stuck in the mud, and Slim met a slow and agonizing death. We are luckier and return safely from this memorable trek. Sadly, we missed the glacier scenery, but the atmosphere of the bear country has permeated us to our fingertips.

Previous pages: The valley where Slim's River flows, cuts through the Kluane range, one of several mountain ranges that make up this enormous national park of the same name. This is an area with one of the densest bear populations in the world and the odds of bumping into a grizzly are high. You can trek on both sides of the river toward the glaciers in the central part of the area. To the right of the picture is where Slim's West Trail runs.

A horn of a bighorn sheep lies on the sandbank, which the river has laid out in front of the Kaskawulsch glacier. The country here is rich in wildlife. Apart from grizzly bears there are wolverines, wolves, lynx, elk, bighorn sheep and mountain goats.

Alpine flowers near the Drei Zinnen in the Dolomites.

Reference

WHAT YOU NEED TO KNOW BEFORE TREKKING

"The basis of all mountaineering is the conservation of energy by three fundamental principles – rhythmic movement, balance and precise placing of the feet."

ERIC SHIPTON in *Upon that Mountain*, 1943

DRINKING WATER

Water is one of the biggest health risks when you are trekking. No matter how clean a stream might seem, you need to be careful. There may be villages and grazing lands far upstream, increasing the risk that disease-carrying bacteria and microbes have spread into the water. Many trekkers have suffered from the gastro-intestinal infection, giardiasis. It is caused by a single-cell animal that is found throughout the world and likes to live in running water.

If there are wells along the way, that is a great help – this is the case, for example, on the Lycian Way – but they do sometimes dry up. If you want to use lakes and streams, colour is not a good indicator. Clear water may be contaminated and cloudy water drinkable. In Fish River Canyon I drank river water that looked almost like mud soup. According to the information we had received the water was pure and risk-free, and we had no problems. Tasmania has lakes and streams that look like tea, but they are extremely clean and healthy. In the Scandinavian fells you can take your drinking water from most of the rivers, which simplifies the trekker's life. But in North America you have to be careful even far out in the wilderness. Waterborne microbes are always a risk. If you are uncertain about the water, it must be treated. In the alpine regions, as a rule I only dare trust the rivers really high up.

There are three practical ways of making water drinkable. It can be boiled for at least one minute, preferably three. Disinfectant can be added, preferably iodine, but that alters the taste. And finally, it can be poured through a china filter with extremely small pores, which removes bacteria and microbes. The last method is the best, and there are small, practical pump filters on the market made for outdoor life.

Drinking constantly while trekking is essential if you are to keep up your energy levels. There are now lightweight and flexible hydration systems of various sizes, which can be compressed when they are not full. In hot and tropical climates you must drink more than usual – also at great heights, where body fluids are lost through exhalation. Ideally, you should take water bottles with a total capacity of around half a gallon (2 to 3 litres) per person. The rule of thumb is always to have at least a quarter of a gallon (1 litre) in your pack. Systems with a bite valve that is readily accessible for a swig are designed to be carried on backpacks.

THE LENGTH OF THE TREK

Treks in foreign countries usually last from a few days to a couple of weeks. When talking about the length of a trip, the time spent is of more importance than the number of miles walked. The relationship between time and distance is not linear. In very mountainous areas such as the Alps and the Himalayas, the differences in altitude are more significant than the horizontal distances. In areas with wide plateaus, for example the Scandinavian fells, Iceland and Tasmania, the opposite is true – the horizontal distance determines the time taken. The accessibility of the path also plays a great part. Well-maintained paths are faster than overgrown ones. Marshy ground and rivers that you have to wade through can slow down a trip.

A guideline for trekking is 2½ miles (4km) per hour if you are walking with a lightweight pack on easily traversed level ground. With a heavy backpack the speed drops to about 2 miles (3km) per hour. On steep paths you need to allow one hour to climb 1,600 feet (500m). Coming down can be quicker, although at the same time it is harder on the legs. But since each individual's capacity varies enormously, these rules of thumb should be taken with a large pinch of salt! When guidebooks say a trail takes a certain amount of days, this means that most trekkers think that this is about the right amount of time. Some would rather walk faster and others, slower.

FOOD

In the wilderness, freeze-dried food is the commonest kind, particularly if you are self-catering. These days there is quite a wide range of meals available and they are generally very tasty. However, you do get tired of them on a long trip. It is still difficult to get freeze-dried food in many countries, mainly in the Third World, so it's a good idea to buy it before you leave and take it with you.

In many areas, especially in Asia, I recommend that you eat local food in the villages you pass through. There is a huge variety, consisting mostly of different kinds of vegetables, which are often served with rice. On organized tours to exotic locations, food – sometimes local dishes, sometimes canned food – is usually included.

ACCOMMODATION

Anyone trekking on paths with huts and inns can make do with a bivi bag, which saves weight. With a proper sleeping bag you are protected for cooler nights. I virtually always take a sleeping bag and a roll mat. It's best to choose something suited to the nature of the trip. In tropical climates the bag does not need to be particularly warm, but in mountain areas it should be able to withstand temperatures down to -5°C. Those filled with artificial fibres are more hardwearing than down-filled bags.

When you are trekking in the wild a tent is essential. The same applies on small expeditions in remote areas using local porters and guides. Even where the expedition passes through inhabited villages, you usually sleep in a tent at night. Tour operators often lend you tents, but it's best to ask beforehand about their condition and quality. I always prefer to have my own, which I am used to handling.

Established tourist areas offer other possibilities for overnight stays. Along trails in the Alps, the Dolomites and the Pyrenees there are huts of various sizes. You can sleep in them, and enjoy catered food and drink. The menus can be very comprehensive and often include beer, wine and spirits. Simple huts are to be found along routes in many parts of the world – for example in Laugavegur, Kungsleden, Pirin, Mount Kenya, Kilimanjaro, Ruwenzori, Gunung Kinabalu, Overland Track, Milford Track, Tongariro and Torres del Paine. These huts are usually intended for self-catering.

When you are trekking in areas in which there are many villages, you can sometimes stay in people's homes. This possibility is most common in parts of the Himalayas and southeast Asia, where there is little tourism. As the number of trekkers increases, tea houses and simple guest houses or "lodges" are opening. This sort of development has taken place along the Everest trail. "Lodge trekking" or "tea-house trekking" has become very popular among those walking independently in the Himalayas. During the trip you stay and eat in these guest houses. They are often simple – built of stone and wood. The menus are becoming more sophisticated, and in addition to local food you can sometimes get Western dishes. The drawback to "lodge trekking" is that it can get crowded. During high season there is sometimes a shortage of rooms, and in the lodges at the highest altitudes the rooms can be small and dirty. With a tent in your pack you always have your own alternative.

MOUNTAINEERING

Mountaineering is the art of getting to the summit with the help of your feet and sometimes also your hands. Climbing is a variant of that. As a climber you tend to choose challenging and steep climbs and the route itself is the goal. Most mountaineers prefer to seek easy and less steep routes, because the summit is the goal. On a lot of mountains in the world – probably most of them – you can reach the highest point without being a climber. Kilimanjaro, for example, only requires you to climb up scree slope, which admittedly is strenuous, but is not at all difficult. There is no climbing involved.

Naturally there are gradations between mountaineering in the form of trekking and actual climbing. The English word "scrambling" signifies something in-between, and the idea is that in some places you have to use your hands. It doesn't require advanced climbing, but by scrambling you have bodily contact with the rock, sharpen your concentration and yet still have the energy to appreciate the landscape. I love this concept. By scrambling you can also climb slightly more difficult mountains without taking along complicated, heavy gear. Only if you are going to traverse glaciers and steep snow fields do you need crampons, ice axes and ropes. As climbing equipment weighs quite a lot and taking it can give you weight problems on aircraft, it is more practical to rent the equipment locally. This is often possible in trekking areas that are also popular among climbers, which is the case in places like Gavarnie in the Pyrenees, Chamonix near Mont Blanc, Namche Bazar along the Everest trail, Huaraz on the Cordillera Blanca and Chaltén close to Fitz Roy, to name but a few.

ALTITUDE SICKNESS

Altitude sickness is caused by low air pressure. The air pressure drops at high altitude, decreasing the level of oxygen in the blood, and you suffer from a shortage of oxygen. The body automatically tries to increase the quantity of air breathed in. The level of carbon dioxide in the blood is also reduced, which increases the pH

value of the blood, and to compensate for this you urinate less. When the oxygen level in the blood drops, the blood vessels' diameters also shrink and this, together with reduced kidney function, can cause fluid to form in the lungs and the brain – oedema. After a while the body produces more red blood cells, which improves the oxygen uptake. The ability to acclimatize varies considerably from one individual to another, to some extent because of hereditary factors.

If you gradually accustom yourself to high altitudes through acclimatization, this counteracts altitude sickness, which can become acute at as low as 9,840 feet (3,000m) above sea level. Climbing a maximum of 985 feet (300m) per day is a good guideline for anyone who is susceptible. The effect of acclimatization is even better if you sleep at a lower level than you have walked at during the day. Stopping one or two days extra at an altitude of around 13,125 feet (4,000m) above sea level is also a good strategy. Acute altitude sickness is life-threatening and demands a rapid descent to a lower level. Anyone who knows they have a problem with altitudes may be able to get their doctor to prescribe a drug such as Diamox for preventive purposes. Altitude sickness can be a problem on the following treks: Garhwal, Mount Everest, Mount Elgon, Mount Kenya, Ruwenzori, Kilimanjaro, Gunung Kinabalu, Cordillera Blanca and the Inca Trail.

DOGS

When you are trekking in inhabited areas, aggressive dogs are the most dangerous animals. They may carry tetanus or rabies, and sometimes they behave in a life-threatening manner. If you are exposed to attack, a trekking pole is a good weapon. Throwing stones is usually effective. The danger of dogs is great in areas where there is a lot of grazing, such as Pirin, Crete, the Lycian Way, Mongolia and the Himalayas. When trekking in such areas, it is useful to take a high frequency whistle, which can stop a dog in its tracks.

SNAKES

You very rarely see poisonous snakes. They are timid animals that usually slither away when anyone approaches. In Australia, the continent that has the most poisonous snakes, it is advisable to be extra careful when choosing a campsite. You should never leave an unattended tent open. The nightmare scenario is a poisonous snake seeking warmth and protection in your sleeping bag! In general, the risk of snake bites is so small that very few trekkers carry antidote serum with them.

LEECHES

Leeches attach themselves to bare skin when you are trekking in tropical rainforests. These creatures are not dangerous and are more of a psychological than physical nuisance. When they are pulled off, you bleed for quite a while. If you walk in long trousers, high boots and a buttoned-up shirt, you don't get so many leeches, but on the other hand, it does make trekking hotter than ever.

FLYING INSECTS

Mosquitoes, flies and gnats may be a pest in northern tracts such as Mongolia, northern Scandinavia and the Yukon, but they are also found in other places, such as at the end of the Milford Track. Strangely enough, there are rarely such large quantities of stinging and biting insects in tropical areas. There, the problems are the diseases that are transmitted by mosquitoes and flies. Of these, malaria is the most well known and widespread. On trekking trails the risks are greater in low-lying tropical areas with forest, wetlands and many grazing animals. At higher levels in the mountains, there is virtually no risk, which you should bear in mind when contacting a vaccination centre before your trip. As prophylaxis against malaria is expensive, has to be taken regularly for a long period, doesn't provide guaranteed protection and in some cases even produces problematical side effects, the benefit is not self-evident, particularly if you are trekking on high ground. Personally, I take a low-key approach, but on some of the trails I have walked, chiefly in East Africa and Borneo, prophylaxis is advisable.

PREDATORS

Large predators are perhaps what you generally think of as the most dangerous animals for trekkers. But in Africa it is very rare to be confronted with predators during a trek.

North America's grizzly and black bears are usually the most problematic of these animals. The level of danger posed by bears is difficult to predict. Experienced wildlife enthusiasts living permanently in bear country usually feel no fear, but they are still cautious. The authorities for the national parks issue general advice. Food and other things with a strong smell, such as toothpaste, must be hung up in bags on branches, 10 feet (3m) above the ground and 7 feet (2m) out from the trunk. Along some trails there are bear poles for the same purpose. Note that you need to take along a 32-foot (10-m) rope for this purpose. Alternatively, you can carry everything that has a strong smell in a bear-proof canteen made of hard plastic, which you lay on the ground a distance away from the tent. While trekking in the Yukon we borrowed such a canteen from Parks Canada. You should also eat a distance away from the tent, but in a different direction from the canteen. Food stores, your cooking area and the tent should ideally form a triangle with 330 feet (100m) between the corners. When you are walking along a trail it is important to make a noise and let the bears know that you are around. These animals normally avoid people, and the risk of an unpleasant meeting with a bear when you're in a big group is minimal. A bell on a trekking pole is not a bad idea, and you can also sing so that your voice echoes around. You should have a pepper spray in your pocket as a last resort if a bear approaches. This so-called "bear repellent" (!) is only useful if the bear is a couple of metres away and obviously it is no good with the wind in your face! If you aim well it is effective – but the grizzly may come back, and the spray doesn't last long.

THE PHYSICAL EFFORT

You walk as long as your legs will carry you and trek as far as your energy lasts. There are, of course, elderly trekkers, but everyone, regardless of age, wonders how much they can manage. Usually it is more than you think, but it's best to take trips suited to your strength. Or should we say your willpower, because there is always a mental side to physical trials of strength. Many people who could manage great efforts are not motivated enough to try.

Trips in areas with well-managed paths and overnight huts require only basic physical fitness. As a rule these trips are less demanding, because you can manage with a lightweight pack. Regular, long walks are a good way to keep fit. On organized trips in remote countries you usually don't have to carry all the luggage yourself, so the effort is manageable. The demands increase when you have a lot to carry in rough terrain. Uphill slopes wear you out more on any trip. And walking in thin air at high altitudes is tough.

Is the physical effort a downside to trekking? No, not if you like feeling good. The human body is made for movement, and trekking is good for your health. However, carrying a backpack weighing over 33 pounds (15kg) is hard for a lot of people. If the pack weighs more than 44 pounds (20kg), the trip can become an ordeal. On the other hand, if you practise with a heavy backpack, 44 pounds (20kg) will become perfectly manageable. But anything weighing more than 55 pounds (25kg) is getting excessive. Naturally, things are different for men and women. Carrying a maximum of 33 pounds (15kg) is good advice for women who have never walked with a backpack before, and for men in the same circumstances, a maximum of 44 pounds (20kg) is advisable. Always try to keep your pack as light as possible.

Practice walks with a full backpack are a good way to prepare. In many ways it is a mental effort. Everyone feels the weight. The pressure of the straps on the shoulders cannot be spirited away, but it is possible to ignore the discomfort. A positive attitude makes any trek more fun. I try to see my backpack as a snailshell that gives me freedom and allows me to enjoy fantastic experiences close to nature. That makes it easier, believe it or not.

DANGEROUS DESTINATIONS

Theft is a risk in many countries. You must always keep an eye on your gear. It's better to be too careful than to end up in difficulties. The risk of theft is usually greatest in more densely populated areas, but along the trails other trekkers may be potential thieves.

Fortunately, trekkers are rarely exposed to mugging and murder, but there have been incidents. If warnings are issued they should be taken seriously. In some regions political conflicts and terrorism are risks that can suddenly flare up or vanish.

A good book to read for advice before trips is *The World's Most Dangerous Places* by Robert Young Pelton. It offers valuable background descriptions and is updated from time to time. Reliable websites with current information include:

U.S. Department of State travel site: www.travel.state.gov/travel

The site for the CIA World Factbook: www.cia.gov/cia/publications/factbook/index.html

British Foreign Office travel advice site: www.fco.gov.uk/travel

ENVIRONMENTALLY FRIENDLY TREKKING

Wilderness etiquette are modern buzzwords. Walking out into unspoilt and pristine areas is not as innocent a pastime for us as it was for the pioneers. There are far more of us now, and that affects the environment. With common sense you can minimize the impact.

WILDERNESS

Anything you take out with you must be brought back. But the question is: what should you do with rubbish and latrine residues? What you can burn you should, provided there is no fire risk. Faeces should be buried, particularly along well-frequented trails. The site should be far from a path or watercourse. In many countries trekkers take a little trowel with them for this purpose. On organized trips the guides and the porters usually dig a big latrine pit for the whole group. It is then filled in again after everyone has used it.

Clearing vegetation for a campsite requires judgment and care. A camp fire is nice but contributes to increased wear on the ground. You rarely prepare food over an open fire for yourself, but it is common on organized trips in inaccessible areas. If there happens to be an old fireplace, that should be used. If you make a new one, you should sweep away the traces before you leave.

Washing up, laundry and personal ablutions are not harmless in unspoilt countryside. Chemicals spilled into streams can contribute to water pollution. Along popular routes this is a real risk. As far as possible I try to clean saucepans and plates with hot water and no detergent. You should only wash with soap and shampoo in streams with a plentiful flow of water, or in large lakes. The same applies to washing clothes.

Leave no traces, take only photographs. This old saying is still valid today. It is not right to take natural items home: stones, flowers or animals. Threatened species on the danger lists should absolutely not be touched. The lists are updated regularly by the international nature conservation organizations.

POPULATED AREAS

In populated areas we must show respect for the local population. It's obvious that you shouldn't just wander into people's yards and gardens. You should always walk around cultivated fields. It is highly inappropriate to disturb the people around you with loud conversation. How you dress is also an important subject in this context. Along many trekking trails the local religion dictates what is appropriate. Women generally need to be more careful than men when it comes to light clothing. If you don't know what the customs are, it's best to avoid shorts and vest tops.

Taking photographs demands sensitivity. Along popular trails the local people are often bothered by tourists wanting to take their photograph. A good guideline is to ask first and never interrupt ongoing ceremonies.

PLANNING

Trips can be set up in different ways. You can follow a well-marked path or walk in trackless wilderness areas. Many people opt to stay a few days in one place and make day trips from there; it may be a campsite, a hut or a tourist resort. You can also make expedition-like trips in trackless areas far from public roads. Most people travel with friends and acquaintances, but organized trips can be fun as you have an opportunity to meet new people.

When planning you need to ask yourself how, where and when, in that order. Expectations are very significant for the trip. How challenging can a trip be? That depends on your experience and fitness. What privations are you prepared to accept? That is a matter for personal choice. How do you want to sleep, what food do you want? Would you rather walk in populated areas or do you prefer untouched wilderness? Is the company of other trekkers important? Can you cope with a lack of oxygen at high altitude? Can you put up with cold and severe weather conditions in exposed mountain areas? Can you cope with humid heat in rainforest or dry heat in the desert? How much are you prepared to arrange yourself?

An organized trip usually costs more than a trek you arrange yourself, but the planning is considerably simpler. Generally, you just have to follow advice and instructions from the organizer. In many places this is actually the only realistic option. The Inca Trail, Kilimanjaro and Ruwenzori are examples of trips that have to be carried out with guides and porters. Trekking with someone who can speak the local language is often a great advantage, indeed in many areas this is a necessity. In some cases the transport to and from the trail may require arrangements that can only be made with the help of a local tour operator. That is the situation in many of Asia's mountains regions – at least away from the most popular trails.

When you are arranging your own trip, it's best to read up on the landscape and the culture. Nowadays there is an enormous amount of information available, partly in guidebooks published with trekking in mind and partly on websites available on the Internet. Some of the most useful guidebooks are:

Bradt Travelguides: www.bradt-travelguides.com
Lonely Planet trekking guides: www.lonelyplanet.com
Trailblazer guides: www.trailblazer-guides.com

There are also a lot of local publications, but these are often hard to get hold of at home. Usually you have to search in well-stocked bookshops when you arrive in the country you are traveling to. In addition, there are masses of useful websites. Most tour operators have their own, with descriptions and facts of various kinds. By searching on the Internet you can often get vast quantities of information about interesting trekking areas.

EQUIPMENT

More people take too much than too little. The old motto "less is more" generally applies to trekking. Many people try to foresee all eventualities and the price they pay is an unnecessarily heavy pack. There is an art to choosing the right things. Previous experience is very important. If you want to go trekking around the world, the gear must be adaptable to the environment, climate and terrain. The type of trip is also significant. I shall offer only a few brief tips as there are many handbooks on the subject.

BOOTS

During my trip to Ruwenzori the guides and several of the porters were wearing rubber boots. I was very interested to see this, as you rarely see rubber boots on trails around the world. It is only in the Scandinavian fells that it is customary to wear them – I did so myself on my first trips there. These boots have the great advantage of being completely watertight and easy to clean, and on muddy paths, such as those in Ruwenzori, they are excellent. However, rubber boots produce the most sweat of any footwear and are not strong enough for walking long distances in stony terrain.

These days I always walk in leather hiking boots with a strong sole and Gore-tex lining, which makes them waterproof but still allows them to breathe. In my experience these work well. Then, there is the question of whether boots should be long or short. With styles that reach more than 8 inches (20cm) above the ankle you can cross most small streams without any risk of letting water in. The short versions are lighter and more flexible on the foot when you step out, not least on the plane, which is something I take into consideration. I always fly with my boots on to save weight at the check-in.

Since my trips to Australia, I have begun to appreciate the combination of short sturdy boots with gaiters. This offers great flexibility. I put the gaiters on if the path is muddy, if we might be walking on a lot of snow and across boulders and if we have to cross a stream that is not too deep.

You should choose your footwear very carefully and walk in them a lot before wearing them on a long trip. Blisters are the commonest ailment among trekkers, but the risk is lowered if the boots are well worn in. For safety's sake you should still take plasters with you. Take something like Nikwax with you too, so that you can grease your boots during the trek. And don't forget that your choice of socks makes a big difference to the comfort of your feet. As spare shoes, I always take a pair of modern sandals to wear in camps and civilized areas.

BACKPACK

The right backpack is just as important to your comfort as your footwear. I prefer a so-called "softpack" – a soft version with the part nearest the back reinforced with ribs, plastic plates or similar. The difference between a backpack that sits well and one that is a constant nuisance is the same as the difference

between good and bad boots – basically the difference between a good trip and a bad one. As your backpack is a personal item, it is important to try out and find a model that suits your build. Be particularly careful about the design of the hip strap. The mobility, softness and stability of this affect your carrying capacity. Even among the smaller day packs there are innumerable models to choose from. Check the padding across the back – an important detail.

How you pack your backpack affects the feel of the load and the pressure on your shoulders. Small adjustments to the contents can alter the balance. The be-all and end-all is the right distribution of the weight; stop immediately and adjust the backpack if it feels unbalanced. An important accessory is the rain poncho, which can be spread over it in persistent rain.

My luggage for flights consists of a large backpack, which I check in, and a day pack, which is my hand baggage. I like to be able to fold up the latter and pack it in the big backpack when I start the trek. I use the day pack for my photographic gear and spare clothes on day trips. Before the big pack is checked in, I put it in a plastic sack, which provides some protection on the flight.

TENT AND STOVE

A camping stove and a tent are necessary pieces of equipment if you are travelling independently. Stoves designed for different types of fuel, so-called "multi-fuel stoves", are the best for trekking around the world. Paraffin is the commonest fuel in international terms, but gas is more practical as it creates the least soot, produces the most heat and is quickest to get going. The stove should work with both types of fuel and preferably petrol as well, because you can always get hold of that at a petrol station.

A tent for trekking should be small, easy to put up and storm-resistant. The tunnel and dome models are the ones usually used now, but there are big differences in quality and weight between the different makes and models. Those consisting of an inner and an outer tent provide the surest protection against steady rain. A two-man tent should not weigh more than 9 pounds (4kg). The one I use weighs less than 7 pounds (3kg).

PERSONAL ITEMS

Don't forget that "less is more", but a torch is an absolute necessity in tropical areas with pitch-black nights, and it's always a good thing to have anyway. The modern types with light diodes are brilliant. They provide a lot of light for their weight. You should always pack some kind of knife. I prefer a multipurpose knife with pliers, a screwdriver, scissors and so on. Don't forget to put it in your backpack for the check-in. If the knife ends up in your hand baggage it will be taken away, usually for good. A small pair of binoculars and an altitude meter (built into my watch) are among the things I can't do without. Sunglasses and a hat or visor are also necessities. A long line to hang your clothes on is often useful. The safety devices you should take with you include a compass, a whistle, a

little wire, sewing thread and an aluminium mirror (for reflecting signals). Toiletries and first aid packs vary from one person to another, but everyone should include a large roll of lavatory paper.

CLOTHES

I prefer to walk in long trousers that can be quickly unzipped to shorts. Make sure they are made of hardwearing fabric. Warm clothes are necessary even in tropical areas – the nights may be cold, particularly at high altitudes. I always take a fleece, a scarf, a hat, long johns and gloves. In addition I have Gore-tex rain gear. Trousers and jackets made of this material can breathe and can also be used if it gets cold. If the trip is more of an expedition, in colder territory an extra sweater, bodywarmer or sometimes a padded jacket may be necessary.

TREKKING POLES

Nowadays I take two poles with me, one for walking and one for safety. There are excellent telescopic models available that take up very little space in your pack. Many people prefer to walk with two poles all the time. Walking with a pole gives you better balance on rocky and snow-covered ground and makes it possible to go a little faster on an ordinary path – important if you need to go far for help. Two poles are also good when you are wading across the larger rivers.

WADING

During trips in northern regions rivers are often an obstacle to be feared. In trackless areas like the Yukon, Sarek and the Altai Mountains they can cause us to change our route. When there is a stream in the way the question arises: to wade or not to wade? It is hard to weigh up racing currents. First you must investigate the force and depth of the water and then you must pinpoint the best place for wading. It is safest to cross where the river is widest.

In mountainous areas with snow and ice the waterflow may vary considerably. One peak might collapse in the spring when the snow melts. Another peak might collapse after periods of steady rain. Rivers may also vary at different times of day. This is particularly true in hot, sunny weather, when the peak flow occurs during the afternoon and evening. So it may be wise to wait until the morning before crossing a fast-flowing river. Wading is deemed difficult if the water reaches above the knees, the current is strong and the bottom is cluttered with large stones that make it hard for you to keep your balance.

The surest way to keep your boots dry is to take them off and wade in trainers or sandals. If the water is cold the disadvantage is that your legs and feet get frozen stiff, which increases the risk of falling over. In really cold water it is much safer to wade with your boots on. You can do it with waterproof trousers on and a strap pulled tight around the ankles. That's often enough to keep your boots dry, at least if there's not far to wade. Alternatively, you can use watertight bags, which you pull on over your feet. With these you can even keep dry when wading through deep water, even if you have short boots. The best are the wading bags that reach over your knees, but of course they do weigh a bit. If you are walking in high rubber boots, wading is problematic only if the water is very deep.

In any difficult wading you should undo the waist tie of your backpack so that you can get it off easily if you take a tumble. A pole is absolutely essential. Walk at an angle against the flow and use the pole both for support and to feel your way. It should preferably be chest-high. If it only reaches your waist you have to bend down, which is a tricky balancing act with a backpack on. To avoid feeling dizzy, don't look down into the water more than you have to.

A long rope can be a help when wading across deep, wide rivers. The person who goes first ties one end around themselves, while the person letting out the rope stands upstream of the wading point. If the wader loses his footing, the rope saves him from being carried away by the water. When the first person has crossed successfully, you swap roles. At deep wading places with a flat bottom, two or more people can cross together. You stand in a line one behind the other, at an angle to the current. Everyone behind the leader holds on to the person in front by putting their hands around the waist. In the water everyone takes a step at the same time. The leader has a pole for support and sets the speed. Everyone moves their right or left leg at the same time, instructed by the leader, and that way the whole line moves as one.

PHOTOGRAPHY

As I write, photography has reached a watershed. Digital cameras are taking over. I have already adopted this new method, but the photos in the book were mainly taken on film cameras. Since the pictures span a long period, I have used many different models of camera and types of film.

Before a trekking trip you need to consider your goals and requirements. The camera, the lens and the film must work together with all the other equipment and it all has to be carried through airports and out on the trails. These requirements are different from when you are driving and can take photos in civilized environments. For a trekking photographer digital technology opens up new possibilities because, among other things, all the equipment can be less bulky, lighter in weight and more practical.

When using a traditional camera, film is a practical problem. I tend to take a lot of rolls on trips (usually of slow, low sensitivity, 50-iso slide film) and apart from the fact that they take up quite a lot of space, it's always a nuisance to have them in your hand baggage at airports. You often have to worry about X-rays and how they may affect the film. Tropical heat is another cause for concern. However, to date I have never experienced any damage either from X-rays or from heat, and my misgivings have diminished over the years. I stopped using black bags to protect the films a long time ago. Digital cameras have swept away all these worries.

During a trek there are good opportunities for landscape and documentary photography. The art of taking powerful images is something you are either born with, or else you have to practise. You can take snaps (holiday subjects), postcards (beautiful scenes such as sunsets, sunny views and so on) and personal pictures (observation of details, picturesque situations, fine light effects and so on). Landscape subjects may be obvious or they may be spotted unexpectedly. For the best results you need a sharp lens and a fine-grained and hence, slow film. It is often necessary to place the camera on a tripod. A certain amount of strategic thinking is needed if you want to produce more than a mere picture postcard. You should be prepared to stop at an interesting view, take time to find angles and maybe wait for the right light. It is important to read the map correctly and to work out suitable sites for photographs in advance. I have obtained the best results with medium-format cameras and rolls of film, but they are heavy and slow to work with.

Documentary pictures of animals and people are often snapshots and demand an awareness of momentary images. You have to use very handy cameras and often a fast (high sensitivity) film. For this genre the ordinary, small picture format has proven universally useful. Previously I carried both a medium-format camera and a small picture one to cope with all types of subjects on my trips. It was a lot to carry!

One advantage of digital technology is that the best models of camera can be used for excellent results in both landscape and documentary photography. The light sensitivity of some digital cameras can be changed. The best ones provide optimum picture quality for the landscape when they have been set to a slow speed and by changing the setting they are quickly adapted to documentary pictures as well. So in future I only need to take one camera. That will save me a lot of equipment and weight. But not everything is better. With digital cameras you are completely dependent on batteries. Batteries with a long life and which tolerate cold and humid heat are, as yet, wishful thinking. Many trails pass through places where you can charge batteries or buy new ones, or more film. It is important to find this out in advance.

A good camera for trekking must be robust. I would also emphasize that the camera is a tool you need to familiarize yourself with, and it is important that it feels good in the hand. Creative needs are often met with two lenses: a wide angle zoom lens and a telephoto zoom lens. During a two-week trek I want to be able to take and store at least 1,000 pictures. That is equivalent to about 30 rolls of film. From now on I shall take a digital camera with extremely high resolution, over 15 megapixels. You need a tripod for poor light conditions and I prefer the lightest-weight, carbon-fibre models. I only take a separate flash if I am trekking through inhabited areas. If a flash is built into the camera, it's an advantage. I also take a small spare camera with 5 megapixel resolution, which I keep handy in my pocket for quick snaps.

The central part of the Canaima National Park in Venezuela offers many untried trekking routes.
Here, we are taking a pioneering trip below Akopan Tepui.

THE WORLD'S BEST TREKKING

EUROPE

In the south the distances between densely populated areas and wild mountain environments are short. But not all the routes are in mountainous areas. The European Ramblers Association is an umbrella organization that has created a network of trails. At present there are eleven long-distance paths on the continent and these often traverse cultivated landscapes, mostly in southern Europe.

Many countries also have their own system of paths. In France the long-distance paths are called "Grandes Randonnées" and are found throughout the country. The path that follows the spine of the Pyrenees is called GR10. In the Cevennes there are some surprisingly remote parts you can trek in, but the French Alps have the country's best-known trails, such as the "Tour du Mont Blanc" and the "Haute Route" between Chamonix and Zermatt in Switzerland. The island of Corsica is known for its wild landscape and excellent trekking paths.

Spain's best trails are located in the mountain ranges – outside the Pyrenees the main ones are Picos de Europa and Sierra de Gredos. But the most famous is the 1,200-year-old pilgrims' way "El Camino de Santiago", which passes through developed areas from the Pyrenees, through the Basque country to Galicia. Portugal's most famous trekking paths are probably those that follow the irrigation channels, the "levados", on Madeira.

The best Italian trails are in the north, in the Alps and the Dolomites. In the latter there is a long-distance path known as the "Alta Via". Here, there are also steep climbing routes, known as *via ferrata*. Picturesque Tuscany has trails suited to easy walking, and further south in the Apennines there are other areas of interest.

The Balkans largely consist of mountainous terrain still relatively unknown to foreign trekkers. However, in hilly Greece, the magnificent Pindos mountains in the north and the steep Olympus mountains in the east are two regions that have become well known, as has the island of Crete where there are several trails. Bulgaria's many mountainous areas also have excellent trails, the most dramatic being in Pirin.

In the northern parts of continental Europe the Carpathian mountains are of great interest. The most dramatic are the Tatra mountains on the border between Poland and Slovakia. Here, there is a high alpine area with many trails similar to those in the Alps – paths between huts and below steep mountains. In Transylvania in Romania, the Carpathian mountains are softer in shape and there are some easy trails.

It is chiefly the fells that attract trekkers in Scandinavia. There are several thousand miles of marked paths in Sweden. The most popular and best known internationally is "Kungsleden" (the King's Way), which extends 275 miles (440km) from Hemavan to Abisko. Sarek National Park is the biggest wilderness area in the European Union and there you

have to carry your own food and tent. West of that is Padjelanta with open heaths and big lakes, and an attractive trekking trail with huts. Norway has an even bigger network of marked paths than Sweden, plus far more overnight huts. Jotunheim is one of the most magnificent areas in Europe, with several paths below very steep, high crags. In northern Norway the bottoms of the mountains are in the sea, but behind the developed coastline there are huge deserted areas for trekking in. Finland too has long paths, chiefly in forested areas resembling wildernesses, for example in Karhunkierros, the "Bear Trail" in Oulanka National Park. The Arctic path extends 500 miles (800km) through the northernmost parts of Finland, Norway and Sweden. In places it overlaps with the Kungsleden.

Iceland is popular for trekking, but there are few charted paths. Apart from Laugavegur there are good trails on Skaftafjell by Europe's biggest glacier. On the north side of the island you can walk a 60-mile (100-km) trail between Myvatn and the Herdubreidar fells.

Great Britain is classic trekking terrritory. The character of the trails varies enormously. The Inn Way in England's Lake District takes you past traditional pubs in the poets' lakeland region. The longest path is the Pennine Way, 267 miles (430km) from the Peak District to the Scottish border, a strenuous trek if you walk the whole length. The trekkers' paradise is really Scotland, where the Southern Upland Way runs right across the southern part from coast to coast. The West Highland Way is probably the best known, running past the highest mountain, Ben Nevis, 4,410 feet (1,344m) above sea level. On the Isle of Skye most of the trekking consists of day trips amid a dramatic landscape.

AFRICA

There are many mountainous areas, but only one genuine mountain range – the Atlas. The treks in many ways resemble those in the Himalayas, although the peaks are not as high. You walk between mountain villages inhabited by Berbers and follow deep valleys between the mountains. The highest peak, Jebel Toubkal, at 13,670 feet (4,167m) above sea level, is encircled by a famous trekking trail. The trip round the mountain takes about nine days on well trodden paths, with small guest houses and huts to sleep in. The area around the second highest mountain, M'Goun, is not so well known and treks there are more like an expedition. Further north, the mountain of Jebel Sirwa, on the edge of the Sahara, is a goal for more remote treks. To the east of the High Atlas lies Jebel Sahro. This mountain chain is largely uninhabited, more barren and has remarkable rock formations. Here, there is scope for really adventurous treks. The Canary Islands, off the coast of North Africa, have trails, particularly the island of Tenerife where you can trek up the great Mount Teide volcano.

Scattered across the mighty Sahara lie mountain massifs that attract a number of trekkers. Tefedest,

Tassili and Hoggar in southern Algeria are the most popular. All consist of rock pinnacles, which in many cases can be ascended without climbing. The desert climate makes the trekking gruelling, but organized tours take place regularly. Along the extensive crags of Dogon Falaise in Mali you can trek for six days between villages offering unique buildings and rich indigenous culture. Air National Park in Niger is another interesting trekking area in the Sahara.

The long Rift Valley extends through East Africa, cutting across Ethiopia in the north and continuing south with two parallel stretches passing through Kenya, Uganda and Tanzania to Lake Malawi. Along this valley there are several volcanoes, some extinct but some still active. Most of the trails are on and around the volcanoes, which are often single, freestanding mountains. Ethiopia is an exception, consisting largely of a high plateau intersected with gorges, which makes it one of the most mountainous countries in Africa. In Demien National Park, you can take a seven-day trek in a strongly undulating landscape. There you will find Ras Dashen, the continent's fourth highest peak, which rises to 15,155 feet (4,620m) above sea level.

The most popular trekking area in Africa is Mount Kilimanjaro. There are several routes up the mountain and they all involve a very demanding trip governed by specific regulations. Tanzania's second highest mountain, Mount Meru, at 14,980 feet (4,566m) above sea level, is quite close and is also a volcano. Many people climb Meru for practice before tackling Kilimanjaro. Mount Kenya is also a classic. You can trek up to the third highest of its peaks, Lenana, and walk round the whole massif. The Aberdare Range in Kenya forms a long ridge of volcanic origin. Here, you have to walk with an armed national park warden to protect you against wild animals. The biggest volcano of all in terms of area is Mount Elgon, which has more trails on the Ugandan side than on the Kenyan side.

Uganda's biggest trekking area is Ruwenzori, which is a fault range, and is often dubbed the "African Alps". The trails are very difficult. Further south in Malawi, rises the freestanding and mighty mountain massif Mulanje, where there are several trails.

On Madagascar, too, you can find interesting areas for trekking. On the Masoala peninsula in the northeast there is a path through a rainforest where you can see some of the island's unique flora and fauna. In the south the Isalo National Park displays an environment to fire the imagination, with wind-polished sandstone mountains and deep ravines. Both long and short treks are possible here.

Southern Africa has several well-tried areas for trekking. The most magnificent mountain formation is the Drakensberg, which forms steep crags and gorges along the edge of a high plateau. The topography is similar to the Ethiopian highlands. The most popular route goes through the northern Drakensberg, from the Royal National Park and south, five days and 40 miles (65km) with no huts and long stretches at high altitude, around 9,840 feet (3,000m) above sea level. South Africa also has a long and magnificent coastline. The well-known Otter Trail passes varying scenery of forests, sandy beaches, cliffs and a river delta over five one-day stages. North of Cape Town there is a mountainous area called Cederbergs, at up to 6,560 feet (2,000m) above sea level. This offers excellent opportunities for trekking on foot or on horseback, among various rock formations in a dry environment.

Namibia has a desert-like landscape. The best-known trek is a trip through Fish River Canyon. A more strenuous trek goes across the Naukluft mountain range. You can take a long trek for eight days or a shorter one that requires half the time. There is a lot of wildlife and there are good chances of seeing antelope. Inland from the fateful Skeleton Coast you can trek along the little Ugab river, 31 miles (50km) in three days.

ASIA
Turkey offers great possibilities, but has few established trails. The landscape is varied, with many mountains, dramatic coasts and large lakes. You can also trek along routes that have historic links with ancient Rome. The country's first long-distance path, the Lycian Way, runs parallel with the south coast. North of the town of Antalya there is another long-distance path, the St. Paul trail. This trail follows ancient Roman routes through mountain areas with big lakes. Both paths are easy to reach from the holiday resorts on the south coast. Further east, in the volcanic, lunar landscape of Cappadocia, you can find easy treks both short and long. In the colourful Taurus Mountains, Aladaglar is a good area for challenging trekking. Even further east in Turkey there are more adventurous trails. The Pontic mountain range along the Black Sea has a high alpine area called Kackar, with steep mountains, more than 12,795 feet (3,900m) above sea level, as well as glaciers. And Noah's Mount Ararat lies where Turkey meets Iran and Iraq. It is possible to trek up this volcano, which is over 16,405 feet (5,000m) high.

Central Asia comprises boundless plains, high mountain ranges and sparsely populated regions. As many of the attractive destinations are hard to get to, relatively few trekkers have found their way here yet. The Tibetan high plateau is a godforsaken environment where trekking still entails real expeditions. There are organized tours to some parts. In the south, bordering on the Himalayas, there is Kailas – the world's most sacred mountain. A steady stream of Hindu and Buddhist pilgrims make their way to the foot of this mountain and they then walk in a circle round the prominent peak, which lies 810 miles (1,300km) west of Lhasa. Experienced trekkers take four days to complete the circle. This is Tibet's most demanding trek and a challenging route at high altitude. Along the northern edge of the Tibetan high plateau runs Kunlun, the most desolate, unknown and inaccessible of the world's really high mountain ranges, with peaks of over 22,965 feet (7,000m) above sea level. Here, too, there

are some organized tours. North of Kunlun extends the Takla Makan, and on the other side of this desert lies the Tienshan mountain range, which is also over 22,965 feet (7,000m) above sea level; this forms the border between China, Kyrgyzstan and Kazakhstan. The landscape consists of verdant alpine valleys with virginal pine forests and impressive mountain peaks. More and more organized treks are coming here.

The Altai Mountains, too, offer a very varied landscape, with steppes and larch forests, alpine peaks and glaciers. The mountain range extends thousands of miles through southern Siberia, Kazakhstan, Mongolia and China. The highest areas are Belukha in Russia and Tavan Bogd in Mongolia, and in both regions there are trekking trails that are beginning to become known. Mongolia is the land of opportunity for trekking, both on foot and on horseback. There are several organized tours every year as it is difficult to trek independently because of the transport problems. The Khangai mountain range runs through the centre of the country, with many as yet untried treks. In the western province of Uvs, apart from the Altai, there is an isolated mountain massif almost 13,125 feet (4,000m) high called Turgen, which can be crossed in a week. The big forests in Khentiin Nuruu, northeast of Ulan Bator, are good for long treks on horseback with a guide.

The Himalayas is the prime area for trekking. The Himalayas stretch from Pakistan in the west to Bhutan in the east, but the high mountains in the west are usually counted as separate ranges with names such as Karakoram, Ladakh and Zanskar. Thanks to its position, Nepal has become a centre for trekking in the Himalayas. You need a trekking permit to walk around the country. In Nepal many people trek independently, but there is a wide range of organized tours on offer. The Everest trail is the most well-known, but the paths around Mount Annapurna in central Nepal are even more popular. The shortest trips there go to the foot of the south face of the massif. You can continue on to Jomosom, close to the border with Tibet, and pass through the 19,685-foot (6,000-m) deep valley of Kali Gandaki west of Annapurna. This return trip is a classic. Many people do a three-week, anticlockwise trip round the massif, crossing high mountain passes. The trip round the Dhaulagiri massif further west is considered to be even more challenging. The Langtang area north of Kathmandu is the most accessible in the country. East of Everest there are fewer trekkers. There you find the less frequented routes to the famous 26,245-foot (8,000-m) mountains of Makalu and Kanchenjunga.

In Bhutan, only organized trekking is allowed. There are several trails and the most popular runs to the country's highest mountain, Chomo Lhari, 24,000 feet (7,315m) above sea level. The opportunities offered by the Indian sector of the Himalayas are pretty much as good as those in Nepal. Garhwal is often called the garden of the Himalayas and there is a famous trail to the "Valley of Flowers". The source of the Ganges at Gangtri is a sacred place for Hindus and a pilgrimage route leads there, which trekkers can also follow. The Curzon trail is famous for its fantastic views. Further

west, in the Indian Himalayas, the landscape changes. The Ladakh–Zanskar area is similar to the dry mountain landscape of Tibet. Here the people live in remote villages. There are no marked paths and there are relatively few visitors – trekking here is more like an expedition. In winter you can follow the river Zanskar through a narrow gorge. The rest of the year that route is impassable.

The Karakoram, the westernmost mountains of the Himalayas are in Pakistan, Here you find the greatest concentration of 26,245-foot (8,000-m) mountains, including K2, the second highest mountain in the world. A well-tried route leads to K2 – this involves an expedition across barren and uninhabited, high mountain terrain, following the Baltoro glacier. The southern part of Karakoram is largely wilderness and trekking there is often tantamount to a small expedition. Apart from the trek to K2, the long trip across the Biafo and Hispar glaciers is among the most magnificent in the world.

The northern parts of Thailand, Laos and Vietnam share similar geography, with undulating mountains and extensive monsoon forests. Various local tribes, who have preserved their traditional culture, live here. You usually trek between villages. The most popular stretches lie in Thailand, particularly in the areas around the town of Chiang Rai. North of Mae Hong Son there are other good areas for village trekking. Several mountain tribes live in the province of Luang Prabang in Laos, and you can make short trips there. The mountainous topography of Laos makes it fun for trekking. The most spectacular area is Khammouane, where limestone mountains rise out of the countryside. On the Bolavan plateau in the south you can trek through rainforest. In Vietnam the area of Sapa, close to the Chinese border, is excellent for trekking. Here you find Fansipan, Indochina's highest mountain at 10,310 feet (3,143m) above sea level, which can be climbed on a five-day trip.

Malaysia, too, has several areas with trails through rainforest. In the centre of the Malacca peninsula lies Tamanegara National Park, where a trip up Gunung Tahan, the peninsula's highest mountain at 7,170 feet (2,186m) above sea level, is a gruelling expedition lasting eight days for the return trip. It is considerably easier to walk up Gunung Ledang (Mount Orphir).

Borneo boasts Gunung Kinabalu, the highest peak in southeast Asia. The trail to it is now popular and usually takes two days. In the Mulu National Park in Sarawak there is the "Head Hunter's Trail", a rainforest path that can be tackled in one to two days. In the same area you can also trek through rainforest up to the top of Gunung Mulu. Indonesia has enormous and largely untried possibilities. In Bromo-Tengger National Park in eastern Java you can trek on active volcanoes.

AUSTRALIA
Although Australia is the flattest of the continents, it has several prominent mountain chains with trekking trails. The 137-mile (220-km long Larapinta trail is well laid-out, running west from Alice Springs, and along and over the MacDonnell mountain range. There are also

attractive paths along the coasts. Apart from the well-known Wilsons Promontory in the southeast, there is a popular coastal path between Eden and Mallacoota, where New South Wales and Victoria meet. The Thorsborne trail on Hinchinbrook Island inside the Great Barrier Reef is a well-known and taxing path along this tropical stretch of coast. Western Australia has its best trekking country in the Fitzgerald River Coast and Stirling Range national parks in the south and on the Hammersley Range in the north. On the tropical northern tip of Australia there is the magnificent Kakadu National Park, which bears the stamp of Aboriginal culture. A well-tried trekking trail leads to the Jim Jim Falls. In the eastern parts of the continent the Great Dividing Range offers great possibilities. The Blue Mountains close to Sydney have several paths for both long-distance and day trips. And the state of Victoria contains the popular areas of the Grampians and the Snowy Mountains. South Australia's prime trails are to be found at Wilpena Pound in the Flinders Range.

It is, above all, Tasmania that has put Australia on the world trekking map. The southwestern part of the island is an impressive wilderness. The South Coast Track follows the coast of this area. The most difficult trails lead over the mountains in Arthur's Range and to the summits of Federation Peak and Frenchman's Cap respectively. The island's most internationally famous path is the Overland Track, which has also become Australia's most popular long-distance trail.

OCEANIA
Of all the islands in and around the Pacific Ocean, New Zealand has the best trekking. At present there are nine trails, including Tongariro and the Milford Track. Other well-known paths are the Routeburn and Kepler tracks, both in the Fiordland National Park. Like the Milford Track, they are very popular and must be booked in advance. The country's mountain environments range from colourful volcanoes to heavily ice-laden peaks. Mount Taranaki, on North Island, is a volcano that is encircled by a trekking trail. The mountain range on South Island is called the Southern Alps. Around Mount Cook, the highest mountain, there are trekking trails of an alpine nature. Here you can also take long-distance glacier walks. Popular routes along the coast are the Heaphy Track and the Abel Tasman Coast Track, both in the northern part of South Island and classified as two of the "Great Walks" – the country's best kept trails.

In New Guinea, the eastern part of the world's second largest island, there are some renowned trails. The most famous is the Kokoda Trail, which crosses the Owen Stanley mountain range. It was first cleared by the gold diggers in the nineteenth century and then became notorious for the hardships suffered by the Japanese army in the Second World War. Up in the mountains there are trails leading to the villages of the diverse tribal groups living on the island.

Several of the Hawaiian islands have interesting trekking trails. On Kauai, apart from the Waimea canyon, the coastal path of Na Pali is a delightful path,

known as the Kalalau Trail. On the main island of Hawaii, you can walk to the top of the volcano of Mauna Loa, a trip of several days up to heights of 13,125 feet (4,000m) and more above sea level; here, you can get caught in sudden snowstorms. On the island of Maui is the famous Haleakala Crater, with a fascinating landscape and trekking trails. Other Pacific islands, such as New Caledonia and Fiji also have trekking trails of note.

SOUTH AND CENTRAL AMERICA
The southernmost part of this continent, Patagonia, is among the wildest areas in the world. The Andes extend down here, but the mountains are not as high as those further north. Most of the peaks are in Chile, while Argentina has the most extensive plains. Patagonia has Torres del Paine and Fitz Roy – two of the earth's most spectacular mountain formations, which the area's best-known trails encircle. In the northern parts, chiefly on the Chilean side and in the district of Araucania, there are several volcanoes with challenging trekking trails. A famous, cross-border region is Patagonia's lake district, with big lakes and volcanic areas. Here, you find the most popular and easily walked trails in this part of the continent.

The Andes mountain range is the second highest in the world, and thanks to its extensive length – from Cape Horn in the south to Venezuela in the north – it covers a wide range of natural conditions. The highest peak, Aconcagua, lies on the border between Chile and Argentina. But it is in Bolivia, Peru and Ecuador that the range is widest, with many high, ice-covered peaks. A trek in this part of the Andes is like a trek in the Himalayas – you walk through inhabited areas and dramatic valleys.

Ecuador has two famous, high volcanoes, Cotopaxi and Chimborazo, which many people try to climb. Chimborazo is the point on earth that juts furthest into space – in other words, it is further from the centre of the earth than Mount Everest. This is because of the asymmetric shape of the earth.

In Peru the highest mountain range is the Cordillera Blanca, and the most popular trail here is the Santa Cruz. Another trail is the Alpamayo Circuit. This path passes in front of the most beautiful face of the world's most beautiful mountain – Alpamayo – but it is a long trip and a demanding one. The Huayhuash range a little further south is considered Peru's most pristine and wildest mountain region, and there is a very taxing trail here that crosses several passes around 13,125 feet (4,000m) above sea level. The country's best-known trail is the Inca Trail, which leads to the mysterious ruined city of Machu Picchu. The surrounding range is the Cordillera Vilcabamba, which offers other trails too. Further south lies the Cordillera Vilcanota, with Peru's biggest glaciers. A trek here offers fine views and many encounters with traditional Indian culture. In Bolivia the Cordillera Real on the eastern shore of Lake Titicaca is considered a gem. The mountain range rises from the Altiplano,and there is a famous trip round the Illampu mountain. There are also several other paths here, among them the Takesi Trail, which

is often called the "Inca Road", and should not be confused with the Inca Trail in Peru.

The northernmost mountain massif in Colombia and Venezuela also has several trekking trails, but in this part of the continent the unique environment of the highlands of Guyana and Venezuela is more attractive to the trekker. In the Canaima National Park, you can walk below the *tepuis* or plateau mountains and even climb some of them. Roraima, the highest, has a well-tried path to the top. In another area you can walk to the world's highest waterfall, the Angel Falls. Along both of these trails you can walk independently, but most people come with organized trips. Climbing up the plateau mountains is a great challenge in very difficult terrain.

The southernmost part of the Panama headland is called the Darien Gap. It is a trackless jungle area with an interesting route from the Atlantic to the Pacific Ocean. There are some organized tours that follow this route. Central America as a whole offers many possibilities for treks, both in tropical rainforest and on high mountains. Costa Rica has an established trail up to the country's highest peak, Chirripo, 12,465 feet (3,800m) above sea level, which is a four day return trip. Mexico boasts several 16,405-foot (5,000-m) high volcanoes that you can climb. Not so far from Mexico City stands Popocatepetl and the more difficult Iztaccihuatl. Further north the immense Copper Canyon attracts considerable interest. It has been "blasted" into the Sierra Madre range and houses a complex world of six long gorges with Indian villages where time stands still. There are organized trips there.

NORTH AMERICA
With its varied landscape and vast expanse, the United States of America is the land of possibilities for trekkers. Most walk independently, but there is a wide range of organized tours available, particularly in the most popular areas such as the Grand Canyon. There are many well-ordered long-distance trails. The United States has a law – the National Trail Systems Act of 1968.– that protects the most important trails. Almost twenty long-distance trails are historically and scenically interesting, and most pass through several states. The Ice Age Trail in Wisconsin leads to sites of geological interest in a forest landscape. The North Country Scenic Trail links interesting places between the Missouri River and the state of New York. In the latter state are the Adirondacks, a mountainous wilderness with an extensive system of trails. The world's first long-distance path was the Appalachian Trail, 2,160 miles (3460 km) along the extensive Appalachian Mountains from Georgia to Maine. Long stretches run through broad-leaved woodland but also over several bare, rounded mountains. In the north the White Mountains are a well-known area for trekkers. Florida, too, has a national trekking trail.

The western United States attracts trekkers from all over the world with its unique landscape. Two long-distance paths here are included in the National Trail System. One is the Pacific Crest Trail, which follows the spine of the ranges along the west coast, and for

This book only offers a small selection of the world's best trekking. In Norway alone there are inexhaustible possibilities. This is Midtmaradalstind, 6,750 feet (2,057m) above sea level.

long stretches it coincides with the John Muir Trail in California's Sierra Nevada. The other is the Continental Divide range, which winds its way over the Rocky Mountains from New Mexico, north to Montana, for more than 31,070 miles (50,000km). The Wind River range in Wyoming provides an overview of much of the Rockies' landscape and is traversed by the Highline Trail. You can walk this path in just ten days. The Glacier National Park in Montana has a comprehensive system of paths, and in Idaho there are the jagged Sawtooth mountains. The Colorado plateau has the most extraordinary landscapes in the United States and the Kaibab and Havasu trails are the most popular paths in the Grand Canyon. In Canyonlands National Park there are short paths in "the Needles" and "the Maze" areas, the latter aptly named because it has very confusing terrain.

Northern North America still lives up to the description "the last frontier lands". Immense, uninhabited wildernesses stretch out for those looking

for expeditions. In the more populous southern parts of Canada it is above all the Rockies that form the trekkers' stronghold. Here, there are paths of every degree of difficulty. The big national park area on the border between Alberta and British Columbia has a highly networked and often well-ordered trail system. It includes parts of the Great Divide Trail, which comes from the USA and ends at the border of the Yukon. You can walk a good week on this trail, past the beautiful Mount Assinboine to the colourful Lake O'Hara. British Columbia also has magnificent coastal paths, the main one being along the seaward side of Vancouver Island. On the mainland there is the Sunshine Coast Trail. As I write, the Trans Canada Trail is being set up, a long-distance path that will pass through all the provinces and territories and connect existing paths with new ones.

The gold-diggers' Chilkoot Trail is well-known and popular. The Yukon has enormous areas with no tracks, but in the immense Luane National Park you

can trek along routes that in some places are marked paths. The Tombstone range in the northern part of the Yukon is a mysterious area with sharp granite pinnacles and interesting possibilities for trekking. On the border with the Northwest Territory, the Canol Heritage Trail extends 217 miles (350km) due east, one of the world's most inaccessible and toughest trekking trails. On Baffin Island there are almost 62 miles (100km) of the Akshayuk Pass Route – an Arctic "King's Way".

Only a few trails have been set up in Alaska. The authorities don't want to make it easy to tour the wilderness. But Alaska is like northern Canada: there are remarkable areas for those who are not afraid to rough it – for example the Brooks Range with the Gates of the Arctic National Park, and the Alaska range with Mount McKinley, the continent's highest mountain. South of Anchorage, on the Kenal peninsula, you will find the Resurrection Trail, the best-known route in the state.

A ROUTE GUIDE TO MY JOURNEYS

It's best to tell it like it is – trekking always entails physical exertion. And trips on a trail can vary considerably, depending on the weather, how much your pack weighs, what mood you are in, your expectations, how you feel on the day, and so on. How we experience the countryside, and its difficulties and challenges is a personal thing. Any itinerary can be experienced in many different ways. Let me mention a good example: I have classified the section of the Lycian Way that I walked as a fairly easy trek. Yet I know that the same stretch has been classified as challenging by people who have walked it with organized tours. My assessment is relative and rates the Lycian Way in relation to other trails I have experienced. For example, I can compare it with the Tour du Mont Blanc, which is far more strenuous than the Lycian Way because of the many mountain passes you have to cross; or Kilimanjaro, which demands a performance on a par with running a marathon. This is the way I have assessed trail after trail and compared them with one another. For such comparisons to be meaningful you need a scale, because you can never describe the conditions of the routes objectively. This means that some people may consider my assessments to be over- or underestimates. However, at least if the same person makes all the assessments, they will be consistent – that has been my aim.

To make the information about my trails easy to understand, I have divided it up under a number of headings.

Organization
A private trip means that you arrange everything yourself. Sometimes you walk completely independently, sometimes with local guides and porters. An organized trip with guides means that a tour operator is responsible for arranging the trip.

Degree of remoteness
This provides an indication of how many other people you may expect to see during your trip. Along popular stretches the degree of remoteness is low, even if the landscape is undeveloped and resembles a wilderness.

Nature conservation
Information about national parks, reserves and world heritage sites that the trail passes through.

Accommodation
When I say a "hut" I mean a roof over your head and no more; a "refuge" means a house offering both accommodation and catered food, and a "guest house" is my term for a simple hotel. When there is no accommodation mentioned you need a tent.

Food
Along most of the trails you need to have your own food, regardless of whether you are trekking privately or with an organized tour. In the latter case you usually don't have to carry or prepare the food. If you are staying in refuges or guest houses you can order catered food

Physical effort
My assessment takes into account the length of the stages, accessibility, the number of slopes and how high above sea level you are trekking. The classification "easy" means that the trail can be managed by anyone with normal physical fitness; "moderate" demands a good basic physical condition; "hard" means you need to be in training; and "very hard" means you should be in extremely good physical condition, plus you need to do some extra training before the trip.

Accessibility
I base this on the type of trail and the terrain. "Easy" means well-trodden paths or ground that is easy to walk on. "Difficult" means there are obstacles in the way – usually muddy or marshy stretches, dense vegetation, major rivers that have to be waded across, rocky ground – or that the paths are little-used, or non-existent.

Sights
A range of interesting things to look out for.

Reminders
A little about the risks, and some practical tips.

Comment
My summing up.

Degree of difficulty
My assessment of the overall difficulty on a scale of 1 to 10, where 1 is "easy", 5 is "moderately difficult" and 10 is "very challenging". Most of the trails have both easy and difficult sections.

Maps
All the maps are shown with north at the top. The scale varies – see each individual map.

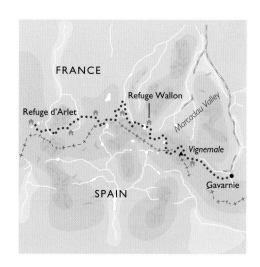

8 miles / 5 km

PYRENEES

A trek on a marked, long-distance path along the crest of the mountain range. A popular stretch is the one from Gavarnie to Lac de Bious d'Artigues in the western region.

Location: on the border between France and Spain

Organization: private/organized tour with guide

Best time: July–September

Time to allow: 45 days for the whole path, 10 for the section mentioned above.

Length: 249 miles (400km) whole path, 43 miles (70km) for this section.

Highest altitude: about 8,860 feet (2,700m) above sea level.

Remoteness: low–moderate.

Nature conservation: Pyrenees National Park and World Heritage site

Accommodation: tent/refuges/guest houses

Food: available in refuges and guest houses, or take your own

Physical effort: easy–moderate

Accessibility: easy

Sights: mountain landscape, flora

Reminders: book refuges in advance; there are alternative paths

Comment: on the whole an easy trail if you avoid the highest passes. Perfect for long day trips from a refuge or a hotel. On longer trips you can buy provisions along the way.

Difficulty: 1–5

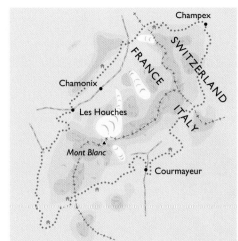

16 miles / 10 km

16 miles / 10 km

8 miles / 5 km

DOLOMITES

A trek on a marked, long-distance path, the Alta Via 4 in the Sesto area, also called Paul Grohmann's High Trail, after a well-known mountaineer.

Location: northeast Italy

Organization: private/organized tour with guide

Best time: July–September

Time to allow: 7–8 days

Length: about 56 miles (90km).

Highest altitude: about 8,200 feet (2,500m) above sea level

Remoteness: low

Nature conservation: Dolomites of Sesto Nature Park

Accommodation: refuges/guest houses/tent

Food: available in refuges and guest houses, or take your own

Physical effort: easy–hard

Accessibility: easy, but the climbing routes are difficult

Sights: extremely jagged mountains, flora

Reminders: climbing routes not advisable if you suffer from vertigo; book refuges in advance

Comment: perfect mountain environment for easy day trips. Long-distance trekking possible without too heavy a backpack. Climbing routes interesting for people who want to try challenging routes.

Difficulty: 1–7

MONT BLANC

A trek on a marked, long-distance trail along traditional paths and roads around Mont Blanc.

Location: borders between France, Italy and Switzerland

Organization: private/organized tour with guide

Best time: July–September

Time to allow: at least 11 days

Length: about 112 miles (180km).

Highest altitude: about 8,870 feet (2,700m) above sea level

Remoteness: low

Accommodation: tent/refuges/guest houses

Food: available in refuges and guest houses, or take your own

Physical effort: moderate–hard

Accessibility: easy

Sights: magnificent mountain landscape

Comment: easy paths, but as a whole a demanding long-distance trek ranging between mountain landscapes and developed environments. People unaccustomed to trekking should opt for the day trips from the tourist resorts.

Difficulty: 5–8

CRETE

A trekking trail on narrow dirt tracks and paths across the Lefka Ori mountain range.

Location: western part of Crete

Organization: private

Best time: April–June, September–October

Time to allow: 2–3 days

Length: about 19 miles (30km).

Highest altitude: about 6,890 feet (2,100m) above sea level

Remoteness: moderate

Nature conservation: Samaria National Park

Accommodation: tent

Food: take your own

Physical effort: moderate

Accessibility: easy

Sights: Samaria Gorge

Reminders: lack of water, oppressive heat, sudden storms

Comment: fairly demanding trekking owing to the climate and the landscape, whether you trek for several days or take day trips.

Difficulty: 5–6

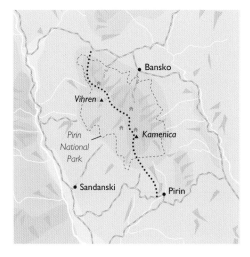

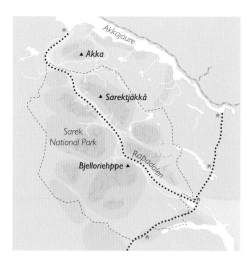

16miles/10 km

16miles/10 km

16miles/10 km

PIRIN MOUNTAINS

A trek along marked paths across the Pirin Mountains.

Location: southwest Bulgaria

Organization: private/organized tour with guide

Best time: July–September

Time to allow: 6–7 days

Length: about 37 miles (60km).

Highest altitude: 9,560 feet (2,915m) above sea level

Remoteness: low–moderate

Nature conservation: Pirin National Park and World Heritage site

Accommodation: tent/refuges

Food: take your own

Physical effort: moderate

Accessibility: easy

Sights: steep mountains, flora

Reminders: if you suffer from vertigo, beware of the northern part; aggressive sheepdogs

Comment: Moderately demanding trek if you avoid the most vertiginous stretches in the north.

Difficulty: 5–6

ISLE OF SKYE

A day trip along various paths in the Black Cuillin.

Location: Inner Hebrides, Scotland

Organization: private

Best time: June–August

Time to allow: 6–9 hours

Length: around 4 miles (6–7 km).

Highest altitude: 3,250 feet (990m) above sea level.

Remoteness: low

Accommodation: tent/youth hostel

Food: take your own

Physical effort: hard

Accessibility: difficult

Sights: jagged mountains, the sea

Reminders: extremely rainy climate; avoid climbing if you suffer from vertigo

Comment: A delightful mountain massif for day trips. If you don't want to climb, the mountain cirques beneath the steep summits are easily accessible.

Difficulty: 6–7

SAREK

A trek along fragmentary paths or map-reading your own route through the many valleys of the area.

Location: northern Sweden

Organization: private

Best time: July–September

Time to allow: at least 9 days

Length: about 81 miles (130km).

Highest altitude: just over 3,280 feet (1,000m) above sea level

Remoteness: very high

Nature conservation: Sarek National Park and Lapponia World Heritage site

Accommodation: tent

Food: take your own

Physical effort: hard–very hard

Accessibility: difficult

Sights: steep mountains, fertile valleys, plenty of wildlife

Reminders: heavy backpack, difficult wading, mosquitoes

Comment: A demanding trek for those used to the outdoor life.

Difficulty: 7–8

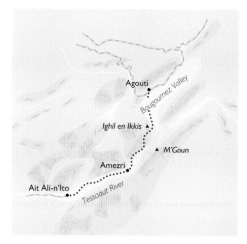

16 miles / 10 km   16 miles / 10 km   8 miles / 5 km

KEBNEKAISE

Cross-country skiing or walking trail across fells traversed by the King's Way.

Location: northern Sweden

Organization: private

Best time: March–April (cross-country skiing), July–September (trekking)

Time to allow: 7–10 days (King's Way, Abisko–Nikkaluokta)

Length: about 62 miles (100km) (King's Way, Abisko–Nikkaluokta)

Highest altitude: about 3,610 feet (1,100m) above sea level

Remoteness: moderate

Accommodation: tent/huts

Food: take your own or can be bought in huts

Physical effort: moderate

Accessibility: easy

Sights: steep mountains; wide open spaces

Reminders: risk of avalanches and snowstorms in winter; mosquitoes in summer

Comment: A fairly accessible area for skiing, with huts that offer shelter in bad weather. In summer the King's Way offers fairly easy trekking in a wildnerness-like mountain landscape.

Difficulty: 5

LAUGAVEGUR

A trek on marked paths from the interior to the coast.

Location: southern Iceland

Organization: private

Best time: July–September

Time to allow: 6 days

Length: 47 miles (75km).

Highest altitude: about 3,610 feet (1,100m) above sea level

Remoteness: moderate–high

Nature conservation: Fjallabak Nature Reserve

Accommodation: tent/huts

Food: take your own

Physical effort: moderate

Accessibility: easy

Sights: volcanic mountains, extraordinary natural formations, waterfalls, hot springs

Reminders: difficult wading at some times

Comment: A fairly easy trek in a colourful landscape resembling a wilderness.

Difficulty: 5

HIGH ATLAS

A trek on traditional paths over mountain passes and along a populated river valley close to the second highest mountain in the range – M'Goun.

Location: central Morocco

Organization: organized tour with guide

Best time: April–May, September–October

Time to allow: about 7 days

Length: 34 miles (55km).

Highest altitude: 11,155 feet (3,400m) above sea level

Remoteness: low–moderate

Accommodation: tent/guest houses/private homes

Food: take your own/local

Physical effort: moderate

Accessibility: easy

Sights: deep ravines, the villages, settlements

Reminders: gorges dangerous in heavy rain

Comment: A fairly demanding route that alternates between deserted and developed tracts.

Difficulty: 5–6

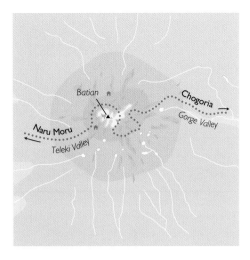

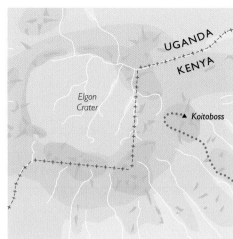

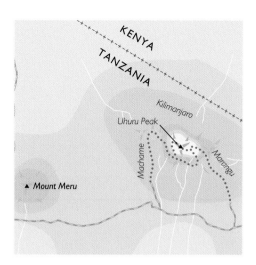

8 miles / 5 km

1¼ miles / 2km

16miles / 10 km

MOUNT KENYA

A trek on well-trodden paths around the mountain. The Chogoria route begins in the east and leads across the third highest peak.

Location: central Kenya

Organization: private, with or without porters/organized tour with guide

Best time: January–February, August–September

Time to allow: 7–8 days

Length: 35 miles (56km).

Highest altitude: 16,355 feet (4,985m) above sea level

Remoteness: low–moderate

Nature conservation: Mount Kenya National Park and World Heritage site

Accommodation: tent/huts

Food: take your own

Physical effort: very hard

Accessibility: easy–difficult

Sights: the majestic mountain; the vegetation; rock hyrax

Reminders: high altitude; warm clothing; park entrance fee

Comment: A demanding trek owing to the rapid ascent to high altitude and a muddy path in some places. In the event of altitude sickness you can make do with walking to the huts. Note that Mount Kenya is said to cause the most cases of altitude sickness of all the mountains in the world.

Difficulty: 7–8

MOUNT ELGON

Day trip on extinct volcano up to Mount Koitoboss.

Location: border between Kenya and Uganda

Organization: private with guide

Best time: December–February, June–August

Time to allow: about 6 hours

Length: about 6 miles (10km).

Highest altitude: about 13,125 feet (4,000m) above sea level

Remoteness: high

Nature conservation: Mount Elgon National Park

Accommodation: tent

Food: take your own

Physical effort: hard

Accessibility: easy–difficult

Sights: mountain plateau in the interior of Africa; the vegetation; caves with elephants

Reminders: high altitude; cattle thieves

Comment: A demanding trip for accustomed trekkers. On the Kenyan side the paths are not obvious in some places.

Difficulty: 6–7

KILIMANJARO

A trek up the mountain's south face to the top. The Marangu route is a return trip and is the most popular. The Machame route, which starts in one place and finishes in another, is more challenging.

Location: northern Tanzania

Organization: organized tour with guide (obligatory)

Best time: December–March, June–September

Time to allow: 5 days Marangu, 6 days Machame

Length: about 31 miles (50km) return trip to peak (Marangu), about 31 miles (50km) across the top (Machame)

Highest altitude: 19,635 feet (5,985m) above sea level

Remoteness: low–moderate

Nature conservation: Kilimanjaro National Park and World Heritage site

Accommodation: tent/huts

Food: take your own

Physical effort: very hard

Accessibility: easy

Sights: the crater; the vegetation; the view

Reminders: high altitude, warm clothing, permit and park entrance fee

Comment: One of the few really high mountains on earth that you can climb without being a mountaineer, but it is very challenging. The rapid ascent to high altitude makes Kilimanjaro more taxing than the Everest trip.

Difficulty: 8–9

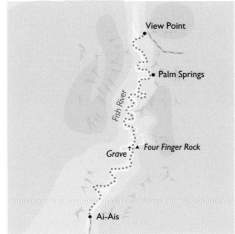

8 miles / 5 km

8 miles / 5 km

19 miles / 30 km

MEDITERRANEAN SEA

RUWENZORI

A circular tour through the mountain massif on well-trodden paths and an ascent of the highest peak.

Location: border between Uganda and Congo

Organization: organized tour with guide

Best time: December–March, June–September

Time to allow: 8 days

Length: about 43 miles (70km).

Highest altitude: 16,730 feet (5,100m) above sea level

Remoteness: high

Nature conservation: Ruwenzori National Park and World Heritage site

Accommodation: tent/huts

Food: take your own

Physical effort: very hard

Accessibility: difficult

Sights: the vegetation; the mountain landscape

Reminders: extremely rainy climate, high altitude, permit and fee

Comment: The most taxing trek you can imagine. You need to be well-accustomed to strenuous trekking.

Difficulty: 9–10

FISH RIVER CANYON

A trek on fragmented paths along the river in a desert-like canyon.

Location: southern Namibia

Organization: private/organized tour with guide

Best time: trail open from mid April to mid September

Time to allow: at least 5 days

Length: about 50 miles (80km).

Highest altitude: about 2,625 feet (800m) above sea level

Remoteness: high

Nature conservation: Fish River Canyon Park

Accommodation: tent

Food: take your own

Physical effort: moderate–hard

Accessibility: easy–difficult

Sights: canyon landscape, fauna

Reminders: oppressive heat; a lot of wading; permit and park entrance fee; medical certificate required

Comment: Quite a demanding trek in desert landscape. Normally no problem with water supplies.

Difficulty: 6–7

LYCIAN WAY

Marked long-distance path following traditional paths and tracks. The section from Ovacik to Bogazici lies to the west.

Location: coast of the Teke Peninsula, southern Turkey

Organization: private/organized tour with guide

Best time: February–May, September–November

Time to allow: at least 30 days (whole path), 5 days (Ovacik–Bogazici)

Length: about 329 miles (530km) (whole path), 37 miles (60km) (Ovacik–Bogazici)

Highest altitude: about 5,905 feet (1,800m) above sea level

Remoteness: low

Accommodation: tent/guest houses/private homes

Food: in guest houses/take your own

Physical effort: easy–moderate

Accessibility: easy

Sights: steep cliffs; ancient monuments; the villages

Reminders: dried up wells; bad-tempered sheepdogs; oppressive heat

Comment: A fairly easy trek with wonderful swimming.

Difficulty: 4–5 (6 if you go down into the Butterfly Valley)

A ROUTE GUIDE TO MY JOURNEYS

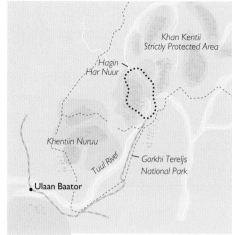

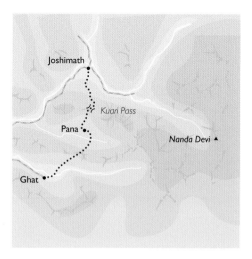

16miles/10km

19mile/30km

16miles/10km

ALTAI MOUNTAINS

A trek on minor paths in the Altai region.

Location: western Mongolia

Organization: organized tour with guide and pack animals

Best time: July–August

Time to allow: at least 9 days

Length: about 62 miles (100km).

Highest altitude: about 9,840 feet (3,000m) above sea level

Remoteness: very high

Nature conservation: Altai Tavan Bogd National Park

Accommodation: tent

Food: take your own

Physical effort: moderate–hard

Accessibility: easy–difficult

Sights: pristine mountain landscape; nomad culture

Reminders: small scale maps; permit and park entrance fee; good fishing

Comment: Quite a demanding trek in an area that is still little known

Difficulty: 5–6

KHENTIIN NURUU

A riding trip or trek through trackless taiga forests.

Location: northern Mongolia

Organization: organized riding trip with guide and pack animals

Best time: June–August

Time to allow: at least 8 days

Length: about 124 miles (200km).

Highest altitude: about 7,875 feet (2,400m) above sea level

Remoteness: extremely high

Nature conservation: Khan Khentiin Nature Conservation Area

Accommodation: tent

Food: take your own

Physical effort: moderate–hard

Accessibility: difficult

Sights: pristine pine forests; flora and fauna

Reminders: small scale maps; a lot of mosquitoes and flies; good fishing

Comment: a real wilderness area for trail-blazers on foot or on horseback. The trips are more like expeditions.

Difficulty: 6–7

GARHWAL

A trek on traditional paths along the Curzon Trail.

Location: northern India

Organization: private, with or without porters, organized tour with guide and porters

Best time: April–June, September–November

Time to allow: 6 days

Length: about 37 miles (60km).

Highest altitude: about 11,810 feet (3,600m) above sea level

Remoteness: low–high

Nature conservation: Nanda Devi National Park and World Heritage site

Accommodation: tent

Food: take your own

Physical effort: moderate–hard

Accessibility: easy

Sights: exquisite mountain views; villages

Reminders: high altitude

Comment: An exquisitely beautiful trip, and not too demanding considering it is in the Himalayas.

Difficulty: 5–6

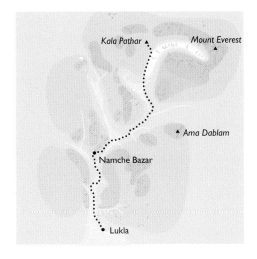

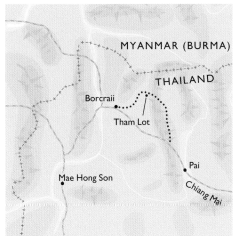

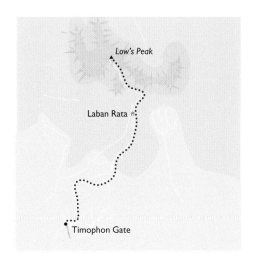

16 miles / 10 km

16 miles / 10 km

½ mile / 1 km

MOUNT EVEREST

A return trip on traditional paths to the world's highest mountain.

Location: eastern Nepal

Organization: private with or without porters/organized tour with guide

Best time: October–November, March–April

Time to allow: at least 12 days

Length: about 75 miles (120km).

Highest altitude: 18,370 feet (5,600m) above sea level

Remoteness: low

Nature conservation: Sagarmatha National Park and World Heritage site

Accommodation: guest houses/tent

Food: in guest houses/take your own

Physical effort: very hard

Accessibility: easy

Sights: the world's highest mountain, the Sherpa culture

Reminders: risk of altitude sickness, shortage of accommodation in guest houses

Comment: quite an easy trek for anyone who can cope with the height.

Difficulty: 5–8

THAILAND

A trek on paths between mountain villages and through dry monsoon forest in the province of Mae Hong Son.

Location: northern Thailand

Organization: organized tour with guide and porters/private

Best time: October–February

Time to allow: 4 days

Length: about 37 miles (60km).

Highest altitude: about 2,625 feet (800m) above sea level

Remoteness: low

Accommodation: private homes/guest houses

Food: take your own/guest houses

Physical effort: easy

Accessibility: easy

Sights: the culture of the mountain tribes

Reminders: choose a reliable guide

Comment: An easy tour that is as much a cultural as a wildlife trek

Difficulty: 1–2

GUNUNG KINABALU

A trek through rainforest and along a rope across the rocky slabs of southeast Asia's highest mountain.

Location: in western Sabah, northern Borneo

Organization: private/organized tour, guide compulsory

Best time: February–May

Time to allow: 2 days

Length: 16 miles (26km).

Highest altitude: 13,450 feet (4,100m) above sea level

Remoteness: low

Nature conservation: Kinabalu national park and world heritage site

Accommodation: guest house

Food: guest house

Physical effort: very hard

Accessibility: easy–difficult

Sights: remarkable granite landscape, rainforest, flora, views

Reminders: high altitude, very slippery slabs in rainy weather, risk of lightning, warm clothing, whistle needed if misty

Comment: An easy-to-walk path through the rainforest but owing to the altitude and the steep slaps the trek is more taxing higher up.

Difficulty: 6–7

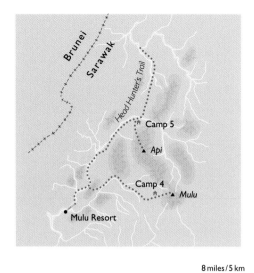

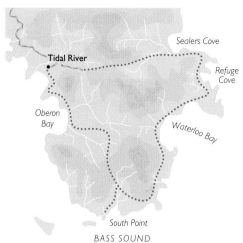

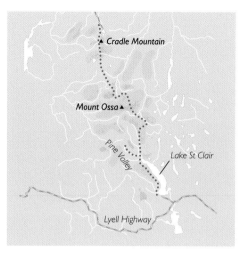

8 miles / 5 km

8 miles / 5 km

8 miles / 5 km

GUNUNG MULU

A trek on cleared trails through the rainforest in the lowlands and up on to the high mountains.

Location: northern Sarawak, Borneo

Organization: private/organized tour

Best time: March–August, October–November

Time to allow: about 8 days

Length: about 31 miles (50km).

Highest altitude: 7,545 feet (2,300m) above sea level

Remoteness: low–high

Nature conservation: Mulu National Park and World Heritage site

Accommodation: huts/shelters

Food: take your own

Physical effort: moderate–very hard

Accessibility: easy–difficult

Sights: rainforest; limestone columns; caves

Reminders: leeches; humid heat; warm clothing (up on Mulu)

Comment: One of the world's most easily accessible trails in genuine tropical rainforest. Fairly easy to walk on the lowlands but the slopes are extremely taxing in the heat.

Difficulty: 6–7

WILSONS PROMONTORY

A trek on well-trodden paths along the beaches and through the forest around a peninsula.

Location: southeastern corner of Australia

Organization: private

Best time: November–March

Time to allow: 4 days

Length: about 25 miles (40km).

Highest altitude: about 985 feet (300m) above sea level

Remoteness: low–moderate

Nature conservation: Wilsons Promontory National Park

Accommodation: tent

Food: take your own

Physical effort: easy

Accessibility: easy

Sights: sandy beaches; vegetation; fauna

Reminders: cheeky wombats; rain; campsite fee

Comment: A wonderful easy coastal trek from one beach to the next.

Difficulty: 1–2

OVERLAND TRACK

Well-known trekking trail through extensive wildernesses.

Location: western Tasmania

Organization: private/organized tour with guide

Best time: November–March

Time to allow: 7–9 days

Length: 45 miles (73km).

Highest altitude: about 3,610 feet (1,100m) above sea level

Remoteness: low–moderate

Nature conservation: Cradle Mountain – Lake St. Clair National Park and World Heritage Site

Accommodation: tent/huts

Food: take your own/provided on organized tours

Physical effort: moderate

Accessibility: easy

Sights: mountain plateaus, vegetation

Reminders: cheeky possums; rain; park/ accommodation charge

Comment: Quite an easy trek revealing a cross section of Tasmania's beautiful landscape. Long stretches in the forest; fine day trips to the peaks.

Difficulty: 5

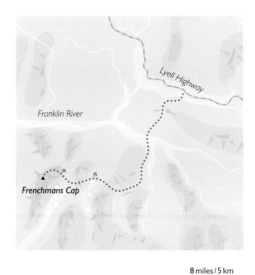

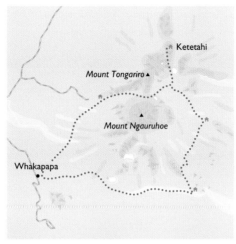

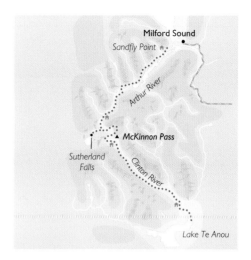

8 miles / 5 km

8 miles / 5 km

8 miles / 5 km

FRENCHMAN'S CAP

A return trip to a very steep mountain.

Location: southwestern Tasmania

Organization: private

Best time: November–March

Time to allow: 3–4 days

Length: about 28 miles (45km).

Highest altitude: 4,745 feet (1,446m) above sea level

Remoteness: moderate–high

Nature conservation: Franklin–Gordon Rivers National Park and World Heritage site

Accommodation: tent/huts

Food: take your own

Physical effort: easy–hard

Accessibility: easy – difficult

Sights: the view from the top

Reminders: park entrance fee

Comment: Quite a demanding trek for accustomed trekkers. The path offers close contact with Tasmania's wildest terrain. Muddy path.

Difficulty: 6–7

TONGARIRO

A circular tour on well-marked paths in a volcanic environment, either round the whole mountain massif or the northern half (Northern Circuit).

Location: in the centre of New Zealand's North Island

Organization: private

Best time: November – April

Time to allow: 4 days (Northern Circuit), 7–9 days (whole trail)

Length: about 31 miles (50km) (Northern Circuit)

Highest altitude: about 5,905 feet (1,800m) above sea level

Remoteness: low–moderate

Nature conservation: Tongariro National Park and World Heritage site

Accommodation: huts/tent

Food: take your own

Physical effort: easy–moderate

Accessibility: easy

Sights: highly colourful landscape

Reminders: changeable weather; accommodation charge

Comment: Easy trek through an unusual volcanic landscape. The trip over the Tongariro volcano may be taken as a day trip (Tongariro Crossing).

Difficulty: 5

MILFORD TRACK

World-famous trekking trail across a pass and through narrow valleys.

Location: southwestern corner of New Zealand's South Island

Organization: private/organized tour with guide

Best time: November–March

Time to allow: 4–6 days

Length: 32 miles (52km)

Highest altitude: 3,520 feet (1,073m) above sea level

Remoteness: low–moderate

Nature conservation: Fiordland National Park and World Heritage site

Accommodation: huts

Food: take your own

Physical effort: moderate

Accessibility: easy

Sights: fjord landscape, rainforest, waterfall

Reminders: a lot of rain, park entrance fee, must be booked in good time

Comment: A fairly easy trek along a magnificent trail. Even on a private trip you walk with a group who all stay overnight at the same place. Good scope for making new friends.

Difficulty: 5

A ROUTE GUIDE TO MY JOURNEYS

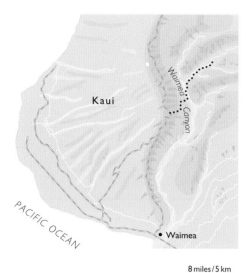

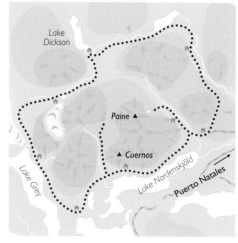

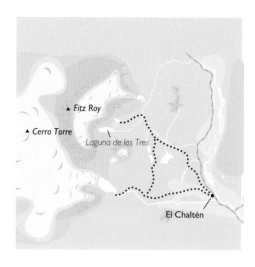

8 miles / 5 km

16 miles / 10 km

8 miles / 5 km

WAIMEA

A return trip down into a deep canyon.

Location: western part of the island of Kauai in the Hawaii group of islands

Organization: private

Best time: April–October

Time to allow: 3–4 days

Length: about 19 miles (30km).

Highest altitude: about 3,280 feet (1,000m) above sea level

Remoteness: moderate–high

Nature conservation: Waimea Canyon State Park

Accommodation: tent

Food: take your own

Physical effort: easy–moderate

Accessibility: easy–difficult

Sights: canyon landscape; vegetation

Reminders: wading, rain causing the river to rise

Comment: Quite a demanding trek in a tropical canyon that can also be reached on day trips from the edge of the canyon. Alternatively, you can trek into the valley from its opening. That means fewer slopes.

Difficulty: 5–6

TORRES DEL PAINE

A long and very varied circular tour around the mountain massif.

Location: Patagonia, southern Chile

Organization: private/organized tour with guide

Best time: December–March

Time to allow: 8–9 days

Length: 62 miles (100km).

Highest altitude: 3,870 feet (1,180m) above sea level

Remoteness: moderate–high

Nature conservation: Torres del Paine National Park

Accommodation: tent/refuges

Food: take your own or available in the refuges

Physical effort: moderate–hard

Accessibility: easy–difficult

Sights: spectacular mountains; glacial lakes with icebergs; fauna; broad-leaved woodlands

Reminders: changeable weather; often a strong wind; park entrance fee

Comment: A demanding tour and one of the most rewarding trekking trails in South America. It is a considerably easier and shorter trip if you just do the "W" path on the south side.

Difficulty: 6–7

FITZ ROY

A trek on the eastern side of a jagged mountain massif.

Location: in southern Argentina, close to the border with Chile

Organization: private

Best time: November–April

Time to allow: about 4 days

Length: about 31 miles (50km).

Highest altitude: about 3,935 feet (1,200m) above sea level

Remoteness: moderate–high

Nature conservation: Los Glaciares National Park and World Heritage site

Accommodation: tent

Food: take your own

Physical effort: moderate

Accessibility: easy

Sights: mountain peaks; fauna; glacial lakes with icebergs

Reminders: strong wind; changeable weather

Comment: Quite an easy trek even though the landscape is extremely spectacular. The tour can be extended north to Los Troncos.

Difficulty: 5–6

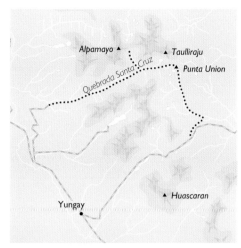

8 miles / 5 km   8 miles / 5 km   16 miles / 10 km

INCA TRAIL

A unique trail along the old stone-paved roads of the Inca Empire.

Location: southern Peru

Organization: organized tour with guide (compulsory)

Best time: June–October

Time to allow: 4 days

Length: 29 miles (46km).

Highest altitude: 13,780 feet (4,200m) above sea level

Remoteness: low

Nature conservation: Machu Picchu's historic conservation area and World Heritage site

Accommodation: tent

Food: take your own

Physical effort: hard

Accessibility: easy

Sights: Inca ruins; rainforest

Reminders: high altitude; arduous stone steps; park entrance fee; must be booked a long time in advance

Comment: A fairly challenging trek across three high passes. Beautiful landscape and many ancient monuments, including the ruined city of Machu Picchu, make this a very popular trail.

Difficulty: 6–7

CORDILLERA BLANCA

A trek along the popular Santa Cruz Trail across the most glaciated mountain range in the Andes.

Location: northern Peru

Organization: private/organized tour with guide

Best time: May–October

Time to allow: 4–5 days

Length: 28 miles (45km).

Highest altitude: 15,585 feet (4,750m) above sea level

Remoteness: low

Nature conservation: Huascaran National Park and World Heritage site

Accommodation: tent

Food: take your own

Physical effort: hard

Accessibility: easy

Sights: jagged snowy mountains; the "world's most beautiful mountain"; flora and fauna

Reminders: high altitude

Comment: Quite a demanding trek which offers a cross section of the Cordillera Blanca. May be walked in either direction.

Difficulty: 6–7

RORAIMA

A trek up one of the highest plateau mountains in the Guyana highlands.

Location: on the border between Venezuela, Guyana and Brazil

Organization: private/organized tour with guide

Best time: December–March

Time to allow: 6 days

Length: about 28 miles (45km).

Highest altitude: 9,185 feet (2,800m) above sea level

Remoteness: moderate

Nature conservation: Canaima National Park and World Heritage site

Accommodation: tent

Food: take your own

Physical effort: moderate–hard

Accessibility: easy–difficult

Sights: mountain walls; the plateaus; the flora; the waterfalls

Reminders: dangerous precipices; a lot of mist; whistle recommended; park entrance fee

Comment: A fairly challenging trek in a mountain landscape that is magnificent in a unique way. There is no other place like it in the world.

Difficulty: 6–7

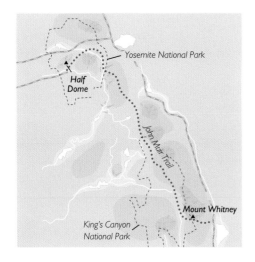

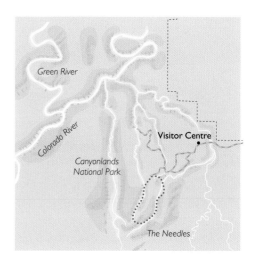

31 miles / 50 km

8 miles / 5 km

8 miles / 5 km

SIERRA NEVADA

Tours and day trips on the John Muir Trail in the Sierra Nevada.

Location: eastern California, USA

Organization: private

Best time: May–October

Time to allow: about 20 days (the whole trail)

Length: about 217 miles (350km) (the whole trail)

Highest altitude: over 13,125 feet (4,000m) above sea level

Remoteness: low–high

Nature conservation: Yosemite National Park and World Heritage site; King's Canyon National Park, federal wildlife areas

Accommodation: tent

Food: take your own

Physical effort: moderate–hard

Accessibility: easy–difficult

Sights: picturesque mountain landscape; giant trees in the forest; fauna

Reminders: you need a permit to stay overnight; forest fires are common; black bears in many places, heavy pack on long trips; altitude sickness in some places.

Comment: Treks on the John Muir Trail are quite taxing. Around the Yosemite valley there are lots of fine day trips. The ascent of Half Dome often takes two days.

Difficulty: 5–6

GRAND CANYON

Tours and day trips down into the world's largest canyon. Kaibab Trail and Havasu Trail.

Location: northwestern Arizona, USA

Organization: private/organized tour with guide and pack animals

Best time: April–June, September–October

Time to allow: 3 days ((both trails)

Length: 22 miles (35km) (Kaibab), 19 miles (30 km) (Havasu)

Highest altitude: 7,220 feet (2,200m) above sea level

Remoteness: low

Nature conservation: Grand Canyon National Park and World Heritage site, Havasupai Indian Reserve

Accommodation: tent

Food: take your own

Physical effort: moderate–hard

Accessibility: easy

Sights: the monumental canyon landscape; waterfalls

Reminders: you need a permit to stay overnight; the heat is a problem

Comment: Fairly demanding treks owing to the climate and the steep slopes. The canyon is 4,920 feet (1,500m) deep. The Havasu Trail is a return trip down to a hidden Eden with a waterfall. The Kaibab Trail combines with the Bright Angel Trail to provide a cross section of the Grand Canyon.

Difficulty: 5–6

CANYONLANDS

Several-day tours and day trips in a fantastic craggy landscape.

Location: southeastern Utah, USA

Organization: private

Best time: May–October

Time to allow: 2–3 days

Length: 3–6 miles (5–10 km).

Highest altitude: about 5,580 feet (1,700m) above sea level

Remoteness: moderate–high

Nature conservation: Canyonlands National Park

Accommodation: tent

Food: take your own

Physical effort: easy–moderate

Accessibility: easy

Sights: the crags

Reminders: you need a permit to stay overnight; the heat is a problem; drinking water

Comment: Fairly easy, short treks over sandstone slabs in a unique craggy landscape.

Difficulty: 3–4

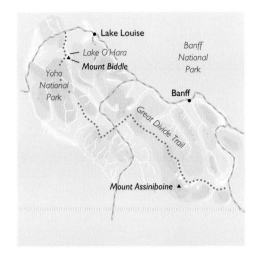

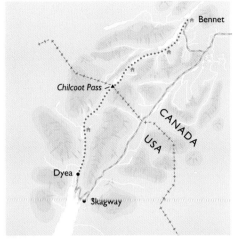

16miles/10 km   8 miles/5 km   8 miles/5 km

ROCKY MOUNTAINS

Several-day tours and day trips around Lake O'Hara.

Location: southeastern British Columbia, Canada

Organization: private

Best time: June–September

Time to allow: one or several days

Length: about 6 miles (10km) (around Lake O'Hara)

Highest altitude: about 7,220 feet (2,200m) above sea level (around Lake O'Hara)

Remoteness: moderate–high

Nature conservation: Yoho National Park and Rocky Mountains World Heritage site

Accommodation: tent/guest houses

Food: take your own or available on the guest houses

Physical effort: easy–hard

Accessibility: easy

Sights: turquoise blue lakes; fabulous mountain scenery

Reminders: controlled access around Lake O'Hara; must be booked in advance; grizzlies and black bears

Comment: Within the envelope of the Canadian Rockies there are many trekking trails, long and short, easy and hard. The area around Lake O'Hara is one of the most beautiful. The Great Divide Trail passes through here.

Difficulty: 4–5

CHILKOOT TRAIL

A trek along the route the gold-diggers took to the Klondike.

Location: southeastern Alaska, USA and northern British Columbia, Canada

Organization: private

Best time: June–August

Time to allow: 5–6 days

Length: 33 miles (53km).

Highest altitude: 3,525 feet (1,074m) above sea level

Remoteness: low–moderate

Nature conservation: Klondike Gold Rush Historic Park (USA)/Chilkoot Trail Historic Park (Canada)

Accommodation: tent

Food: take your own

Physical effort: hard

Accessibility: easy–difficult

Sights: relics of the gold rush; the mountain landscape; flora

Reminders: park entrance fee; campsites must be booked; changeable weather; grizzlies and black bears

Comment: Quite a challenging trek that combines magnificent wildlife sightings with an experience of some of the tribulations of the gold rush.

Difficulty: 5–6

YUKON

A trek on the Slim's West Trail which is partially marked as far as Observation Mountain.

Location: northwestern Yukon, Canada

Organization: private

Best time: June–August

Time to allow: 3–4 days

Length: about 37 miles (60km).

Highest altitude: 6,970 feet (2,125m) above sea level (Observation Mountain)

Remoteness: very high

Nature conservation: Kluane National Park and World Heritage site

Accommodation: tent

Food: take your own

Physical effort: hard

Accessibility: difficult

Sights: magnificent mountain landscape with big glaciers

Reminders: tricky wading; quicksands; high population of grizzlies; bear canteens for food stores are a must; treks must be registered.

Comment: A fairly taxing trek in a wonderful mountain valley. The trek suits people who want to trek in bear country and feel close to the wild animals.

Difficulty: 6–7

Index

Further Reading

For the bibliography I have chosen a number of books that offer inspiration and/or information about trekking, trails and experiences in the world's great mountain regions.

Abbey, Edward. *Desert Solitaire*. McGraw-Hill Book Company: New York, 1968

Amin, Mohamed et al. *On God's Mountain: The story of Mount Kenya*. Hunter Publishing: Massachussetts, 1992. (Big picture book.)

Ardito, Stefano. *Trekking in Africa: A guide to the finest routes*. Swan Hill Press: Shrewsbury, 1996. (Well illustrated guide to 16 trekking trails.)

Ardito, Stefano. *Trekking in the Himalayas: A guide to the finest routes*. The Crowood Press Ltd: Marlborough, 1995. (Well-illustrated guide to 15 trekking trails.)

Ardito, Stefano. *Walking and climbing in the Alps*. Swan Hill Press: Shrewsbury, 1995. (Well-illustrated guide to 18 trekking trails.)

Bernabaum, Edwin. *Sacred Mountains of the World*. Random House: New York, 1990.

Birkett, Bill. *Classic Treks: The 30 most spectacular walks in the world*. Bulfinch Press: Boston, 2000. (Big picture book).

Blessed, Brian. *Quest for the Lost World*. Boxtree: London, 1999. (About Roraima.)

Briggs, John. *Mountains of Malaysia: A practical guide*. Longman Malaysia: Malaysia, 1988.

Brown, Hamish. *Hamish's Mountain Walk*. Gollancz: London, 1978. (About Scotland.)

Chester, Jonathan. *The Himalayan Experience: An introduction to trekking and climbing in the Himalayas*. Simon & Schuster: Australia, 1989.

Cleare, John. *Distant Mountains: Encounters with the world's greatest mountains*. Duncan Baird Publishers: London, 1998. (Big picture book.)

Cleare, John. *Mountains of the World*. Publishers Group West: California, 1997. (Big picture book.)

Crane, Nicholas. *Clear Waters Rising: A mountain walk across Europe*. Viking Press: New York, 1996.

Douglas, Ed. *Chomolungma Sings the Blues: Travels round Everest*. Constable and Robinson: London, 1997.

Fedden, Robin. *The Enchanted Mountains.: A quest in the Pyrenees*. John Murray: London, 1962 (reprinted 2002).

Fletcher, Colin. *The Man who Walked through Time*. Alfred A. Knopf: New York, 1967. (About the Grand Canyon.)

Fletcher, Colin. *The Complete Walker III*. Alfred A. Knopf: New York, 1984. (About outdoor pursuits techniques.)

Fletcher, Colin. *The Secret Worlds of Colin Fletcher*. Alfred A. Knopf: New York, 1989. (Essays.)

Grundsten, Claes and Peter Hanneberg. *Our Magnificent Wilderness: 40 of the greatest natural World Heritage sites*. Duncan Baird Publishers: London, 2004.

Jackson, Jack. *The World's Great Adventure Treks*. New Holland Publishers: London, 2003. (Big picture book about 20 trails.)

Kelsey, Michael R. *A Climber's and Hiker's Guide to the World's Mountains and Volcanoes*. Brigham Distributing: Utah, 2001.

Langmuir, Eric: *Mountaincraft and Leadership*. British Mountaineering Council: London and Edinburgh, 1984. (About outdoor pursuits techniques.)

Macfarlane, Robert. *Mountains of the Mind: A history of a fascination*. Granta Books: London, 2003. (About humankind's relationship with the mountains.)

Matthiessen, Peter. *The Snow Leopard*. Viking Press: New York, 1978.

Napier, Eloise. *A Place to Walk: Unforgettable walking holidays from around the world*. Conran Octopus: London, 2003. (About easy treks in 25 areas.)

Noland, David. *Trekking*. Outside Books/WW norton: New York, 2001. (Commentary on 20 trails throughout the world.)

O'Connor, Bill. *The Trekking Peaks of Nepal*. Cloncap Books: Seattle, 1989.

Perry, Julian. *The Mountains of Bulgaria: A walker's companion*. Menasha Ridge Press: USA, 1995.

Potton, Craig. *Classic Walks of New Zealand*. Craig Potton Publishing: New Zealand, 1998. (Big picture book about 9 trails.)

Rankin, Robert. *Classic Wild Walks of Australia*. Robert Rankin Publishing: Brisbane, Australia, 1989. (Big picture book about 25 trails.)

Razzetti, Steve. *Top Treks of the World*. New Holland Publisahers: London, 2001. (Big picture book about 29 trails.)

Reader, John. *Kilimanjaro*. Elm Tree Books: London, 1982. (Big picture book.)

Reynolds, Kev. *Walks and Climbs in the Pyrenees*. Cicerone Press: Dublin, 1988.

Reynolds, Kev. *Tour of Mont Blanc*. Cicerone Press: Dublin, 2002.

Rowell, Galen. *The Yosemite*. Sierra Club: California, 1989. (Big picture book with text by John Muir.)

Schandy, Tom. *Magnificent Africa: animals, birds, plants, landscapes*. Duncan Baird Publishers: London, 2003. (Big picture book.)

Shipton, Eric. *Six Mountain and Travel Books*. Baton Wicks Publications: London, 1999. (Collected work of classics, such as *Nanda Devi*, *Blank on the Map* and *Upon that Mountain*.)

Solnit, Rebecca. Wanderlust. *A History of Walking*. Verso Books: London, 2002.

Stevenson, Andrew. *Annapurna Circuit: a Himalayan journey*. Constable and Robinson: London, 1997.

Thomson, Hugh. *Nanda Devi: A journey to the last sanctuary*. Weidenfled & Nicolson: London, 2004.

Tilman, H.W. *Seven Mountain and Travel Books*. Baton Wicks Publications: London, 2003. (Collected work of classics, such as *Snow on the Equator* and *When Men and Mountains Meet*.)

Townsend, Chris. *The Advanced Backpacker: A handbook for year-round, long-distance hiking*. HarperCollins: New York, 2001.

Unsworth, Walt. *Classic Walks of the World*. Oxford Illustrated Press: Oxford, 1985. (Picture book about 17 trails.)

Unsworth, Walt. *Classic walks in Europe*. Oxford Illustrated Press: Oxford, 1987. (Picture book about 17 trails.)

Acknowledgments

On my way to Jomosum in the Himalayas, I began a lifelong trek. It was the year 1972 and the trip was my first far-away trek. After just one and a half years I was already making my way back to that alien environment for fresh trips. Even before that I had already been trekking in mountains for many years – in the Swedish fells. After my teenage adventures, I accumulated more and more experience and now I have collected the essence of it in this book. The question is what is it that drives me, or what in general terms makes people trek for miles, climb mountains, seek out new places and strange cultures, and what in my case attracts me to outdoor pursuits we were not made for? If I knew the full answer perhaps I would stop, but my love for wild places is deeply rooted and sincere. There, I find a beauty worth the telling. And I was born with a lust for adventure. The contrast with everyday life tickles my fancy. A double life. But I also have the dreams I have always dreamed. It's those mystic, perhaps romantic, nostalgic or even childish things which I have still not precisely pinpointed. As long as my legs will carry me, I want to go on investigating them. I also want to help spread the word, which I believe is so important to the human race, that nature, the outdoor life and trekking constitute an excellent route to physical and mental health. They are not just a luxury.

This book would never have been produced without the cooperation of many people, either directly or indirectly. My beloved family, Jill, Måns and Catrin, have meant a lot, of course, and have even come with me on many of my trips. A bear hug goes to them.

The editor Gösta Mineur at *Check-in* travel magazine has been my faithful partner for many years, while I have written reports on the various trekking trails. In order to enable me to carry out some of the trips a number of companies have given me backing, and various people have helped – see list, top right. And last, but not least, my warmest thanks go to the traveling companions and friends who have accompanied me on these trips – see list, bottom right.

Claes Grundsten

Grateful thanks to:

Ulf Amundsen
Tomas Bergenfeldt
Lotta Borgiel
Peter Hunger
Ola Skinnarmo
Lottie Sundelöf
Jan Wigsten
Haglöfs AB
Hilleberg The Tentmaker AB
Primus AB
Utemagasinet
Äventyrsresor AB

Rolf Bardon
Eva Carleberg
Anders Eriksson
Björn Esping
Suzanne Insulander
Arne Larsson
Örjan Nyström
Göran Palmgren
Gordon Sanders
Katarina Villner
Björn Wessman
Lars-Olof Österström
Those who came on my photo safari to Sarek in 2000
Those who came on the Äventyursresor Altai trek in 2003